THE BEATLES THE MUSIC AND THE MYTH

Exclusive Distributors
Music Sales Limited, 14/15 Berners Street, London, W1T 3LJ.

Music Sales Corporation,
257 Park Avenue South, New York, NY 10010, USA.

Macmillan Distribution Services,
56 Parkwest Drive, Derrimut, Vic 3030, Australia.

Cover and book design by Fresh Lemon.
Picture credits:
Text pages: all images LFI, except page 72 –
Rex Features and page 173 – Getty Images
Colour section: all images LFI, except: page 2: Cavern
Club, page 3: group picture including Stuart Sutcliffe,
page 4: New York arrival, page 5: Shea Stadium,
Washington Coliseum, page 7: John & Yoko and
page 8 portrait of Paul Mccartney – Getty Images.
Page 7: Paul & Linda – Rex Features.

Every effort has been made to trace the copyright
holders of the photographs in this book but one or two
were unreachable. We would be grateful if the
photographers concerned would contact us.

Printed by Gutenberg Press Limited, Malta.

A catalogue record for this book is available from the
British Library.
Visit Omnibus Press on the web at
www.omnibuspress.com

THE BEATLES
THE MUSIC AND THE MYTH

PETER DOGGETT & PATRICK HUMPHRIES

OMNIBUS PRESS

LONDON / NEW YORK / PARIS / SYDNEY / COPENHAGEN / BERLIN / MADRID / TOKYO

1940
JULY 7

Richard Starkey (Ringo Starr) born in Liverpool, the birthplace of all four Beatles.

1954
SEPTEMBER

George starts at the Liverpool Institute.

1953
SEPTEMBER

Paul enters the Liverpool Institute.

1940
OCTOBER 9

John Winston Lennon born.

1942
JUNE 18

James Paul McCartney born.

1952
SEPTEMBER

John starts at Quarry Bank High School, having left Dovedale Primary School in July.

1943
FEBRUARY 24

George Harrison born.

1956
APRIL

John buys his first single, Lonnie Donegan's skiffle hit, 'Rock Island Line'.

1957

George's mother buys him a guitar from a boy at school for £3.

1957
MARCH

Inspired by Lonnie Donegan and fired up by Elvis Presley's 'Heartbreak Hotel', John and his school friend Pete Shotton start a skiffle group which they call The Blackjacks, soon to become The Quarrymen.

1956
JUNE 18

For his 14th birthday, Paul's father buys him a trumpet which he swaps for a Zenith acoustic guitar, priced £15.

1957
JULY 6

John and Paul meet for the first time, at the Woolton Parish Church Garden Fete, held at St. Peter's Church where The Quarrymen are performing.

1956
OCTOBER 31

Paul's mother dies of breast cancer. Within a few weeks of his mother's death, Paul has written his first song, 'I Lost My Little Girl'.

1957
OCTOBER 18

Paul plays his first gig with The Quarrymen.

1958
FEBRUARY 6
George joins the Quarrymen.

1960
AUGUST 16
The Beatles leave Liverpool for their first season in Hamburg.

1958
JULY 15
John's mother, Julia, is killed in a road accident.

1959
MID-OCTOBER
The group change their name to Johnny & The Moondogs.

1960
JANUARY 17
John's friend Stuart Sutcliffe is persuaded by John to buy a bass guitar and join Johnny & The Moondogs.

1960
AUGUST 6
The Beatles invite Pete Best to be their drummer.

1960
MAY
Stuart suggests The Beetles as a new name for the group. John decides on Beatles.

1961
JANUARY

Paul takes over on bass.

1961
JUNE 22 /23

The Beatles, with Paul on bass
and Stuart Sutcliffe watching but
not playing, back Tony Sheridan
on a recording session for German
producer and orchestra leader
Bert Kaempfert.

1961
FEBRUARY 9

They play their The Cavern
under the name of The
Beatles. The club would
become forever associated
with the group.

1961
DECEMBER 6

The Beatles' accept Brian
Epstein as their manager.

1961
APRIL 1

The start of a three-month,
13-week season at the Top Ten
Club, Hamburg.

1962
JANUARY 1

The Beatles audition for
Decca Records but are
turned down.

1960
DECEMBER 27

At a show at Litherland
Town Hall, The Beatles play
their Hamburg set which
has an electrifying effect on
the young audience.

1961
NOVEMBER 9

Brian Epstein see The
Beatles for the first time
at the Cavern.

1962
MAY 9
George Martin meets with
Brian Epstein at Abbey Road.

1962
APRIL 10
Stuart Sutcliffe, who had
remained in Hamburg,
is rushed to hospital with
a brain haemorrhage,
but dies in the ambulance.
He was 22.

1962
AUGUST 15
Pete Best plays his last
shown with the group.

1962
APRIL 13-30
The Beatles play a seven-week
season at the Star-Club.

1962
AUGUST 23
John marries
Cynthia Powell.

1962
JUNE 6
The Beatles recorded four
numbers in Abbey Road studios
but George Martin does not like
Pete Best's drumming.

1962
SEPTEMBER 4
The Beatles record
'Love Me Do'.

1962
AUGUST 18
Ringo joins The Beatles.

1963
FEBRUARY 11

Abbey Road. All ten new tracks needed to make the *Please, Please Me* album are recorded in one ten-hour session

1962
DECEMBER 18 – 31

The Star-Club, Grosse Freiheit, Hamburg. The Beatles' fifth and final residency in Germany.

1963
MARCH 22

The album Please, Please Me is released in the UK

1962
DECEMBER 27

'Love Me Do' reaches number 17 in the Record Retailer's Top 50 charts, its highest position.

1963
APRIL 11

'From Me To You' is released in the UK.

1962
OCTOBER 5

'Love Me Do' is released.

1963
FEBRUARY 2

The Beatles' first UK tour opens at the Gaumont Cinema, Bradford. They are effectively bottom of the bill.

1963
JANUARY 11

'Please, Please Me' is released in the UK. The Beatles appeared on ABC TV's *Thank Your Lucky Stars,* performing 'Please Please Me'.

1963
AUGUST 23

'She Loves You' is released in the UK
and reaches number one where it stays
for seven weeks.

1963
OCTOBER 23

The Beatles fly to Stockholm,
arriving to a scene of
screaming fans and
uncharacteristic Swedish
chaos.

1963
AUGUST 3

The Beatles' last
performance at the
Cavern club.

1963
OCTOBER 31

The Beatles return to London
where hundreds of screaming
teenage girls gather on the roof
of the Queen's Building at
Heathrow to welcome them
back. Scenes like this occur at
airports worldwide for the next
three years.

1963
JULY 1

The Beatles record
'She Loves You'.

1963
OCTOBER 13

The Beatles top the bill at ATV's Val Parnell's
Sunday Night At The London Palladium,
transmitted live from the theatre to an audience
of 15 million viewers. Outside the Palladium fans
stop traffic. It is the birth of 'Beatlemania'.

1963
NOVEMBER 1

The first night of The Beatles'
Autumn Tour, their first series
of concerts as unchallenged
headliners. Box-office chaos
erupts everywhere.

1963
OCTOBER 17

The Beatles record 'I Wanna Hold Your Hand'.

1963
NOVEMBER 29
'I Want To Hold Your Hand'
is released.

1964
MARCH 2
The Beatles begin filming
A Hard Day's Night.

1964
FEBRUARY 7
The Beatles fly to New York City
on Pan Am flight 101, where 3,000
fans are waiting at JFK airport.

1963
NOVEMBER 22
The album *With The Beatles*
is released.

1964
FEBRUARY 11
They make their US live debut
at the Washington Coliseum,
protected by 362 police officers.

1964
FEBRUARY 9
The Beatles appear on the *Ed Sullivan Show*.
The Nielsen ratings show that 73,700,000
people had watched The Beatles on
Ed Sullivan, not just the largest audience
that Sullivan had ever had, but the largest
audience in the history of television.

1964
JANUARY 17
In Paris The Beatles learn that
'I Want To Hold Your Hand' has
reached number one in America.
It had taken only three weeks to
reach the top position.

1964
FEBRUARY 22
The Beatles arrive back in London at
8:10 am to a tumultuous welcome.

1964
JULY 10

'A Hard Day's Night' and the album of the same name are released in the UK.

1964
DECEMBER 4

The album *Beatles For Sale* is released.

1964
SEPTEMBER 20

The US tour closes with a charity concert at the Paramount Theater, Broadway, New York City.

1964
APRIL 4

In the *Billboard* Hot 100 chart for the week of April 4, The Beatles occupy no fewer than 12 places, including the top five, an unprecedented achievement that is unlikely ever to be equalled.

1964
AUGUST 18

The Beatles set off on their 25-date American tour.

1964
MARCH 20

'Can't Buy Me Love' is released in the UK.

1964
JUNE 3

Drummer Jimmy Nicol is recruited to stand in for ill Ringo during the first week of a tour to Denmark, Holland, Hong Kong, Australia and New Zealand. In Adelaide police estimate that 200,000 people line the ten-mile route of their motorcade from the airport to the city centre.

1965
FEBRUARY 11

Ringo marries Maureen Cox in London.

1964
AUGUST 28

After a show at the Forest Hills Tennis Stadium, Bob Dylan visits The Beatles at their New York hotel where they smoke grass together.

1965
MAY 27

Paul writes the lyrics to 'Yesterday' in the car on the way from the airport.

1965
MARCH 27

John takes LSD for the first time.

1965
AUGUST 6

The album *Help!* is released.

1965
FEBRUARY 22

The Beatles fly to the Bahamas from Heathrow to begin filming *Help!;*

1965
AUGUST 13

The Beatles arrive at JFK Airport to begin their third US tour.

1965
AUGUST 15

The Beatles play Shea Stadium, the biggest rock in history at that time.

1965
APRIL 5

The Beatles film an Indian restaurant sequence at Twickenham, and George is introduced to Indian music for the first time.

1965
APRIL 9

'Ticket To Ride' is released.

1965
OCTOBER 26

The Beatles are invested with their MBEs.

1966
JULY 8

The Beatles arrive back in London. George: "We're going to have a couple of weeks to recuperate before we go and get beaten up by the Americans."

1966
JANUARY 21

George marries Pattie Boyd at the Leatherhead & Esher Register Office, Surrey.

1966
JUNE 23

The Beatles begin their final world tour in Germany.

1966
MARCH 4

The London *Evening Standard* publishes an interview with John Lennon in which he says: "We're more popular than Jesus now." His words upset no-one in Great Britain but when they were reprinted in the US, Christian fundamentalists react with hate and outrage.

1966
MAY 1

The Beatles last stage appearance in the UK at the *NME* Poll Winners concert at Wembley.

1966
JULY 3

The Beatles fly to the Philippines where they inadvertently offend Imelda Marcos, the wife of the President, by failing to attend a party. The next day they are spat at, insulted and jostled as they run the gauntlet to get to their plane.

1965
DECEMBER 3

The single 'Day Tripper' and album *Rubber Soul* are released.

1966
JUNE 30

The tour continues in Japan.

1966
AUGUST 11

The Beatles fly to the US, fort their final tour. In Chicago John is forced to apologise for something which the Americans had taken out of context. The tour proceeds amidst assassination threats.

1967
FEBRUARY 17

'Penny Lane' backed with 'Strawberry Fields Forever' is released.

1966
SEPTEMBER 10

The album *Revolver* reached number one on the *Billboard* Hot 100 charts, where it remains for six weeks.

1967

For the first four months of the year the Beatles are at Abbey Road recording *Sgt Pepper's Lonely Hearts Club Band.*

1966
SEPTEMBER 28

Japanese artist Yoko Ono makes her first public appearance in Britain, during an art symposium in Covent Garden, London.

1966
AUGUST 29

The last ever Beatles concert, at Candlestick Park, San Francisco.

1966
JULY 29

The American magazine *Datebook* publishes John interview in which he said, "We're bigger than Jesus now." A DJ in Birmingham, Alabama, organises an immediate boycott of The Beatles' music, and broadcast his intention to conduct a 'Beatle-burning' bonfire of the group's records.

1966
NOVEMBER 9

John meets Yoko Ono at the Indica Gallery, Mason's Yard, London.

1967
AUGUST 24

John and Cynthia, Paul and Jane, and George and Patti attend a lecture by the Maharishi Mahesh Yogi at the London Hilton on Park Lane.

1967
JUNE 1

Sgt Pepper's Lonely Hearts Club Band is released.

1967
AUGUST 27

Brian Epstein is found dead in his London house.

1967
JUNE 25

The Beatles perform 'All You Need Is Love' on the BBC *Our World* live worldwide TV link-up watched by 200 million viewers.

1967
DECEMBER 8

The EP *Magical Mystery Tour* is released in the UK.

1967
AUGUST 26

The Beatles inform the national press, who were besieging the Maharishi's meditation centre in Bangor, that they have renounced the use of hallucinogenic drugs.

1967
DECEMBER 26

Magical Mystery Tour is given its world premiere on BBC Television and is panned by the critics, The Beatles first public 'failure'.

1967
SEPTEMBER 11

Filming for *Magical Mystery* Tour begins.

1968
NOVEMBER 22

The 'White Album' is released.

1968
MAY 14

John and Paul give a press conference at the Americana Hotel on Central Park West to announce the formation of Apple.

1968
NOVEMBER 28

John pleads guilty possession of cannabis at Marylebone Magistrates' Court. This conviction was to haunt John for years as it was used by the Nixon administration in repeated attempts to deny him a Green Card for residence in the US.

1968
MAY 19

John begins his relationship with Yoko Ono.

1968
FEBRUARY 15

George, Patti, John and Cynthia fly from London Airport to India, followed a few days later by Paul, Jane, Ringo and Maureen. In India, at the Maharishi's retreat, they write a number of songs.

1968
OCTOBER 18

Officers from the drugs squad raid John and Yoko's London flat and find cannabis. They are charged with possession and obstructing the police.

1968
MAY 30

Abbey Road. Work began on what will to become the double album *The Beatles,* usually known as the 'White Album'.

1969
MARCH 20

John and Yoko are married in Gibraltar.

1969
JANUARY 30

The Beatles, with Billy Preston, perform live on the flat roof of the Apple offices on Savile Row in central London. Traffic is brought to a halt as the lunchtime crowds gather on the pavement below. John ends the set, and The Beatles' live career, with the words "I'd like to say thank you on behalf of the group and ourselves and I hope we passed the audition."

1969
APRIL 11

'Get Back' is released.

1969
JANUARY 2

Under pressure from Paul to return to live performance, The Beatles begin rehearsals for a proposed film, which will become *Let It Be,* at Twickenham Film Studios.

1969
MARCH 12

Paul and Linda are married at Marylebone Register Office.

1969
JULY 1

Abbey Road sessions begin.

1969
JANUARY 28

John and Yoko meet with Allen Klein, and John decides on the spot to make him his personal adviser.

1969
MARCH 21

Allen Klein is appointed business manager of Apple.

1969
AUGUST 22

The Beatles pose together for a photo session in the grounds of John's mansion Tittenhurst Park, the last ever Beatles photo shoot, and their last appearance together at any Beatles event.

1970
MAY 8

Let It Be is released.

1969
SEPTEMBER 26

Abbey Road is released.

1969
AUGUST 8

The now famous photograph of The Beatles walking across the zebra crossing near the Abbey Road recording studio is taken.

1970
MARCH 23

Paul finishes off the master tapes of his solo album *McCartney.*

1970
APRIL 1

Ringo becomes the last Beatle to play at a Beatles recording session, adding a drum part to 'I Me Mine'.

1970
JANUARY 27

Phil Spector is invited to complete the *Let It Be* project.

1969
SEPTEMBER 11

During a meeting at Apple, John informs Allen Klein that he is quitting The Beatles.

1970
APRIL 10

Paul effectively quits The Beatles by stating, in a press release that he does not foresee a time when he and John will become an active songwriting partnership again.

The Beatles revolutionised pop music in the Sixties. A cliché? Yes, of course. But it's become a cliché simply because it's true, and because a cliché is the only possible response to something as overwhelming and staggering as The Beatles' career. In the artificially-hyped multinational media world of the twenty-first century,

Not only that, they never ceased to stretch and broaden the palette of pop and rock – incorporating the lyrical poetry of folk singers like Bob Dylan, the psychedelia of the American West Coast, the jangle of folk-rock and the gutsiness of roots genres like blues and country, without sounding for a second like anyone but themselves. Masters of pastiche, they were also the most original and experimental artists in rock history – eager always to push at boundaries, to find out what might happen if you played *that* instrument in *that* room with the tape running backwards and all pre-conceptions left outside the door.

RODUCTION

The Beatles' sales figures will be, and are being, outclassed by entertainers with barely a fraction of their talent and artistry. But those achievements wouldn't have been possible in the first place without The Beatles, who rescued a brand of popular music that was in danger of fading into oblivion, and turned it into a medium that produced million-dollar returns – and art. That, finally, is The Beatles' greatest claim to fame. Working under immense pressure, to schedules that would baffle the sedentary superstars of the modern era, they produced thirteen great albums, and more than 20 singles, in a little over seven years.

Incorporating influences from every branch of popular music, and even beyond to the classical world, they returned the compliment in full, inspiring musicians in rock, pop, folk, jazz, R&B, country and blues in a way that will never be possible in the future. Their fashions, argot and habits were imitated by millions. They set the social agenda for the West's most playful and adventurous decade of the last century. They provided the soundtrack for a generation. And they also taped about 200 of the greatest pop records of all time, examined in the following pages, CD album-by-album.

Few artists in any field affect a generation beyond their own. To survive more than 20 or 30 years after your death requires a combination of genius and luck. After that, it's in the lap of the gods. But alone of the pop performers of the 20th Century, it's safe to predict that The Beatles' music will live forever.

PART I
THE ORIGINAL ALBUMS

PLEASE PLEASE ME

Parlophone CDP7 46435 2
Released April 1963

It requires a leap of the imagination to return to the innocent days of 1963, when The Beatles recorded and released their first two long-playing albums. The common currency of teenage pop was the three-minute single, or at a stretch the two-for-the-price-of-two 45rpm extended player (EP). Albums, or LPs as they were universally known in the early Sixties, were regarded as being beyond the financial reach of most teenagers; and with the oldest of The Beatles themselves no more than 22 when their first album was recorded, the teen audience was definitely EMI's target.

Only adult performers like Frank Sinatra and Ella Fitzgerald were allowed to use the 30- or 40-minute expanse of the LP as a personal artistic statement. For the rest, the LP was unashamedly a cash-in – either for a film, or else for die-hard supporters entranced by a hit single or two. Hence the full title of The Beatles' début album, which defined its selling points precisely: *Please Please Me, Love Me Do and 12 Other Songs*.

Much has been made of the fact that 10 of the record's 14 tracks were recorded during one day; but that was the way the pop business operated in 1963. This haste was proof of The Beatles' junior status at EMI, and also of the company's desire to rush an LP onto the market before teenage Britain found a new set of heroes. Remember that the band had yet to score their first No. 1 when the album was recorded: the extended session represented a commendable act of faith on the behalf of producer George Martin.

Four of the album's titles were already in the can, via their first two singles, 'Love Me Do'

and 'Please Please Me'. The rest – a mix of originals and covers – was a cross-section of their typical concert fare, with one exception: the group's penchant for covers of Chuck Berry and Little Richard rock'n'rollers was ignored, presumably because George Martin believed the era of rock'n'roll was past.

Recorded on two-track at Abbey Road, the album was mixed into mono and very rudimentary stereo – the latter format claiming only a tiny proportion of the market in 1963. Until 1968, The Beatles regarded the mono versions of their albums as the authentic representation of their work; and if they'd been asked, they would no doubt have agreed with George Martin's decision to prepare the CD mix of *Please Please Me* in mono. But stereo-philes, particularly in America, regarded this decision as barbarism in disguise, and continue to lobby for the release of the CD in stereo.

I SAW HER STANDING THERE
(John Lennon/Paul McCartney)
Recorded 11 February 1963
With a simple count-in, Paul McCartney captured all The Beatles' youthful exuberance in the opening seconds of their début album. Lyrically naïve, melodically unpolished, 'I Saw Her Standing There' was still classic Beatles' rock'n'roll – Lennon and McCartney trading vocals as if they were chewing gum between syllables, the falsetto 'ooos' that soon became a Beatles trademark, the rising chords of the middle eight that promised some kind of sexual climax, and the tight-but-loose vigour of the playing. And the record ended with a triumphant clang of a guitar chord matched by a whoop from McCartney. No doubt about it, The Beatles had arrived.

MISERY
(John Lennon/Paul McCartney)
Recorded 11, 20 February 1963
Right from the start of their recording career, The Beatles were encouraged by manager Brian Epstein to work as a songwriting factory, turning out hits to order for other artists. By February 1963, their reputation had yet to acquire its later power, and fellow performers more often than not turned them down. Helen Shapiro was offered this Lennon composition the week before The Beatles recorded it themselves, but her management declined. Unabashed, Lennon and McCartney romped through what was supposed to be a declaration of lovelorn anguish like two schoolboys on half-day holiday. Never has a song about misery sounded so damn cheerful.

Trivia note: the sheet music for this song, as copied by Kenny Lynch's early cover version, gives the first line as: "You've been treating me bad, misery." Lennon and McCartney sang something much more universal: "The world's been treating me bad".

ANNA (GO TO HIM)
(Arthur Alexander)
Recorded 11 February 1963
If The Beatles had been allowed more than a day to make this album, they would no doubt have re-recorded the instrumental backing for this rather laboured cover of an Arthur Alexander R&B hit. But there was no faulting Lennon's vocal, which had already hit upon the mixture of romantic disillusionment and supreme self-interest that became his trademark when tackling a love song. It was almost sabotaged, though, by the pedestrian nature of McCartney and Harrison's backing vocals.

CHAINS
(Gerry Goffin/Carole King)
Recorded 11 February 1963
At The Beatles' Decca audition in January 1962, George Harrison threatened to surface as their prime lead vocalist. A year later, he'd already been relegated to cameo appearances, as on this charmingly cheerful cover of The Cookies' New York girl-group hit, which The Beatles had only recently added to their repertoire.

BOYS
(Luther Dixon/Wes Farrell)
Recorded 11 February 1963
If George was restricted to cameos, Ringo Starr's vocal contributions to The Beatles' recording career were purely tokens, to keep his fans from causing a fuss. He bawled his way through The Shirelles' 1960 US hit with enthusiasm if not subtlety, nailing the song in just one take. Presumably nobody in 1963 stopped to wonder why Ringo was singing a lyric that lauded the joys of boys, rather than the opposite sex. The song, a raucous 12-bar rock'n'roller, had been a Beatles standard for a couple of years, Ringo having inherited the number from former drummer Pete Best.

ASK ME WHY
(John Lennon/Paul McCartney)
Recorded 26 November 1962
Unlike Paul McCartney, John Lennon took time to slide into the conventions of pop songwriting. 'Ask Me Why' illustrated what happened before he acquired the knack. From the difficult rhythm of the opening lines to the cut-and-paste structure of the middle section, it was a song that seemed to have been constructed painfully, bar-by-bar, rather than flowing naturally like McCartney's early efforts. Careful study of his role models, like Smokey Robinson and Arthur Alexander, soon rewarded Lennon with a keen grasp of the essentials of composing, though not in time to prevent this number being consigned to the flipside of 'Please Please Me'.

PLEASE PLEASE ME
(John Lennon/Paul McCartney)
Recorded 26 November 1962
Though no evidence remains on tape, The Beatles' original arrangement of 'Please Please Me' was apparently closer to a Roy Orbison ballad than a beat group number. It was attempted during the group's second EMI session in September 1962, George Martin remembering it as "a very dreary song". He suggested that the group soup up the arrangement – something that was done to such effect that it became their first No. 1 at the end of February 1963.

In up tempo form, it became an overt sexual invitation on Lennon's part, and a clear sign that The Beatles were more than just another pop group. Their harmonies, the opening harmonica riff, and Ringo's accomplished drumming testified to a remarkable surge in confidence since their first EMI sessions.

As with 'Love Me Do', there are two different versions of this song on EMI releases. The stereo mix, unavailable on CD, utilised an alternate take on which Lennon and McCartney messed up their vocals. Quite how that blatant a mistake escaped the notice of George Martin remains to be answered.

LOVE ME DO
(John Lennon/Paul McCartney)
Recorded 11 September 1962
Despite the claim on the album cover, this track wasn't the one issued on the first Beatles single. It was the same song, true enough, but not the same recording. At the group's début session, on 4 September 1962, they had struggled through more than 15 takes of 'Love Me Do' before George Martin was remotely satisfied. A week later, they returned to London, to find session drummer Andy White ready to take Ringo Starr's place. Having only recently replaced Pete Best in the band, Ringo must have wondered whether his own days were numbered. White duly handled the sticks on a remake of the song, with Ringo dejectedly

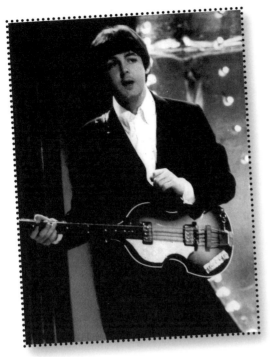

immediately after. McCartney's 'P.S. I Love You' dated from the early months of 1962, and had the slightly forced feel of 'Love Me Do' and 'Ask Me Why' – with only Paul's swoop into the upper register for the last middle section to suggest that any great genius was on display. Like 'Ask Me Why', it qualified for the album solely because it had appeared on the flipside of a single.

BABY IT'S YOU
(Hal David/Burt Bacharach/Barney Williams)
Recorded 11, 20 February 1963
Lennon may have sounded slightly ill-at-ease on his own songs, but with covers, he already had the confidence of a born interpreter. The group's boyish harmonies didn't distract him from giving another Shirelles hit a commanding vocal performance that marked him out as The Beatles' most distinctive voice.

DO YOU WANT TO KNOW A SECRET?
(John Lennon/Paul McCartney)
Recorded 11 February 1963
Given away simultaneously to fellow Brian Epstein protégé Billy J. Kramer (for a hit single), and to George Harrison (for this LP), 'Do You Want To Know A Secret?' was a Lennon composition - inspired by a line he remembered from a Disney song that his mother used to sing. "I thought it would be a good vehicle for George because it only had three notes and he wasn't the best singer in the world," Lennon explained charitably in later years.

A TASTE OF HONEY
(Ric Marlow/Bobby Scott)
Recorded 11 February 1963
In Hamburg and Liverpool, The Beatles were required to work up a sheaf of ballads and standards, which would melt the hearts of even the most anti-rock audience they would be forced to entertain. McCartney was the Beatle with the heritage in pre-Elvis pop, and it fell to him to perform the group's token demonstration of 'sophistication' – an American song recorded most notably by

banging a tambourine on the sidelines. For reasons that remain unclear, it was the initial version of 'Love Me Do' which appeared as the group's first 45. But when their album was assembled, George Martin elected to use the Andy White recording instead – presumably because the tape of the single had been sent overseas to an EMI subsidiary. Later in 1963, the decision was made to use the White take on all future pressings of the single, as well; and from then until 1982, Ringo's recording début with The Beatles remained officially unavailable.

The song itself was a genuine Lennon/McCartney collaboration, its plodding beat enlivened by Lennon's harmonica solo. That was a gimmick he picked up from Bruce Channel's spring 1962 hit, 'Hey Baby', and proceeded to use many times over the next two years. Without the gimmick, 'Love Me Do' hadn't previously been regarded as one of the highlights of the group's original repertoire.

P.S. I LOVE YOU
(John Lennon/Paul McCartney)
Recorded 11 September 1962
There's a clear division in The Beatles' early work between the songs they wrote before 'Please Please Me', and the ones that came

Lenny Welch, but fast becoming a favourite among sedate jazzmen and big bands around the world.

In retrospect, the inclusion of this song seems laughable – the Stones would never have made such a blatant cop-out – but in McCartney's capable hands, 'A Taste Of Honey' became another slice of Beatle music. The group didn't much care for the song, though: when they performed it live, Lennon invariably changed the chorus to 'A Waste Of Money'.

THERE'S A PLACE
(John Lennon/Paul McCartney)
Recorded 11 February 1963
Forget the theory that John Lennon only started singing about himself when he starting taking drugs. Listen to the words of this cheery beat tune, and you'll find his first piece of self-analysis: "There's a place where I can go, when I feel low, when I feel blue. And it's my mind, and there's no time, when I'm alone." No-one – not even Bob Dylan – was writing songs like that in 1963. But nobody told John Lennon that. The result: the first self-conscious rock song, beating The Beach Boys' equally self-obsessed 'In My Room' by several months.

TWIST AND SHOUT
(Bert Russell/Phil Medley)
Recorded 11 February 1963
"I couldn't sing the damn thing, I was just screaming." So said John Lennon, about the first take of the final song recorded during The Beatles' marathon 11 February session. His voice shot by the rigours of the day's schedule, and unable to fall upon the twin crutches of pills and booze which had fuelled The Beatles on their night-long gigs in Hamburg, Lennon simply shredded his vocal cords in the interests of rock'n'roll.

Until McCartney matched it with 'Long Tall Sally' a year later, this was the supreme Beatles rocker – a cover, ironically enough, of a tune that the Isley Brothers had rescued from an abysmal original recording by Phil Spector's charges, The Top Notes. In that one take, Lennon cut Britain's best rock'n'roll record to date, and the band kept pace with him, right down to Ringo's exultant flourish on the drums as The Beatles reached home.

WITH THE BEATLES

Parlophone CDP7 46436 2
Released November 1963

Four months after they released their début album, The Beatles began work on their follow-up. By the time it was released, in November 1963, the group were the hottest product in British show-business. Second time around, there was no need to sell the album on the reputation of a recent hit single: with Christmas on the horizon, EMI knew the fans would buy anything The Beatles released. What they didn't realise, though, was that *With The Beatles* would prove to be such a giant step beyond their hastily assembled début.

The cover artwork immediately revealed that more thought had gone into this album than its predecessor. Whereas *Please Please Me* used the standard smiling pop pose as its cover design, *With The Beatles* boasted a much artier Robert Freeman photo, with the group's heads arranged in careful line, shot in half-light. It emerged later that this trick was simply borrowed from much earlier pictures of the group, taken by the German photographer Astrid Kirchherr. But as far as the public was concerned, the artwork was startlingly new.

Musically, too, *With The Beatles* announced that the revolution had arrived. The Beatles kept faithfully to the same mix of originals and outside songs that had filled their first long-player, but they were already beginning to play the studio as an instrument. On *Please Please Me*, they'd briefly discovered the potential joys of overdubbing. Now, with more time on their hands, they went to town. "The first set of tricks was double-tracking on the second album," John Lennon admitted many years later. "We were told we could do it, and that really set the ball rolling. We double-tracked ourselves off the second album." And they did it without sacrificing an ounce of the freshness and exuberance that had become The Beatles' hallmark – audible most clearly on the mono mix of the record, which was again favoured by George Martin for the CD release.

IT WON'T BE LONG
(John Lennon/Paul McCartney)
Recorded 30 July 1963
Throughout their career, The Beatles never lost sight of the importance of having hit singles. Certainly in 1963, their continued production of hits was their passport to the future, and they blatantly concocted potential chartbusters as and when required.

Lennon and McCartney competed for the honour of winning an A-side, with only pride and prestige at stake – the songwriting royalties for all their songs were split equally between them, after all.

Like 'She Loves You', the single they recorded a month earlier, Lennon's 'It Won't Be Long' was built around a 'yeah, yeah' chorus. Two singles with the same gimmick would have become a straitjacket, so 'It Won't Be Long' was 'relegated' to the position of lead track on the album, where it was every bit as effective a hook as 'I Saw Her Standing There' had been on *Please Please Me*.

ALL I'VE GOT TO DO
(John Lennon/Paul McCartney)
Recorded 11 September 1963
Compare this song to 'Ask Me Why', written around a year earlier, and the rapid maturity in Lennon's songwriting is immediately apparent. John singled out Arthur Alexander (the man who'd written 'Anna', plus several other Beatles stage favourites) as his prime inspiration for this soulful ballad. He stretched the word 'I' over seven syllables in the opening line, using all the melismatic flair of Sam Cooke or Jackie Wilson, and proved how well he understood the power of melody by shifting into a higher register for

the final chorus as a cry of passion. It was a remarkably assured performance, which would have been beyond anyone else in the group at this early stage of their career.

ALL MY LOVING
(John Lennon/Paul McCartney)
Recorded 30 July 1963

While Lennon was converting emotion into music, McCartney was writing unforgettable melodies. Classical students claim there's a tune of Tchaikovsky's buried in 'All My Loving', but it's an irrelevant point, as the finished song is pure Beatles – the most commercial song they recorded in 1963 that wasn't issued as a single. Often maligned as musicians, The Beatles prove their worth on this song: Harrison's lead break is beautifully tidy and restrained, while Lennon's lightning rhythm guitar playing is the powerhouse of the arrangement.

DON'T BOTHER ME
(George Harrison)
Recorded 12 September 1963

"That was the first song that I wrote, as an exercise to see if I could write a song," George Harrison confessed in his autobiography, *I Me Mine*. "I don't think it's particularly good." Faced by two prolific bandmates, Harrison was envious of their ability and their royalty cheques. Liverpool friend Bill Harry nagged George on the subject while he was ill in bed during a Beatles tour, and Harrison responded by turning his reaction into a slightly clumsy but reasonably accomplished song. Interestingly, it didn't sound anything like his own musical heroes, Carl Perkins or Goffin & King, but came out as a facsimile of what Lennon & McCartney were writing – just as beat groups across the country were doing in their bedrooms.

LITTLE CHILD
(John Lennon/Paul McCartney)
Recorded 12 September, 3 October 1963

Even The Beatles occasionally sounded like tired hacks, though this early in their career, they could always summon the enthusiasm to hide their lack of inspiration. Five years later, this contrived but chirpy pop tune would have been classed as bubblegum. But on *With The Beatles*, Lennon and McCartney's dynamic vocals and Lennon's chest-expanding harmonica solo turned a piece of hackwork into 106 seconds of pure energy.

TILL THERE WAS YOU
(Meredith Willson)
Recorded 30 July 1963

Standards time again, as Paul filled the 'A Taste Of Honey' slot with the hit song from the Broadway musical, *The Music Man*. He sang the song as if he meant every word, and George Harrison contributed an accomplished acoustic guitar solo – so accomplished, in fact, that some cynics have questioned whether he actually played it. But the solo on the rendition they recorded onstage in Hamburg was equally dextrous, so unless they'd smuggled a session man into the Star-Club, George was the man.

PLEASE MR. POSTMAN
(Dobbin/Garrett/Garman/Brianbert)
Recorded 30 July 1963

During 1963, the American stable of Motown labels, owned by Berry Gordy, began to enjoy regular distribution for their youthful soul records in Britain. The Beatles were instant fans, to the extent that three of the tracks on *With The Beatles* were covers of recent Motown hits.

On their first album, 'Chains' and 'Anna' had been enthusiastic renditions of outside songs, without threatening to become definitive. On 'Twist And Shout', however, and again with The Marvelettes' 'Please Mr. Postman', Lennon's performance was so magical that it made the original sound like an imitation. The Beatles tightened up The Marvelettes' vocal arrangement, while Lennon's lead dripped with authority and self-confidence. It was a thrilling conclusion to the first side of the album, which had already seen the group tackling everything from soul to rock to balladry with ease.

ROLL OVER BEETHOVEN
(Chuck Berry)
Recorded 30 July 1963

Even before there was a Beatles, Lennon, McCartney and Harrison had been performing this Chuck Berry rock'n'roll standard from 1956. During 1961, the song passed from John's hands to George, who also had to double as lead guitarist – fine in the studio, when he could overdub the solo, but prone to being more erratic onstage. Despite their heritage as a rock'n'roll band, The Beatles sounded strangely uncomfortable the first time they cut an authentic American rock song in the studio, hurrying the pace to the point that George had problems fitting all the words into each line.

 ### HOLD ME TIGHT
(John Lennon/Paul McCartney)
Recorded 12 September 1963

During the sessions for their first album, The Beatles had taped and then abandoned a version of this self-composed beat number – and the tape was subsequently destroyed. If the take that *was* considered good enough for release is anything to go by, the original must have been disastrous, as this remake has a McCartney vocal that strays distressingly off key, to the point that neighbouring dogs are likely to howl with distress. Only a handful of Beatles recordings can be said to be below par, but this is one of them.

 ### YOU REALLY GOT A HOLD ON ME
(William 'Smokey' Robinson)
Recorded 18 July 1963

Not so 'You Really Got A Hold On Me', Lennon's second brilliant hijacking of a Motown song. Sublime though The Miracles' original is, it's easily outclassed by The Beatles' effortless interpretation. John's vocal could be used as a dictionary definition of reluctant infatuation, while the decision to dramatise the phrase 'tied up' with a repeated break in the rhythm was a stroke of genius. The response vocals challenged George's limited range to the hilt, but sheer enthusiasm won the day, as The Beatles stole another American song for their own.

 ### I WANNA BE YOUR MAN
(John Lennon/Paul McCartney)
Recorded 11, 12, 30 September, 3, 23 October 1963

By the time The Beatles finished work on this song, they knew that The Rolling Stones were issuing it as their second single. As the story goes, Stones manager Andrew Oldham spotted Lennon and McCartney in a London street, bundled them into his car, and requested a song for his new band.
The Beatles played the Stones the chorus of 'I Wanna Be Your Man', then went into another office to finish the bridge – emerging an hour or so later to display the completed effort to their visibly impressed juniors.
The Stones played the song as an R&B tune; The Beatles gave it to Ringo, whereupon it became his usual concert showcase for the next three years. Amusingly, on the road Ringo usually managed to forget that the song had all of two verses, and ended up repeating the first one over and over again.

 ### DEVIL IN HER HEART
(Richard Drapkin)
Recorded 18 July 1963

Aficionados of the American girl-group sound, The Beatles borrowed this tune from The Donays – probably the most obscure song they ever covered in the studio. It was George Harrison's choice, and he responded with an energetic if not always convincing

lead vocal, backed by the superb chorus harmonies of Lennon and McCartney.

 NOT A SECOND TIME
(John Lennon/Paul McCartney)
Recorded 11 September 1963
'Not A Second Time' reinforced John Lennon's status as the most adventurous of The Beatles when it came to composing. The rhythm of this piano-based song seemed to be on the verge of imminent collapse, but whereas this was a flaw on 'Ask Me Why', it suited the emotional disruption of the lyric this time around. Usually, John sounded completely in control of every romantic situation, even when the lyrics asserted otherwise, but everything about 'Not A Second Time' announced that Lennon was simply a pawn in her game – predating the more blatant emotional masochism of 'Norwegian Wood' by two years.

 **MONEY
(THAT'S WHAT I WANT)**
(Berry Gordy/Janie Bradford)
Recorded 18, 30 July, 30 September 1963
The third and last of the Motown classics moulded into pure John Lennon songs, Barrett Strong's hit 'Money' took on a new life in this interpretation. The tentative delivery of the original was knocked off the pavement by Lennon's steamroller vocal, every bit as tonsil-shredding as 'Twist And Shout' had been. As on 'I Wanna Be Your Man', George Martin came into his own on keyboards: on the earlier track, he'd played Hammond organ, while this time he supplied the piano which was the root of the song.

But the piano wasn't the only difference between this performance, and the far less convincing version of the same tune at The Beatles' January 1962 audition. At Decca, Lennon had simply been singing Barrett Strong's song. At EMI nearly two years later, he was living it, howling the lyrics as a piece of psychotherapy. And as many critics have noticed, he widened the context of the song by adding a single, throwaway phrase to the final choruses: "I wanna be free," he cried, a prisoner to the passion that the rest of the song denied.

Trivial note: mono and stereo mixes of this song once again have slightly different Lennon vocals. And once again, the definitive version is included on the mono-only CD.

A HARD DAY'S NIGHT

Parlophone CDP7 46437 2
Released July 1964

The transition from pop stars to film actors was already a well-trodden route by 1964. The pop business hadn't yet cottoned on to the potential riches of international merchandising, but a hasty and cheap black-and-white movie was the next best thing. It also enabled The Beatles to be seen in towns and countries that they had no intention of visiting in person. It's probably not a coincidence that The Beatles staged only one further lengthy UK tour after the *A Hard Day's Night* film was released.

Although the film grossed millions of dollars in America, it was originally conceived as an entirely British phenomenon. The Beatles had been approached in the autumn of 1963, at which stage their fame had scarcely spread beyond their native land. Hence the low budget and black-and-white film: if United Artists had realised the movie would ever be shown in America, they would almost certainly have ensured it was made in colour.

"We were a bit infuriated by the glibness of it and the shittiness of the dialogue," John Lennon complained in 1970. But Alun Owen's script was a work of remarkable realism by the previous standards of British pop films. The Beatles played caricatures of themselves, in caricatures of their everyday situations – on the road, in concert, and rehearsing for a TV show. Several scenes in the movie featured the group's earlier hits, but the contract called for the band to supply director Dick Lester with seven new songs; and EMI soon made the decision to release a soundtrack album, which would feature the film songs alongside another batch of new recordings.

Returning from their first visit to the States, The Beatles were faced with a ridiculously tight schedule. They had less than two weeks to write and record the songs for the film; then, during the subsequent shooting, they had to knock off the remaining numbers for the album. If ever there was an excuse for recording cover versions, this was it: instead, for the first and only time in The Beatles' career, John Lennon and Paul McCartney wrote the entire album between them. "Between them" was hardly correct, in fact, as Lennon contributed no fewer than ten of the thirteen tracks, dominating the LP more than any one Beatle was ever allowed to do thereafter.

Once again, The Beatles okayed the mono mix of the album, and then left George Martin to prepare a hasty stereo version; and once again, Martin utilised the mono tracks on EMI's CD release.

A HARD DAY'S NIGHT
(John Lennon/Paul McCartney)
Recorded 16 April 1964
Ringo Starr, recalling some wordplay of John Lennon's, inadvertently christened The Beatles' first film, saving it from the fate of going into history as *Beatlemania*. Once the title was fixed, The Beatles had to provide a song to match, and quickly: within a week, Lennon (with help from McCartney on the middle section) had prepared this sturdy piece of songwriting-to-order.

The unforgettable opening – George Harrison striking a G suspended 4th chord on his 12-string Rickenbacker – took a few takes to get right, but eventually made this record one of the few that can be recognised by its opening two seconds alone.

For the first time, Lennon and McCartney settled into the pattern they would follow for the rest of the group's lifetime, each man singing the section of the song he'd written. Fans had an early chance to distinguish between McCartney's in-born lyrical optimism, and Lennon's grudging cynicism. And there was another revolution in the air, as The Beatles discovered the joys of fading their singles out, rather than ending in a single climactic chord. After double-tracking and overdubbing, fade-outs became the next favourite toy in The Beatles' studio cupboard.

I SHOULD HAVE KNOWN BETTER
(John Lennon/Paul McCartney)
Recorded 26 February 1964
Even when he was functioning as an admitted hack writer, composing Beatles songs to a tight deadline, the John Lennon of 1964 succeeded effortlessly in concocting memorable melody lines. 'I Should Have Known Better' was built around the simplest of two-chord rhythms, with puffing harmonica to match, but it had an effervescence that touched everything The Beatles recorded in the heady spring of 1964.

IF I FELL
(John Lennon/Paul McCartney)
Recorded 27 February 1964
In 1964, no-one had yet noticed any split in songwriting styles between Lennon and McCartney, so this delicate and melodic ballad was greeted as just another Beatles song. Only in retrospect was it seen as early proof that there was more to John Lennon's armoury than rock'n'roll, acid imagery and cynical wit. In structural terms, this was by far the most complex song John had written to date, and its terrifyingly high harmony line briefly floored McCartney, whose voice cracked under the strain on the mix released on the stereo album. On the CD and the

On the set of 'A Hard Days Night', 1964

mono LP, however, Paul walked the tightrope without missing a note.

 ### I'M HAPPY JUST TO DANCE WITH YOU
(John Lennon/Paul McCartney)
Recorded 1 March 1964

John Lennon wrote this song, but thought so little of it that he passed it over for George Harrison to sing – The Beatles' lead guitarist having failed to meet with group approval for any of his latest efforts at songwriting. Lennon would no doubt have regarded the song's theme as too tame for his more rugged image – though he *had* just reached the top of the American charts by saying he wanted to hold his girl's hand – but Harrison's charmingly naïve vocal delivery caught the mood of the song perfectly. As usual, The Beatles patched up the thinnest of material with a superlatively commercial arrangement.

 ### AND I LOVE HER
(John Lennon/Paul McCartney)
Recorded 27 February 1964

Even under pressure, The Beatles refused to settle for anything but the best when recording this McCartney love song for his girlfriend of the time, actress Jane Asher. For three days running, they attempted different arrangements, eventually nailing it in the same three-hour session in which they cut 'Tell Me Why'. Simple, evocative and gentler than any Lennon/McCartney song they'd recorded up to that point, 'And I Love Her' was treated to a predominantly acoustic arrangement.

Trivia note: several different edits of this song were released in different parts of the world, the variations coming in the number of times the closing guitar riff was repeated.

 ### TELL ME WHY
(John Lennon/Paul McCartney)
Recorded 27 February 1964

Another delicious piece of hackwork, 'Tell Me Why' was almost Beatles by numbers – a beefy chorus, a wonderfully cool Lennon vocal, even a self-mocking falsetto section towards the end, and all wrapped up in a fraction over two minutes.

 ### CAN'T BUY ME LOVE
(John Lennon/Paul McCartney)
Recorded 29 January 1964

The Beatles' first single of 1964 was taped almost as an afterthought, at the end of the group's one and only EMI studio session outside Britain. Their visit to Pathé Marconi Studios in Paris had been arranged so they could reluctantly concoct German-language versions of two of their biggest hits. With less than an hour remaining, the group cut this

Paul McCartney song in just four takes – completely reworking the arrangement between their first, R&B-styled attempt and the more polished final version.

'Can't Buy Me Love' came closer than any of The Beatles' singles thus far, to matching the rock'n'roll music that they'd been playing since the mid-Fifties. Its lyrics neatly reversed the theme of 'Money' from their previous album, and the track gave George Harrison a splendid opportunity to show off his guitar skills. He added his solo as an overdub, having already proved on that tentative first take that unrehearsed improvisation wasn't exactly his forte.

ANY TIME AT ALL
(John Lennon/Paul McCartney)
Recorded 2 June 1964
Tight for time, as they were at every session in 1964, The Beatles began recording this song before John Lennon had finished writing it. Thankfully, they eventually realised the fact, though not before they'd attempted seven takes. Lennon added a gentle middle section to this otherwise tough rocker during their afternoon tea-break, and the song was in the can well before bedtime.

I'LL CRY INSTEAD
(John Lennon/Paul McCartney)
Recorded 1 June 1964
Though The Beatles' sound is commonly regarded as a mix of American rock'n'roll, pop and R&B, country music became a vital part of the equation from 1964. Under a constant barrage of encouragement from Ringo Starr, the rest of the group started listening to records by Buck Owens, George Jones and other Nashville stars, and the influence began to filter through to the songwriting – particularly Lennon's.

For such a simple song, 'I'll Cry Instead' proved tough to record. Eventually The Beatles gave up trying to perform it live, and divided it into two sections, which George Martin edited together as the final record. Its divided nature explains why it was so easy for the song to be artificially extended for the US album release.

'I'll Cry Instead' inadvertently spawned a genre of Beatles and solo songs: lyrics which had Lennon, usually the masterful romantic hero, sitting head in hands, indulging himself in an ocean of self-pity. For much of the last decade of his life, this pose of guilt and sorrow became something of a straitjacket around his songwriting.

THINGS WE SAID TODAY
(John Lennon/Paul McCartney)
Recorded 2 June 1964
McCartney's contributions to *A Hard Day's Night* may have been few in number, but they were impressively strong. Like John, Paul was experimenting with writing around minor chords, and quickly realised that they lent themselves to lyrics that were reflective rather than celebratory. John took the formula a stage further by writing almost all his songs for this album in the key of G.

WHEN I GET HOME
(John Lennon/Paul McCartney)
Recorded 2 June 1964

Like much of his work on this album, 'When I Get Home' doesn't bear too much critical examination – except that from a hastily assembled song, The Beatles were able to make a state-of-the-art pop record by 1964 standards. The track began as if in mid-performance, with a catchy vocal hook, and then romped along merrily enough for another two minutes, without ever suggesting that Lennon meant a word he was singing.

YOU CAN'T DO THAT
(John Lennon/Paul McCartney)
Recorded 25 February, 22 May 1964

Of all the songs on this album, John Lennon was proudest of this. Not at all coincidentally, it was the roughest, least polished number he'd recorded up to that date. It was blatantly inspired by the R&B songs coming out of Memphis, and (as rock critic Lester Bangs wrote years later), "built on one of the bitterest and most iron-indestructible riffs ever conceived". Lennon handled the lead guitar himself, hammering out a wiry solo which grew into a furious flurry of chords, totally unlike anything that George Harrison had performed on the rest of the album.

I'LL BE BACK
(John Lennon/Paul McCartney)
Recorded 1 June 1964

At the end of a record that was a brilliant collection of sometimes less than brilliant songs, John Lennon's 'I'll Be Back' harked back to the strange construction of some of his earlier efforts. Like 'Ask Me Why' and 'All I've Got To Do', it was pure Lennon, owing nothing to what was happening in the pop world around him. For the moment, he hadn't hit on the knack of combining these unsettling melodies with words that carried any emotional weight, so 'I'll Be Back' ended up another superb song about a fictional romance. But the moment of liberation wasn't far away.

BEATLES FOR SALE

Parlophone CDP7 46438 2
Released November 1964

It's been noted before that the tired, glazed expressions of the four Beatles on the cover of their fourth album was a simple response to circumstances. Unlike the pampered stars of the Nineties, they had no chance between 1963 and 1965 to bask in their wealth and fame. They toured almost non-stop throughout 1963, breaking only for an occasional week's rest – during which they were expected to write and record, tape radio shows for the BBC, and meet the press.

1964 began the same way: two weeks in a Christmas Show at the Astoria, Finsbury Park, then three weeks in France, a fortnight in the States, a week to start work on the soundtrack to *A Hard Day's Night*, and then an intensive two months of filming. Aside from a holiday in May, their year followed this hectic course right to the end, encompassing a second visit to America, a tour of Australia and New Zealand, a quick jaunt across Europe, summer seaside dates in Engand, and finally a five-week series of UK concerts in October and November.

Into that schedule had to be squeezed the recording of the aptly titled *Beatles For Sale*. It was thrown together on off-days between concerts over a period of almost three months, so it wasn't altogether surprising when the record seemed to take a step back from the stylistic unity of their earlier LPs.

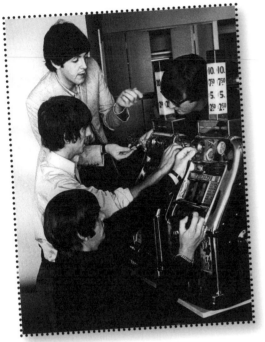

The return to a blend of original material and covers hinted at the strain the group were under; the generally perfunctory nature of their covers rammed the message home. But the eight Lennon/McCartney songs on the album displayed a growing maturity, and betrayed a new set of influences which would very soon whisk The Beatles beyond the reach of their beat group contemporaries.

One of the prime inspirations for the *Beatles For Sale* songs was country music – first noted on 'I'll Cry Instead' on the third album, and a constant point of reference through their work in 1965. The group had grown up on rockabilly, itself deeply rooted in country, but it took Ringo's continual championing of Nashville's contemporary stars to inspire songs like 'I Don't Want To Spoil The Party' and 'Baby's In Black'.

More lasting was the creative impact of Bob Dylan, to whom The Beatles had been listening since the end of 1963. At first, Lennon, McCartney and Harrison picked up on the style and sound of Dylan's records. Once the American singer had introduced them to the pleasures of dope, however, they began to respond to the artistic freedom that his songwriting made possible. Without

Dylan, or drugs, the path from *Beatles For Sale* to *Revolver* might have been too tangled for The Beatles to follow.

NO REPLY
(John Lennon/Paul McCartney)
Recorded 30 September 1964
"I remember Dick James coming to me after we did this one," John Lennon recalled shortly before his death, "and saying, 'You're getting much better now – this is a complete story'. Apparently, before that he thought my songs tended to sort of wander off." Music publisher Dick James soon found his own tastes outstripped by the adventurous spirit of The Beatles; by 1966, no-one was looking to their songs for "a complete story". But James was right on one score: even though the song was plainly a piece of romantic fiction, it had a watertight structure and a powerful melody, and The Beatles skills as vocal arrangers were on open display. On tracks like this, *Beatles For Sale* sounds like the pinnacle of British beat music, polished to an icy sheen in preparation for being shattered by The Beatles and the Stones, among others, over the next 12 months.

'No Reply' would go on to become the favoured track for owners of answerphones to record on their machines 20 years later.

I'M A LOSER
(John Lennon/Paul McCartney)
Recorded 14 August 1964
Looking back at this song, Lennon recognised it as a milestone. "Instead of projecting myself into a situation," he explained, "I would try to express what I felt about myself. I think it was Dylan who helped me realise that." And the Dylan influence was obvious in other ways, too, from the acoustic guitars powering the song to the use of the harmonica as a statement of passion.

Like 'I'll Cry Instead', 'I'm A Loser' soon drifted into naked self-pity – and anyway, the raw emotions of the song were dressed up in a strong pop format. But for a while, at least, Lennon was delighted at his discovery that he could channel his innermost thoughts into music, as well as the free-form linguistic pleasures of his books. As for the song's message, Lennon summed up his ambivalence perfectly in 1970: "Part of me thinks I'm a loser and part of me thinks I'm God Almighty."

BABY'S IN BLACK

(John Lennon/Paul McCartney)
Recorded 11 August 1964
A heavy waltz with a vague country influence, 'Baby's In Black' was one of the last genuine Lennon/McCartney collaborations – composed during a head-to-head session over acoustic guitars, the way they'd been doing since the late Fifties. Its rather maudlin lyric suggests that it might originally have been a Lennon idea, but the performance is pure Beatles – and pure 1964. Numbers like this, which invested a little romantic difficulty with the importance of a world crisis, gradually faded from The Beatles' repertoire over the next twelve months.

ROCK AND ROLL MUSIC

(Chuck Berry)
Recorded 18 October 1964
Not for the first time, The Beatles took a classic American record and cut it to shreds. Chuck Berry's original Chess recording – which set up rock'n'roll as an antidote to boredom with every other musical style – only hinted at the raw power of the genre. With Lennon, McCartney and producer George Martin trebling up the keyboard part, The Beatles turned every hint of that promise into reality. Berry wrote and performed brilliant rock songs, but it took Lennon to sing this one the way it was meant to be heard.

I'LL FOLLOW THE SUN

(John Lennon/Paul McCartney)
Recorded 18 October 1964
As early as 1960, the pre-Beatles Liverpool band, The Quarry Men, were experimenting with a tentative arrangement of this McCartney song, making it just about the earliest Lennon/McCartney composition which they ever recorded. Simple but effortlessly melodic, it proves that Paul was

born with the gift of writing memorable tunes, while John Lennon's ability as a tunesmith evolved only with practice.

MR. MOONLIGHT

(Roy Lee Johnson)
Recorded 18 October 1964
On Friday August 14, 1964, The Beatles recorded one of the strongest rock'n'roll performances of their career. Sadly, this wasn't it. But it could have been: the group eventually decided to jettison their electrifying interpretation of Little Willie John's R&B standard, 'Leave My Kitten Alone' (which remains officially unreleased) in favour of this bizarre, mediocre version of another song from black America, Dr. Feelgood & The Interns' 'Mr. Moonlight'.

John Lennon had taken to the song immediately he heard it, and it was swiftly incorporated into their Cavern repertoire. But the recorded version, which required two separate sessions to 'perfect', had none of the spontaneity or humour of their live performances. It shambled along rather apologetically, and the half-hearted vocal support from McCartney and Harrison left Lennon's impassioned lead sounding faintly ridiculous. Asked to pick the weakest track The Beatles ever recorded, a fair percentage of fans would opt for 'Mr. Moonlight'.

KANSAS CITY / HEY, HEY, HEY, HEY

(Jerry Leiber/Mike Stoller; Richard Penniman)
Recorded 18 October 1964
Like Little Richard before them, The Beatles covered Leiber & Stoller's early Fifties R&B song and added a frenetic call-and-response routine to the end. Richard had already reworked the original arrangement to his own specifications, and Paul McCartney followed that revamp to the letter. For this recording, The Beatles simply blasted the song the way they did on stage. This late 1964 rendition may be tighter than the performance from December 1962 captured on the *1962 Live Recordings* CD, but the approach is almost identical.

EIGHT DAYS A WEEK
(John Lennon/Paul McCartney)
Recorded 6, 18 October 1964

A few months earlier, The Beatles had been delighted by the discovery that they could fade their recordings out. Now they went a stage further, and made pop history by fading this song *in*. Ironically, the track had a conventional ending – though that was edited onto the tape after the basic recording was finished.

Like 'Baby's In Black', 'Eight Days A Week' was a Lennon/McCartney collaboration, though again with Lennon's influence to the fore. It would have made a perfect hit single, and may even have been written with that idea in mind, as its title obviously has some link with the working name of their second movie, scripts for which had already been submitted by October 1964: *Eight Arms To Hold You*.

HONEY DON'T
(Carl Perkins)
Recorded 26 October 1964

The second change came with this Carl Perkins rockabilly favourite – traditionally sung by John Lennon on stage, but passed over amiably to Ringo Starr as his token vocal cameo on the album. The switch gave Ringo the chance to utter one of his trademark invitations to George as Harrison launched into the guitar solo.

EVERY LITTLE THING
(John Lennon/Paul McCartney)
Recorded 30 September 1964

Though it's one of the least well-known songs they ever recorded, John Lennon's 'Every Little Thing' was as impressive as anything on *Beatles For Sale*, with all the trademarks of their 1964 work – a laconic, yet affectionate Lennon vocal, some Harrison guitar that looked forward to the as-yet-unrecorded sound of The Byrds, and a

> ## "People like me are aware of their so called genius at ten, eight, nine... I always wondered, why has nobody discovered me? In school,. Didn't they see that I was cleverer than anybody in this school?" – John

WORDS OF LOVE
(Buddy Holly)
Recorded 18 October 1964

Two standards from The Beatles' pre-fame live repertoire went through a change of ownership during these sessions. Back at the Cavern in 1961 and 1962, it had been Lennon and Harrison who shared the close harmony vocals on this Buddy Holly song – the only number by one of their favourite writers that they ever recorded. On the record, though, which kept strictly to Holly's arrangement, McCartney elbowed Harrison out of the limelight. Nevertheless, George's contribution – the lovely chiming guitar licks throughout – is pretty impressive.

stunningly melodic chorus that stuck instantly in the brain. Ripe for rediscovery by someone like Tom Petty (and covered in 1969 by Yes, of all people), it justifies the claim that almost every Lennon/McCartney song on The Beatles' early albums would have made a convincing hit single.

I DON'T WANT TO SPOIL THE PARTY
(John Lennon/Paul McCartney)
Recorded 29 September 1964

Influenced partly by rockabilly, partly by mainstream country, and partly by the general air of melancholy that seeped into several of his songs in 1964, John Lennon

wrote this vaguely self-pitying account of romantic disappointment. Proof of The Beatles' increasing sophistication as arrangers came with the middle eight, on which Paul's harmony moved subtly away from the simple line he might have sung a year earlier.

WHAT YOU'RE DOING
(John Lennon/Paul McCartney)
Recorded 26 October 1964

With 'I'll Follow The Sun' having been written in the late Fifties, 'What You're Doing' proved to be Paul McCartney's only new solo contribution to the *Beatles For Sale* album. After out-stripping Lennon as a songwriter in the group's early years, Paul was now going through a fallow period, just when John was at his most prolific. A couple of years later, the situation would be dramatically reversed.

The song itself was built around a simple guitar riff, but as often proves to be the case, simplicity proved difficult to perfect. The Beatles devoted two sessions to taping the song before junking the results and then re-cutting it on the last possible day of recording.

EVERYBODY'S TRYING TO BE MY BABY
(Carl Perkins)
Recorded 18 October 1964

Cut in a single, echo-swamped take, this second Carl Perkins cover allowed George Harrison the chance to pay his respects to one of his all-time musical heroes. The combination of the disorientating echo and Harrison's scouse drawl made Perkins' overtly Tennessean lyrics almost impossible to decipher: without access to a lyric sheet, in fact, Harrison may simply have been reproducing the sound of what the American rocker was singing, rather than exactly the same words. Either way, it made for a strange ending to a disjointed album.

HELP!

Parlophone CDP7 46439 2
Released August 1965

A vastly increased budget, colour stock, exotic overseas locations, and a lavish publicity campaign – The Beatles' second feature film had everything except the one quality which had made its predecessor so successful, realism. John Lennon later dismissed *Help!* as "bullshit", which was unjustly harsh. But though its script crackled with jokes and The Beatles wisecracked their way through the full 100 minutes, complete with striking musical interludes, *Help!* didn't have the magic of *A Hard Day's Night*.

That's not to say it wasn't a successful movie by its own lights. It grossed an impressive figure, in Britain and around the world, and it stands up today as a glossy, semi-satirical period piece, perfectly in keeping with the wacky Beatles image that the world initially mistook for the real thing. By 1965, though, The Beatles were losing interest in refuelling their image. Through the use of soft drugs, they were beginning to glimpse an artistic purpose beyond Beatlemania and the production-line of hit records. John Lennon, in particular, managed in 1965 to find his own lyrical voice, and started to use The Beatles as a vehicle to express his increasingly confused feelings about his role in the group, and his personal relationships.

In one important respect, the preparations for *Help!* were identical to those for the previous year's movie. The decision was

HELP!
(John Lennon/Paul McCartney)
Recorded 13 April 1965

"The only true songs I ever wrote were 'Help!' and 'Strawberry Fields'," John Lennon claimed in December 1970. "They were the ones I really wrote from experience and not projecting myself into a situation and writing a nice story about it, which I always found phoney. The lyric is as good now as it was then. It makes me feel secure to know that I was that sensible, aware of myself back then. But I don't like the recording that much, we did it too fast, to try to be commercial." In the same week he gave that interview, Lennon actually attempted to re-record the song, slowing it to funereal pace as a piano ballad. His efforts merely exposed what a smooth and powerful piece of work The Beatles' rendition was – to the point that the surface sheen and production expertise successfully disguised any hint of authentic anguish in Lennon's vocal. The record turned out nothing more or less than a perfect Beatles single, and an ideal theme tune for their movie.

made in advance to divide the 'soundtrack' album between one side of songs that would appear in the film, and another of non-movie tunes. And as before, the film songs had to be completed before the shooting began. The Beatles' flight for the Bahamas left on February 22: just seven days earlier, the group arrived for their first movie session at Abbey Road. By the time their plane set off for their film location, they had recorded no fewer than 11 songs — although two of these, 'If You've Got Trouble' and 'That Means A Lot', were destined to remain unreleased.

At that stage, the film was still untitled, and it wasn't until The Beatles had returned to Britain at the end of March that they were informed that it would be called *Help!*. A title song was commissioned and delivered almost overnight, while the soundtrack album was eventually completed during breaks in the filming, just six weeks before its release date.

Trivia note: the single and LP versions of this song feature slightly different Lennon vocals.

THE NIGHT BEFORE
(John Lennon/Paul McCartney)
Recorded 17 February 1965

Studio finesse was second nature to The Beatles by February 1965 – and so too was commercial songwriting. John Lennon's first flirtation with electric piano (which was a constant feature on this album) was the only novel moment on this fluent and ultra-appealing McCartney pop song.

YOU'VE GOT TO HIDE YOUR LOVE AWAY
(John Lennon/Paul McCartney)
Recorded 18 February 1965

After the tentative Dylan-isms of 'I'm A Loser', John Lennon made his debt to the American singer-songwriter entirely clear on this song. Too self-pitying for Dylan himself, it was nonetheless a piece of personal expression for its composer, who still automatically equated writing from the heart with songs about romantic disappointment.

For two musical reasons, this track stood out from earlier Beatles recordings. First of all, it was an entirely acoustic performance from an electric rock'n'roll band. Secondly, it featured a guest musician from outside The Beatles' circle. George Martin had been adding keyboards to the group's records from the start, but this song featured a flute solo by arranger John Scott, though his contribution wasn't noted on the sleeve.

I NEED YOU
(George Harrison)
Recorded 15, 16 February 1965
For only the second time, The Beatles recorded a George Harrison composition – earlier efforts like 'You'll Know What To Do' having been rejected by Lennon/McCartney. An otherwise unexceptional song was punctuated by brief, slightly hesitant bursts of guitar noise, controlled by a foot pedal soon to become famous as the wah-wah.

ANOTHER GIRL
(John Lennon/Paul McCartney)
Recorded 15, 16 February 1965
Though the songs themselves broke few boundaries, the recording sessions for the *Help!* album found The Beatles gradually exploring new techniques and instrumental combinations. On his own 'Another Girl', for instance, Paul played the twisting lead guitar line – as he did on 'Ticket To Ride', recorded at the same session. George Harrison's misgivings about his diminished role on these tracks were presumably dampened by the fact that the third song taped that day was one of his own.

YOU'RE GONNA LOSE THAT GIRL
(John Lennon/Paul McCartney)
Recorded 19 February 1965
A beautifully compact piece of songwriting, 'You're Gonna Lose That Girl' illustrated that Lennon was every bit McCartney's match when it came to producing quality pop tunes to order. Tempted though he must have

been, Paul let George play lead guitar this time around, contenting himself with adding piano to the basic track.

TICKET TO RIDE
(John Lennon/Paul McCartney)
Recorded 15 February 1965
John Lennon once described this song, The Beatles' first single of 1965, as the precursor to heavy metal. "It was pretty fucking heavy for then," he boasted, "if you go and look at what other people were making. It doesn't sound too bad." Indeed not: from Lennon's brilliantly deadpan vocal to Ringo's cross-beat drumming and McCartney's lead guitar flourishes, 'Ticket To Ride' was musically the strongest record The Beatles had made up to that point.

ACT NATURALLY
(Johnny Russell/Vonie Harrison)
Recorded 17 June 1965
Ringo's usual vocal appearance on this album was originally supposed to be 'If You've Got Trouble', a dire Lennon/McCartney composition which The Beatles attempted twice before recognising its canine qualities. By way of compensation for being saddled with such a loser, Ringo was allowed to record an American country hit, co-written by comedian Johnny Russell, and recently débuted by one of the giants of the Bakersfield sound, Buck Owens. With its "they're gonna put me in the movies" lyric, the song fitted the bill perfectly. More than two decades later, Ringo and Buck combined forces to re-record the number.

IT'S ONLY LOVE
(John Lennon/Paul McCartney)
Recorded 15 June 1965
Asked to select his least favourite Beatles songs, John Lennon went unerringly for 'Run For Your Life' and this mawkish number – which was still considered strong enough to qualify for heartfelt cover versions by vocalists as diverse as Bryan Ferry and Gary 'US' Bonds. Listen out again for George Harrison on wah-wah guitar, this song being one of the least likely candidates for such an effect in the entire Beatles catalogue.

YOU LIKE ME TOO MUCH

(George Harrison)
Recorded 17 February 1965
American rock critic Lester Bangs noted that
this George Harrison composition was
"probably the first song in rock history whose
lyrics admitted that neither party loved the
other but neither had the guts to call it
quits". Harrison's unsentimental attitude to
love resurfaced on the next album with
'If I Needed Someone'. At the time, though,
more attention was paid to George's
increasing confidence as a vocalist, and to
the two-men-at-one-piano trick of Paul and
George Martin.

TELL ME WHAT YOU SEE

(John Lennon/Paul McCartney)
Recorded 18 February 1965
More electric piano, and another McCartney
pop tune, slightly more laboured than its
contemporaries on this record. The *Help!*
album was the last occasion on which
The Beatles felt able to indulge themselves
in a set of entirely fictional teen-romance
songwriting. By the time they reconvened for
the *Rubber Soul* sessions at the end of
1965, the concept of lyric-writing as a form
of intimate confession had taken hold.

I'VE JUST SEEN A FACE

(John Lennon/Paul McCartney)
Recorded 14 June 1965
A folk song taken at bluegrass tempo, 'I've
Just Seen A Face' was a McCartney gem,
given an entirely satisfactory acoustic
arrangement. The fact that it was taped
during the same three-hour session as Paul's
screaming rocker, 'I'm Down', makes its
discreet assurance even more remarkable.
To the delight of the older fans in his
audiences, Paul resurrected this song during
the Wings' tours of the mid-Seventies.

YESTERDAY

(John Lennon/Paul McCartney)
Recorded 14 June 1965
"I really reckon 'Yesterday' is probably my
best song," said Paul McCartney in 1980.
"I like it not only because it was a big
success, but because it was one of the most
instinctive songs I've ever written. I was so
proud of it. I felt it was an original tune – the
most complete thing I've ever written.
It's very catchy without being sickly."

Despite his initial misgivings about the
song's sentimentality, John Lennon
eventually agreed, picking 'Yesterday' as one

of Paul's strongest compositions. Its origins have passed into the realms of legend: McCartney awoke one morning with the melody in his head, set some nonsense words to the tune to make sure he remembered it (working title: 'Scrambled Egg') and then played it to all and sundry, convinced that a song which had come so easily must have been stolen from something else. No one could identify the source, and Paul was eventually convinced that 'Yesterday' had sprung fully-formed from his own imagination.

In 1965, the song evoked some controversy, when it was revealed to the press that Paul had recorded it without any help from the rest of the group, the only instrumental support coming from his own acoustic guitar and a string quartet arranged by George Martin. American magazines listed the song as a McCartney solo release, and when it topped the US singles charts there was speculation that Paul would soon opt for a career outside the group. So he did, but not for another five years.

RUBBER SOUL

Parlophone CDP7 46440 2
Released December 1965

"I think *Rubber Soul* was the first of The Beatles' albums which presented a new Beatles to the world," reckons George Martin, who was close enough to the proceedings to know. "Up till then, we had been making albums rather like a collection of singles. Now we were really beginning to

 ### DIZZY MISS LIZZY
(Larry Williams)
Recorded 10 May 1965
Larry Williams emerged from the same Specialty Records stable as Little Richard, and his best records shared Richard's frenetic marriage of rock'n'roll and R&B. McCartney handled the Little Richard covers in The Beatles, while the Larry Williams songs became Lennon's responsibility. The group had been performing 'Dizzy Miss Lizzy' on stage since their first trip to Hamburg in 1960, though Harrison's slightly erratic guitar fills showed that they hadn't played it for a while before this session. But Lennon cruised through the vocal like the natural rock'n'roller he was.

He illustrated his love for the song by reviving it at his first major post-Beatles concert appearance in Toronto four years later. Meanwhile, 'Dizzy Miss Lizzy' became the last cover version that The Beatles ever released.

think about albums as a bit of art on their own. And *Rubber Soul* was the first to emerge that way."

John Lennon concurred: "We were just getting better, technically and musically, that's all. We finally took over the studio. On *Rubber Soul*, we were sort of more precise about making the album, and we took over the cover and everything. It was Paul's album title, just a pun. There is no great mysterious meaning behind all this, it was just four boys, working out what to call a new album."

There's no real disagreement, among fans, musicians and critics alike. *Sgt. Pepper* may have been The Beatles' production extravaganza, and *Revolver* their first post-acid celebration, but *Rubber Soul* was the record on which they revealed clear signs of fresh thinking – not just in musical or lyrical terms, but also philosophically. If *Beatles For Sale* marked the pinnacle of British beat, and *Help!* a consolidation of the past, *Rubber Soul* was a step into the future.

It's important to remember that The Beatles weren't pioneers in their quest for new artistic experiences. Bob Dylan had already recorded and released *Bringing It All Back Home* and *Highway 61 Revisited* by the time the group began work on *Rubber Soul*. But The Beatles were the first to introduce Dylan's free-form wordplay into the tight constraints of the three-minute pop song. Weeks before The Byrds discovered the joys of being 'Eight Miles High', the Liverpudlians announced that "the word is love".

Equally important to remember is that, unlike *Pepper* or the 'White Album', *Rubber Soul* wasn't a carefully considered studio creation. As they had been the previous autumn, The Beatles were trapped on a deadline-powered treadmill. When they arrived at Abbey Road studios on October 12, they knew that their next single, and album, had to be ready for release at the start of December. In the event, they cut it right to the bone: the final songs weren't written or recorded until mid-November. Just 18 days after the album was mixed, copies were on sale in the shops.

Despite the determinedly trend-setting approach of the album, one thing hadn't changed: The Beatles still intended *Rubber Soul* to be heard in mono, rather than stereo. In order to make both this record and *Help!* acceptable for modern digital audiences, George Martin remixed them both into 'proper' stereo for the CD releases.

DRIVE MY CAR
(John Lennon/Paul McCartney)
Recorded 13 October 1965
For all John Lennon's reputation as a rock'n'roller, it was Paul McCartney who wrote The Beatles' most raucous songs of 1965 – 'I'm Down' (the flipside of the 'Help!' single) and then this sly piece of sexual innuendo. What's most noticeable about the song at this distance, though, is the sparseness of the production. At a time when their nearest rivals, The Rolling Stones, were experimenting with dense, murky soundscapes, The Beatles cut this album with the maximum of separation between individual instruments, creating a feeling of space rather than tension.

NORWEGIAN WOOD
(THIS BIRD HAS FLOWN)
(John Lennon/Paul McCartney)
Recorded 21 October 1965
At the time it was released, Paul McCartney described this Lennon composition as "a comedy song". In the same debunking spirit, George Harrison admitted that the arrangement was "an accident as far as the sitar part was concerned". And not until 1970 did John Lennon explain: "I was trying to write about an affair without letting my wife know I was writing about an affair."

The sitar wasn't an accident, as George had played the instrument on the first still-unreleased version of the song on October 12. And the lyrics certainly weren't comedy, though they had their moments of humour. In oblique, memorable imagery, Lennon conjured up a romantic encounter that rapidly moved beyond his control – a theme that would soon become an obsession in his work.

YOU WON'T SEE ME
(John Lennon/Paul McCartney)
Recorded 11 November 1965
From reality to fantasy, in one fell swoop: no-one would claim McCartney's 'You Won't See Me' as a piece of self-revelation. But it was a supreme piece of commercial songwriting, recorded during the last, frantic day of sessions to complete the album. Note the superb falsetto harmonies, and McCartney's confident piano playing.

NOWHERE MAN
(John Lennon/Paul McCartney)
Recorded 21, 22 October 1965
Sitting bored in his Surrey home suffering writer's block, John Lennon suddenly envisaged himself as the "nowhere man, thinking all his nowhere plans for nobody". As the composer, Lennon wrote himself a message of hope: "nowhere man, the world is at your command". The Beatles translated the song into gorgeous Byrdsian 1965 pop, showing off another set of delicious vocal harmonies, and George added a jangly guitar solo that resolved on a memorable harmonic chime.

THINK FOR YOURSELF
(George Harrison)
Recorded 8 November 1965
George Harrison's spiritual investigations would soon initiate an entire genre of songwriting. 'Think For Yourself' was the first sign that he had a voice of his own, every bit as cynical as Lennon's about the trappings of everyday life, but holding out the study of the mind and the universe as a panacea. "Try thinking more, if just for your own sake," he sang, in a line which summed up his philosophy for the next few years.

THE WORD
(John Lennon/Paul McCartney)
Recorded 10 November 1965
Meanwhile, John and Paul considered that "the word is love" – their first tentative step into the shimmering waters of drug-enhanced freedom and meditation. At the time, McCartney was more impressed by the song's simple musical form: "To write a good

song with just one note in it – like 'Long Tall Sally' – is really very hard. It's the kind of thing we've wanted to do for some time. We get near it in 'The Word'."

MICHELLE
(John Lennon/Paul McCartney)
Recorded 3 November 1965
Songs become standards when they sound as if they've been around forever the first time you hear them. 1965 saw Paul McCartney unveiling the two songs that have been covered more often than anything else he has ever written – first 'Yesterday' and then this romantic Gallic ballad, complete with in-built French translation. Every bit as much a hook as the chorus was the descending bass-line, as Paul explained to Mark Lewisohn: "I'll never forget putting the bass line in because it was a kind of Bizet thing. It really turned the song around."

WHAT GOES ON?
(John Lennon/Paul McCartney/Richard Starkey)
Recorded 4 November 1965
"That was a very early song of mine," John Lennon explained, "but Ringo and Paul wrote a new middle eight together when we recorded it." That gave Ringo his first ever composing credit, the group having turned down his solitary composition up to that point, 'Don't Pass Me By'. On *Rubber Soul*, 'What Goes On' performed exactly the same function as 'Act Naturally' had on *Help!* – opening the second side of the LP with a lightweight, country song in preparation for the meatier fare to follow.

GIRL
(John Lennon/Paul McCartney)
Recorded 11 November 1965
Written overnight for the last session of the album, 'Girl' was the song that illustrated just how far John Lennon had travelled since 'I Feel Fine' a year earlier. "'Girl' is real," he explained in 1970." It was about that girl, who happened to be Yoko in the end, the one that a lot of us were looking for. And I was trying to say something about Christianity, which I was opposed to at the

time." With its biting attack on Catholic values, and its thinly veiled mixture of lust and disgust, 'Girl' was Lennon's most personal statement of disillusionment to date.

I'M LOOKING THROUGH YOU
(John Lennon/Paul McCartney)
Recorded 10, 11 November 1965
For almost the first time, Paul McCartney used this song as a vehicle for a personal message, rather than an attempt to write a hit single. He'd fallen out with his girlfriend of the time, Jane Asher, and 'I'm Looking Through You' was his response – half apology, half accusation. The Beatles first recorded the song without its melodic middle section, substituting a harsh guitar solo. Ever the tunesmith, Paul had written the missing lines by the time they finally recorded the released version.

IN MY LIFE
(John Lennon/Paul McCartney)
Recorded 18, 22 October 1965
"In the early days, George Martin would translate for us," Lennon remembered in 1970. "In 'In My Life', there's an Elizabethan piano solo. He would do things like that." In musical terms, that was the most striking thing about 'In My Life'. But it acquired a new resonance in the wake of Lennon's death in 1980, when it took on the role of a personal epitaph, a warm-hearted salutation to friends and lovers down the years. That's the way it was intended in 1965, as well, with John feeling sufficiently removed from his upbringing to be able to feel nostalgic about the world he'd left behind.

WAIT
(John Lennon/Paul McCartney)
Recorded 17 June,
11 November 1965
Desperate needs require desperate remedies, and for the second time ('Hold Me Tight' being the first) The Beatles plugged a gap on a new album by returning to a reject from a previous session. At least 'Hold Me Tight' had been re-recorded, though: for 'Wait', the group called up the tape of a song

which they'd attempted during the sessions for *Help!*, and decided wasn't up to scratch. With more vocal harmonies, percussion and vocals, they salvaged it, though the song's naïve enthusiasm still sounds out-of-place amid the more worldly lyrics of other *Rubber Soul* songs.

IF I NEEDED SOMEONE
(George Harrison)
Recorded 16, 18 October 1965
By far the best song George Harrison had written up to that point, 'If I Needed Someone' left its mark for several reasons. It boasted stunning three-part harmonies, the tightest they'd yet achieved on record; it had a jingle-jangle guitar sound obviously borrowed from The Byrds, in exactly the same way as The Byrds had developed their sound from listening to The Beatles; and it featured lyrics that were not so much anti-romantic as totally realistic. 'If I Needed Someone' may be the first pop song written from the jaded, though not quite exhausted, viewpoint of a man who had women lined up outside his hotel door in every city of the world.

RUN FOR YOUR LIFE
(John Lennon/Paul McCartney)
Recorded 12 October 1965

The first song to be recorded for *Rubber Soul* appeared last on the album – and on its composer's list of preferences. "I always hated that one," John Lennon admitted in later years. "It was one I knocked off just to write a song, and it was phoney." It was also a mildly nasty rocker with a central threat stolen from an Elvis Presley classic. The line, "I'd rather see you dead little girl than to be with another man", first surfaced on Elvis's revolutionary revamp of the blues standard 'Baby, Let's Play House' back in 1955. Lennon never sought to disguise the theft; but in 1965, most reviewers and fans hadn't been schooled in Elvis's Sun sessions, which were then available only scattered across long-deleted albums, and the lyrical debt went unnoticed.

REVOLVER

Parlophone CDP7 46441 2
Released August 1966

The Beatles were supposed to begin 1966 by making their third feature film in as many years. But no-one could agree on a script, or even a theme, and instead The Beatles enjoyed an unprecedented three-month break at the start of the year.

They were already convinced that their enervating routine of tour-film-record-tour had to be broken, and had completed their British tour at the end of 1965, assuming it would be their last. They were already contracted to undertake one final jaunt around the world in June, but mentally they were beginning to metamorphose into post-touring states of mind.

With the exception of their last British concert at the *NME* Pollwinners' Show on May 1, The Beatles had more than two months on their schedule to record their next LP. They began on April 6 with the most revolutionary track on the album, Lennon's 'Tomorrow Never Knows', and ended just over eight weeks later with one of the two most brilliant pop albums ever recorded up to that point. Its rival was The Beach Boys' *Pet Sounds*, a masterpiece of melody, harmony and orchestral arrangement that undoubtedly affected the final sound of The Beatles' LP.

What time and mental space in the studio gave The Beatles was the chance to experiment (although most of the *Revolver* songs went through remarkably little change of approach once the sessions began), and the freedom to choose exactly the right sound for each track. *Revolver* was where The Beatles became a consummate studio band – ironically enough, in the same year that they proved completely unable (or maybe unwilling is closer to the point) to perform their more complex material on stage. Listen to *Revolver*, and then to the tuneless performances they gave on tour a few weeks later, and it's hard to imagine that they are the same band.

The Beatles' state of mind during that final tour is aptly summed up by this quote from Paul McCartney: "I was in Germany on tour just before *Revolver* came out. I started listening to the album and I got really down because I thought the whole thing was out of tune. Everyone had to reassure me that it was OK." And so it was.

TAXMAN
(George Harrison)
**Recorded 21, 22 April,
16 May 1966**

"'Taxman' was when I first realised that even though we had started earning money, we were actually giving most of it away in taxes." So said George Harrison, cementing forever the public perception of him as the Beatle most obsessed with money (an interesting sideline to his other clichéd role as the mystic Beatle).

Groomed for years by manager Brian Epstein to stay out of political controversy, The Beatles began in 1966 to comment on issues like the war in Vietnam. 'Taxman' was a more universal protest – George fingered both the Conservative and Labour leaders in his lyrics – but the song had a political message, nonetheless. It also had a remarkably powerful lead guitar riff, played (ironically enough) not by George but by Paul.

ELEANOR RIGBY
(John Lennon/Paul McCartney)
**Recorded 28, 29 April,
6 June 1966**

"I wrote a good half of the lyrics or more," claimed John Lennon in later years of this archetypal Paul McCartney song. True or not, it was a sign that Lennon realised the strength of what Paul had written. It was a short story with a moral, all packaged within little more than two minutes. Aside from the backing vocals, McCartney was the only Beatle featured on the track, accompanied by a string section scored by George Martin – one of his most obvious and effective contributions to a Beatles record. The song later inspired the most memorable segment of the *Yellow Submarine* movie, as the craft drifts above the lonely, dingy streets of Liverpool.

I'M ONLY SLEEPING
(John Lennon/Paul McCartney)
Recorded 27, 29 April, 5, 6 May 1966

Half acid dream, half latent Lennon laziness personified, 'I'm Only Sleeping' was a joyous celebration of life without pressure. It also conformed to one of the key instructions of the acid trippers, that explorers of the mind should relax and let thoughts come to them, rather than forcing them to appear.

The other-worldly feel of the song was created by artificial means – first speeding up Lennon's vocal to make it sound as if he was singing from beyond the physical plane, and then playing the tape of Harrison's guitar interjections backwards. During the editing

process, a fistful of different mixes were prepared, and variations on the basic stereo CD version can be found on vinyl releases scattered around the globe.

LOVE YOU TO
(George Harrison)
Recorded 11, 13 April 1966
Lester Bangs called it "the first injection of ersatz Eastern wisdom into rock", but George Harrison's translation of the Buddhist spiritual texts he'd been reading in recent months simply reinforced the message of 'Think For Yourself' on the previous album. As far as the public were concerned, though, Harrison had "gone Indian" overnight, an impression reinforced as he took sitar lessons from Ravi Shankar, encouraged the rest of the group to study under the Maharishi Mahesh Yogi, and offered Eastern-sounding songs to the group for the next 18 months.

'Love You To' sounded astonishing alongside the electrifying pop of the *Revolver* album, where it proved that The Beatles could tackle any genre they wanted. It also inaugurated a less happy tradition, of John Lennon not contributing to the recording of Harrison's songs. One man who did appear, however, was Indian tabla player Anil Bhagwat.

HERE, THERE AND EVERYWHERE
(John Lennon/Paul McCartney)
Recorded 14, 16, 17 June 1966
For the third album running, Paul McCartney turned up with a song that became an instant standard. He credited its original inspiration to multiple hearings of The Beach Boys' *Pet Sounds* LP, though there's little melodic similarity between them. But the romantic simplicity of the song shone like a beacon through the cynicism and uncertainty that fuelled most of the album.

YELLOW SUBMARINE
(John Lennon/Paul McCartney)
Recorded 26 May, 1 June 1966
A simple children's song intended for the equally simple public persona of Ringo Starr,

'Yellow Submarine' still received the full-scale studio treatment. Mark Lewisohn's definitive account of The Beatles' sessions documents the various effects and gimmicks that were recorded for the song, and then rejected. 'Yellow Submarine' was, in business terms, the most important song on the *Revolver* LP, as it inspired the cartoon movie which solved the enduring problem of the third film that The Beatles had owed United Artists since the summer of 1965.

SHE SAID SHE SAID
(John Lennon/Paul McCartney)
Recorded 21 June 1966
Another major Lennon song on an album dominated by his paranoid acid visions, 'She Said She Said' was inspired by a doom-laden, LSD-driven remark by actor Peter Fonda, who buttonholed Lennon at a celebrity party with the words "I know what it's like to be dead". 'Tomorrow Never Knows' captured the horror of that statement; 'She Said She Said' turned it into an early piece of Lennon autobiography, the first step on the journey to his *Plastic Ono Band* album. And all this turmoil and angst was contained within a brilliant three-minute pop song.

GOOD DAY SUNSHINE
(John Lennon/Paul McCartney)
Recorded 8, 9 June 1966
Perfect summer pop for the era, McCartney's 'Good Day Sunshine' had enough melodic twists and turns (note the harmonic shifts in the final chorus) to put it beyond the reach of most would-be cover artists. Simple, effective and stunning, it was the ideal complement to the darker *Revolver* songs.

AND YOUR BIRD CAN SING
(John Lennon/Paul McCartney)
Recorded 26 April 1966
John Lennon described this song as "another horror", and he wrote it, so he should know. It's full of the fake wisdom of those philosophically lightweight days when it seemed as if the world could be turned on its axis by a tab of acid and a few seconds' thought. Musically, though, it's one of the highlights of the album, powered by

a twisting, insidious guitar riff and featuring one of Lennon's most deadpan, off-hand vocals. Rich and mysterious, the track may have been fancy paper round an empty box, but the package sounded so good that no-one cared.

FOR NO ONE
(John Lennon/Paul McCartney)
Recorded 9, 16, 19 May 1966
Just two Beatles appeared on McCartney's 'For No One', Ringo playing percussion, and Paul singing and playing keyboards and the lovely descending bass line. The French horn, allowed a lengthy solo in George Martin's score, was performed by Alan Civil from the London Philharmonia. The song itself was another remarkable McCartney ballad, melodically sophisticated and lyrically mature.

DOCTOR ROBERT
(John Lennon/Paul McCartney)
Recorded 17, 19 April 1966
Named without any hint of disguise after a London 'doctor' who could be guaranteed to supply rock stars with exotic drugs on demand, John Lennon's 'Doctor Robert' was hinged around the same rough-edged guitar as 'And Your Bird Can Sing'. And once again, his lead vocal oozed cynicism and emotional distance, like the world-weary survivor of three years' hard Beatlemania that he was.

I WANT TO TELL YOU
(George Harrison)
Recorded 2, 3 June 1966
Allowed three songs on any Beatles album for the first time (and also the last, with the exception of the double 'White Album'), George Harrison had the chance to expose several different facets of his songwriting talent. Like 'If I Needed Someone', 'I Want To Tell You' was hinged around The Beatles' superb harmonies (Lennon and McCartney seemed to relish the role of backing singers, relieved of the pressure to carry the song). Once again, Harrison unwrapped an awkward, determinedly realistic view of relationships, in which failed communication was the order of the day. Throughout The

Beatles' career, George never wrote a straightforward love song: all his portrayals of romance were surrounded in misunderstanding and the dreadful prospect of boredom, and this was no exception.

GOT TO GET YOU INTO MY LIFE
(John Lennon/Paul McCartney)
Recorded 8, 11 April, 18 May, 17 June 1966
Revolver revealed The Beatles as master of any musical genre they cared to touch. Having satirised white musicians' desire to play black musical styles in the title of *Rubber Soul*, Paul McCartney turned his hand to the 1966 soul boom with ease, concocting this fabulous piece of mock-Stax, with five brassmen providing the final Memphis-style touches. The hand of control was evident throughout, with the brass sound deliberately 'limited' to create a faintly unreal sound.

Trivia note: compare the fade-outs of the mono and stereo versions of this song, and you'll find entirely different McCartney ad-libs.

TOMORROW NEVER KNOWS
(John Lennon/Paul McCartney)
Recorded 6, 7, 22 April 1966
Almost five months after The Beatles added their final vocals to the charming 'I'm Looking Through You', they were back in the studio – to create three minutes of turmoil that envisaged the death of the conscious mind and the triumph beyond death of the universal spirit. What had happened between November 1965 and April 1966? John Lennon had been on a dual voyage of discovery – experimenting with the hallucogenic powers of LSD, and finding that it was possible to match the chaotic visions he saw on his chemically-fuelled trips with collages of sound.

Both Lennon and McCartney began creating mind movies at their home studios, extended webs of noise that were based around tape loops and 'found sounds'. McCartney was the pioneer in this regard, and it was he who supervised the addition of the almost supernatural squawks and howls that punctuated the song. But the concept was Lennon's, taken from his reading of *The Tibetan Book Of The Dead*. Like Harrison, Lennon noted the similarity between the imagery of Eastern spirituality, and the beyond-consciousness experiences of the acid trip. 'Tomorrow Never Knows', with its eerie 'treated' vocal, droning drums and terrifying soundscape, was the ultimate expression of his discovery – and of the enormous change in The Beatles since they'd finished *Rubber Soul*.

SGT. PEPPER'S LONELY HEARTS CLUB BAND

Parlophone CDP7 46442 2
Released June 1967

"The biggest influence on *Sgt. Pepper* was *Pet Sounds* by The Beach Boys," said Paul McCartney in 1980. "That album just flipped me. When I heard it, I thought, 'Oh dear, this is the album of all time. What the hell are we going to do?' My ideas took off from that standard. I had this idea that it was going to be an album of another band that wasn't us – we'd just imagine all the time that it wasn't us playing. It was just a nice little device to give us some distance on the album. The cover was going to be us dressed as this other band in crazy gear; but it was all stuff that we'd always wanted to wear. And we were going to have photos on the wall of all our heroes."

That's the standard view of *Sgt. Pepper*, from the man who almost single-handedly created the album, and its legend. In this reading, *Pepper* is the best pop record of all time – the album that customarily wins critics' polls, the masterpiece that first persuaded 'serious' musical critics pop was worth their consideration.

There's a rival view of the whole affair, however, and it was put forward most cogently by McCartney's supposed partner, John Lennon. "*Paul* said 'come and see the show' on that album," he moaned a few years after its release. "I didn't. I had to

knock off a few songs so I knocked off 'A Day In The Life', or my section of it, and 'Mr Kite'. I was very paranoid in those days. I could hardly move."

More than any other Beatles album bar *Abbey Road*, *Sgt. Pepper* was a Paul McCartney creation. He it was who dreamed up the concept, the title, the idea behind Peter Blake's remarkable cover, the orchestrations, and the device of pretending that the entire LP was the work of another band entirely – which in turn became one of the major themes of the *Yellow Submarine* movie, then in its pre-production stages.

Meanwhile, John Lennon was deep in a creative trough. For the first time, Lennon and McCartney appeared – to Lennon, at least – to be in competition rather than on the same side. Since The Beatles had played their final live shows in August, McCartney had been composing – first the musical themes for the film *The Family Way*, then the songs that would appear on the next Beatles album. Lennon had also been involved in film work, but as an actor, in Dick Lester's *How I Won The War*. Required for the part to shed his Beatle locks, he adopted the granny specs that soon became his trademark, stared into the mirror, and wondered what the future might bring for an unemployed Beatle. Back in England at the end of the filming, Lennon regarded McCartney's enthusiasm to get into the studio as a threat. Aware that he was likely to be outnumbered in the songwriting stakes, he raised the emotional barriers and took against the *Pepper* album from the start.

In the end, Lennon came up with the requisite number of songs for the album, but he never warmed to the concept. On *Revolver*, and again on the majestic 'Strawberry Fields Forever', cut early in the sessions, he'd experienced the relief and satisfaction of writing from the heart. For *Pepper*, he was back where he'd been in 1964, writing songs to order. Hence the sarcastic, dismissive comments he reserved for this album throughout the rest of his life.

Whatever else *Sgt. Pepper* may or may not have been, it was certainly an event. It unified British pop culture in a way no other occasion could match. Maybe in hindsight it wasn't The Beatles' strongest album, but it had an impact unlike any record before or since. It literally revolutionised the direction of pop, helping to divide it between those who were prepared to follow the group along the path of experimentation (thus creating 'rock') and those who mourned the loss of the less significant Beatles of yore (the champions of 'pop'). After *Pepper*, nothing was ever the same again – within or without The Beatles.

SGT. PEPPER'S LONELY HEARTS CLUB BAND
(John Lennon/Paul McCartney)
Recorded 1, 2 February, 3, 6 March 1967
Complete with the appropriate sound effects, the album's up-tempo title track introduced the record, the concept and the Club Band. It performed the function of an overture in an opera, preparing the audience for what was to follow, and introducing the themes that supposedly unified the piece.

WITH A LITTLE HELP FROM MY FRIENDS
(John Lennon/Paul McCartney)
Recorded 29, 30 March 1967
Beatles official biographer Hunter Davies watched Lennon, McCartney and their associates completing work on Paul

McCartney's original idea, aware from the start that this would be a vehicle for Ringo Starr – or 'Billy Shears', as he was billed in the opening seconds of the song. Though the song's theme was tailored towards Ringo's warm public image (right down to the line "what would you say if I sang out of tune", a real possibility), at least one observer saw a hidden meaning. Speaking in 1970, US Vice-President Spiro Agnew told an audience that he had recently been informed that the song was a tribute to the power of illegal drugs – news to its composers, perhaps.

Not often did other performers outclass The Beatles with cover versions of their songs, but Joe Cocker's gut-wrenching version of 'Friends' in 1968 left Ringo floundering.

LUCY IN THE SKY WITH DIAMONDS

(John Lennon/Paul McCartney)
Recorded 1, 2 March 1967

The minor furore over the meaning of 'Friends' had nothing on the frenzied response to this piece of whimsy from the pen of John Lennon. "I was consciously writing poetry," he admitted, shifting blame for the line about "newspaper taxis" to his nominal co-writer. But the *Alice In Wonderland* style imagery, supposedly inspired by a drawing John's son Julian had brought home from nursery school, was widely believed to be a description of an acid trip. As soon as someone noticed the initials of the song's title (LSD), that seemed to clinch the story – except that Lennon continued to deny it until his dying day. Having owned up to so much else down the years, there was no reason for him to lie – especially over a song which he always felt was "so badly recorded".

GETTING BETTER

(John Lennon/Paul McCartney)
Recorded 9, 10, 21, 23 March 1967

Based on a favourite saying of Beatles friend/chauffeur Terry Doran, 'Getting Better' was a McCartney song augmented by Lennon, who contributed the self-accusing

verse that began "I used to be cruel to my woman". Ever since Lennon's death, McCartney has bemoaned his inability to find a co-writer who, like John, would answer a line like "it's getting better all the time" with "can't get much worse". Even in the midst of what was intended to be a concept album, McCartney could turn out a song that was clever, melodic, memorable and universal in its application.

FIXING A HOLE

(John Lennon/Paul McCartney)
Recorded 9, 21 February 1967

For the first time in England, The Beatles left Abbey Road studios for the session that provided the basic track for this fine McCartney song, often overlooked by critics and fans alike. EMI's studio was fully booked for the night, so the group moved to Regent Sound in the West End, where The Rolling Stones' early hits had been taped.

While John Lennon's writing veered between fantasy and obvious self-revelation, McCartney's skirted from the romantic to the delightfully oblique. This song definitely fell into the latter category, with lyrics that unveiled as many mysteries as they solved. Instrumentally, too, 'Fixing A Hole' was a minor classic, from McCartney's opening trills on the harpsichord to Harrison's lyrical guitar solo.

SHE'S LEAVING HOME

(John Lennon/Paul McCartney)
Recorded 17, 20 March 1967

"Paul had the basic theme for this song," said John Lennon, "but all those lines like 'We sacrificed most of our life... We gave her everything that money could buy', those were the things Mimi used to say to me. It was easy to write." Paul's rather precious piece of fictional writing wasn't helped by Mike Leander's ornate score for the song, one of the few occasions when The Beatles were left sounding pretentious. It took the realism of Lennon's answer-lines to cut through the sweetness of the piece.

BEING FOR THE BENEFIT OF MR. KITE
(John Lennon/Paul McCartney)
Recorded 17, 20 February, 28, 29, 31 March 1967

A masterpiece of ingenuity rather than inspiration, 'Mr Kite' was written when John transcribed the wording from a vintage circus poster into verse form, and recorded with the help of scores of small segments of fairground organ tape, tossed into the air and then stuck back together to produce the eerie noise that dominates the instrumental sections. Lennon dismissed it as a throwaway – which, when you remember how it was made, is pretty apt.

WITHIN YOU WITHOUT YOU
(George Harrison)
Recorded 15, 22 March, 3, 4 April 1967

Though it was John Lennon who resented Paul McCartney's domination of the *Pepper* sessions, George Harrison probably had more cause to be aggrieved. He was restricted to just one number on the LP, his other contribution ('Only A Northern Song') being rejected.

Like 'Love You To', 'Within You, Without You' blatantly displayed George's infatuation with Indian culture. Recorded with the assistance of several Indian musicians, plus Beatles aide Neil Aspinall on tamboura, the song required no help from any other member of the group. "It was written at Klaus Voorman's house in Hampstead, one night after dinner," George explained a decade later. "I was playing a pedal harmonium when it came, the tune first, then the first sentence." Some thought it a masterpiece, some a prime example of mock-philosophical babble. Either way, it was pure Harrison.

WHEN I'M SIXTY-FOUR
(John Lennon/Paul McCartney)
Recorded 6, 8, 20, 21 December 1966

Paul began writing this song when he was a teenager, needing only to add the middle sections for this revival of a ten-year-old melody. Within the concept of the album, it fitted the image of the Edwardian Pepper band, whereas it would have seemed mawkish on any of the group's earlier LPs. The addition of clarinets to the mix heightened the pre-First World War feel.

LOVELY RITA
(John Lennon/Paul McCartney)
Recorded 23, 24 February, 7, 21 March 1967

The anthem for traffic wardens ("meter maids") everywhere, 'Lovely Rita' was a glorious throwaway, full of musical jokes and brimming with self-confidence. Nothing on the record expressed that as fully as the piano solo, ironically played by keyboard maestro George Martin.

GOOD MORNING, GOOD MORNING
(John Lennon/Paul McCartney)
Recorded 8, 16 February, 13, 28, 29 March 1967

Using a TV commercial for Kellogg's cereal as his starting point, John Lennon concocted a wonderfully dry satire on contemporary urban life. Several points to watch out for here: the reference to the popular BBC TV sitcom, *Meet The Wife*; the ultra-compressed brass sound provided by members of Sounds Incorporated; a stinging Harrison guitar solo; and the cavalcade of animals, in ascending order of ferocity, which segues into a reprise of the next track.

SGT. PEPPER'S LONELY HEARTS CLUB BAND (REPRISE)
(John Lennon/Paul McCartney)
Recorded 1 April 1967

For the first but definitely not last time, Paul McCartney topped and tailed a set of songs by reprising the opening melody, in true Hollywood musical fashion.

A DAY IN THE LIFE
(John Lennon/Paul McCartney)
Recorded 19, 20 January, 3, 10, 22 February, 21 April 1967

Delete 'A Day In The Life' from *Sgt. Pepper*

and you'd have an elegant, playful album of pop songs. With it, the LP assumes some kind of greatness. Some might vote for 'Hey Jude' or 'Strawberry Fields Forever' as the finest ever Beatles recording, but 'A Day In The Life' would run anything close – and it's certainly the best ever collaborative effort between Lennon and McCartney.

Lennon wrote the basic song, its verses a snapshot from his own life and the world around him – the death of a friend in a car crash, a newspaper cutting about the state of the roads in Blackburn, Lancashire. The tag line "I'd love to turn you on" brought a broadcasting ban in Britain: more importantly, it led twice into an overwhelming orchestral assault, with 40 musicians headed helter-skelter up the scales towards a crescendo of silence. First time around, the barrage leads into McCartney's stoned middle-eight, another day in another life; second time, there's a pause, and then a piano chord that resounds for almost a minute. Then bathos: a whistle only dogs could hear, followed by the locked-groove gibberish that brought the side to a close, and is sampled briefly at the end of the CD. Stunning, magnificent, awesome: there's nothing in rock to match it.

MAGICAL MYSTERY TOUR

Parlophone CDP7 48062 2
Released as six-track EP December 1967, as LP December 1976

Early in April 1967, with *Sgt. Pepper* not yet complete, Paul McCartney flew to America for a week's holiday. On his return flight, he drafted out his idea for a TV special which would involve a mystery tour on a coach – not the usual British seaside trip to a less than exotic location twenty miles down the coast, but a voyage into the imagination.

By mid-April, McCartney had written the title tune for the project, and the four Beatles had agreed a tentative format for

The Beatles with Jimmy Savile

the programme. What with the intervention of the Maharishi Mahesh Yogi, and the unexpected death of Brian Epstein, the project wasn't completed until almost the end of the year. When it was ready for public screening, it was scheduled for prime-time viewing on BBC TV, as part of the programming for Boxing Day 1967. Used to a stodgy diet of sitcoms and variety shows, the great British public responded to the frequently bizarre and often amateurish *Magical Mystery Tour* with bewilderment bordering on anger. The professional reviewers were equally damning, and the film passed into history as The Beatles' first major flirtation with public disapproval.

The reasons for the failure were varied. The film was originally shown in black-and-white, thereby losing the visual impact of many of the sequences. The public hadn't known what to expect, and many viewers were assuming that the show would be the kind of song-and-dance spectacular that the closing 'Your Mother Should Know' sequence satirised. Mostly, though, the criticisms were justified. For all its brilliant set pieces, *Magical Mystery Tour* desperately required professional editing and direction. Self-indulgent and unrestrained, it showed The Beatles that they didn't have an automatic lock on the public's taste.

As usual with a McCartney idea post-1966, John Lennon felt resentful about the entire project. "Paul had a tendency to come along and say, well, he's written his ten songs, let's record now," he moaned in 1970. "And I said, well, give us a few days and I'll knock a few off. He set *Magical Mystery Tour* up and had worked it out with [Beatles roadie] Mal Evans, and then he came and showed me what his idea was, the story and how he had it all, the production and everything. George and I were sort of grumbling, you know, 'Fuckin' movie, oh well, we better do it'."

Six new songs were written and recorded for the film. The Beatles finally elected to release them as a double-EP package, at twice normal single price, complete with a cartoon book vaguely telling the story of the film. The American market wasn't geared up for EPs, however, so Capitol turned the two EPs into an LP, adding in the earlier Beatles singles from 1967. In that format, the album was heavily imported into Britain, and eventually won a full release here in the late Seventies. When EMI prepared The Beatles' albums for CD, *Magical Mystery Tour* automatically took its place in the line-up, between *Pepper* and the 'White Album'.

MAGICAL MYSTERY TOUR
(John Lennon/Paul McCartney)
Recorded 25, 26, 27 April, 3 May, 7 November 1967
Aside from some vocal additions in November, the title track from the *Magical Mystery Tour* film was completed before *Sgt. Pepper* was released. It was a McCartney effort from start to finish, embellished by the use of session brass players, and with Paul himself acting as a carnival barker at the start to drag the punters in.

No fewer than three different versions of the track were made available to the public at the end of 1967. The film mix remains unavailable on record, but both the mono and stereo versions were included when EMI issued a boxed set of The Beatles' EPs on compact disc. The CD album, meanwhile, has the stereo version.

THE FOOL ON THE HILL
(John Lennon/Paul McCartney)
Recorded 25, 26, 27 September, 20, 25 October 1967
Maintaining his record of writing an instant standard on every mid-Sixties Beatles album, Paul McCartney composed this touching, beautiful ballad late in the proceedings, cutting a solo demo at the piano, and then concocting a deliciously light and airy arrangement for the final version. Three flute players added to the atmosphere (once again the mono and stereo mixes differ, most notably in their placement of the flute interjections).

The Beatles with George Martin at Abbey Road Studios during the recording of 'Hey Jude', 1968

FLYING
(John Lennon/Paul McCartney/
George Harrison/Richard Starkey)
Recorded 8, 28 September 1967
No other Beatles recording underwent such drastic editing as this instrumental with vocal backing. Intended to support a psychedelic section of the film, rich in shifts of colour and texture, it was suitably eerie – and bizarre, apparently ending with a jazz section borrowed from elsewhere in The Beatles' collective record library. All that was removed as the track was sliced from ten minutes to little more than two, leaving 'Flying' as an off-the-wall EP-filler — the only instrumental The Beatles issued on EMI, and also their first four-man composition.

BLUE JAY WAY
(George Harrison)
Recorded 6, 7 September,
6 October 1967
George Harrison was at his rented home on Blue Jay Way in Los Angeles, waiting for former Beatle aide Derek Taylor to arrive for dinner. Taylor, fortuitously, was late, and Harrison turned his mild concern and irritation into this song. What could have been a simple, maudlin ditty was transformed by The Beatles' studio prowess into an exotic, almost mystical journey. Harrison's vocal was treated until it sounded as if it was coming from beyond the grave, though with none of the ghostly threat of Lennon's similarly altered voice on 'Tomorrow Never Knows'. Backwards tapes, droning organs, and a cello combined to heighten the Eastern atmosphere – without a single Indian instrument being employed.

YOUR MOTHER
SHOULD KNOW
(John Lennon/Paul McCartney)
Recorded 22, 23 August, 29 September 1967
Simple and nostalgic alongside the calculated experimentation of the other film soundtrack songs, 'Your Mother Should Know' inspired one of the great *Magical Mystery Tour* set pieces, as The Beatles waltzed down a huge staircase in white suits, like refugees from a 1930s Hollywood musical.

I AM THE WALRUS
(John Lennon/Paul McCartney)
Recorded 5, 6, 27, 28, 29
September 1967
"I was the Walrus, whatever that means. The Walrus was a big capitalist that are all the fucking oysters, if you must know. I always had this image of the Walrus in the garden and I loved it, so I didn't ever check out what the Walrus was. But he's a fucking bastard, that's what he turns out to be. Everybody presumes that means something, that just because I said I am the Walrus, it must mean I am God or something, but it's just poetry."

That's John Lennon in 1970, attempting to debunk all the theories that had been inspired by the oblique lyrical stance of his sole contribution to the *Magical Mystery Tour* soundtrack. He revealed many years later that 'Walrus' had been a deliberate effort to mystify his critics and followers alike, by stringing together violently dissimilar images without a shred of continuity. Lennon enjoyed watching the outside world interpreting his nonsense verse, and relished the recording of the song, which – like 'Blue Jay Way' – became the vehicle for another bout of studio experimentation. (As was often the case with The Beatles' most unusual recordings, several slightly different mixes of 'Walrus' were issued aound the world.)

Among the delights on offer were a mellotron, heavily used by Lennon at home and in the studio in 1967; a 12-piece string section; 16 members of the Mike Sammes Singers, chanting "Oompah, oompah, stick it up your number"; and several lines of Shakespeare's *King Lear*, lifted from a BBC radio drama production being broadcast during the mixing session.

HELLO GOODBYE
(John Lennon/Paul McCartney)
Recorded 2, 19, 20, 25 October, 2 November 1967

To John Lennon's disgust, his epic 'I Am The Walrus' was issued on the flipside of this commercial but rather inconsequential McCartney composition – three minutes of contradictions and meaningless juxtapositions, with a tune that was impossible to forget. More interesting than the song were The Beatles' four promotional films, shot at London's Saville Theatre, none of which was able to be shown on British TV at the time because of Union rules about miming.

STRAWBERRY FIELDS FOREVER
(John Lennon/Paul McCartney)
Recorded 29 November, 8, 9, 10, 21, 22 December 1966

The greatest pop record ever made? Almost certainly it is, though it shares with its partner, 'Penny Lane', the less glorious fate of having broken a run of Beatles No. 1 hits that went all the way back to 'Please Please Me' four years earlier. In what is arguably the most disgraceful statistic in chart history and to the eternal shame of the British record buying public, Engelbert Humperdinck's vacuous ballad 'Release Me' prevented The Beatles' double-sided slab of genius from reaching the top.

Ostensibly inspired by a Liverpool children's home familiar from his boyhood, 'Strawberry Fields Forever' was actually an attempt by John Lennon to chart the process of consciousness and understanding, through fragmented lyrical images. The story behind the finished record is familiar: two different renditions of the song, in entirely different moods and keys, were cleverly edited together by George Martin via the use of variable tape-speed. If ever a song deserved such serendipity, it was this one – a record that never dates, because it lives outside time.

PENNY LANE
(John Lennon/Paul McCartney)
Recorded 29, 30 December 1966, 4, 6, 9, 10, 12, 17 January 1967

"'Penny Lane'/'Strawberry Fields Forever' was the best record we ever made," reckoned Beatles producer George Martin. McCartney's nostalgic 'Penny Lane' didn't have the psychic tension of Lennon's 'Strawbery Fields', but it was every bit as imaginative and lyrical. No other single displays the complementary talents of the Lennon/McCartney pairing so well.

While John's song was locked in the mind, Paul's roamed the streets of Liverpool with a smile on its face. The music matched that sense of freedom, with the crowning touch supplied by David Mason's piccolo trumpet solo. A closing Mason flourish was removed from the song in the final mix, though only after an early mix had been sent to the States, for use on promo copies of the single.

BABY YOU'RE A RICH MAN
(John Lennon/Paul McCartney)
Recorded 11 May 1967

"We just stuck two songs together for this one," admitted John Lennon, "the same as 'A Day In The Life'." The final effect wasn't quite as grandiose, but 'Baby You're A Rich Man' certainly took less time to record – being started and finished in a single six-hour session. Rumours that the song's final choruses contain a hidden 'tribute' to Brian Epstein – "baby you're a rich fag Jew" – appear to be groundless. But it is true that the number was originally intended for the *Yellow Submarine* soundtrack, though it ended up being released a year before the film on the flipside of 'All You Need Is Love'. The instrument punctuating the song that sounds like a manic trumpet is a primitive synthesiser called a Clavioline, incidentally.

ALL YOU NEED IS LOVE
(John Lennon/Paul McCartney)
Recorded 14, 19, 23, 24, 25 June 1967

In 1967, satellite technology finally allowed instant visual communication between every corner of the globe. To celebrate this achievement, international broadcasting organisations united to stage *Our World*, a programme which would bring together segments from every continent, as part of a multi-national live TV show.

The Beatles were invited to contribute to the British section of the show, performing a new song. With universal appeal in mind, John Lennon wrote 'All You Need Is Love', one of the anthems of the Sixties. The decision was made to broadcast the actual recording of the song live – or so the public were

informed, though Lennon and the other Beatles sang and played along to a pre-recorded backing track, and John actually re-cut his lead vocal a few hours later. The broadcast passed without incident, and remains one of the strongest visual impressions of the summer of love, as a mini-orchestra and many of the group's friends from the pop aristocracy congregated in the cavernous Studio One at Abbey Road.

THE BEATLES (THE WHITE ALBUM)

Parlophone CDS7 46443 8
Released November 1968

On one hand, *The Beatles* – the 'White Album', as all but pedants call it – was the most diverse record that The Beatles, or probably any pop band in history, has ever made. On the other, as Paul McCartney remembered, "That was the tension album. We were all in the midst of that psychedelic thing, or just coming out of it. In any case, it was weird. Never before had we recorded with beds in the studio and people visiting for hours on end: business meetings and all that. There was a lot of friction during that album. We were just about to break up, and that was tense in itself."

Lester Bangs described it perfectly: "The first album by The Beatles or in the history of rock by four solo artists in one band." In doing that, he was simply following John Lennon's lead: "If you took each track, it was just me and a backing group, Paul and a backing group – I enjoyed it, but we broke up then."

During the course of the sessions, Ringo Starr actually quit the group for more than a week, before ambling back when he realised that the others were continuing the album without him. Ringo is unlikely to have been at the centre of the dissension in the ranks: the main arguments were between George and Paul (Harrison reckoning that McCartney was treating him as a junior member of the band) and John and the rest of the band (over, on one side, Lennon's insistence on Yoko Ono joining the group in the studio and, on the other, her treatment at the hands of Paul and George).

There were plenty of other pressures at work. The lack of central management in the group's career since the death of Brian Epstein in August 1967 had presented them with additional financial and business decisions to worry about, ignore and occasionally even make. McCartney's keen interest in maintaining a steady ship rubbed up against Lennon and Harrison's more *laissez-faire* attitude to events.

The creation of Apple, their multi-genre business empire that was intended as a fantasy come true but rapidly disintegrated into chaos, took its toll on the group's unity and enthusiasm. So too did the aftermath of the Maharishi episode, with even the most meditation-friendly of The Beatles suffering extreme disillusionment after their idyll with the Indian guru mutated into farce. Most of all, though, the group were individually and collectively aware that without leadership or a definite direction, they had no unifying purpose. From the start of 1968 onwards, they seemed to work to a 'two steps forward, three steps back, one step into another dimension' policy – with results that were often inspired, and just as often muddle-headed.

It's some kind of proof of their genius, then, that the 'White Album' was so brilliant, and so vast. Producer George Martin always wanted the group to throw away the chaff and trim the 30-track, 90-minute epic into a tight 40-minute LP of polished gems.

But half the attraction of the 'White Album' is its sprawling chaos. Such a giant canvas allowed The Beatles, more often than not one at a time, to show off every aspect of their music. For the first and probably last time in pop history, a group demonstrated on one release that they could handle rock'n'roll, reggae, soul, blues, folk, country, pop and even the avant-garde with consummate ease – and still come out sounding like The Beatles. As a handy history of popular music since 1920, or simply a rich mine of battered gems, *The Beatles* is impossible to beat.

For the last time, both mono and stereo mixes of this double-album were prepared, and The Beatles took great delight in making them as different from each other as possible. Almost every song on the 'White Album' has variations between the two mixes: in one extreme case, the mono version is 20 seconds shorter than the stereo.

behaviour at the Maharishi's Indian retreat, when Lennon was deputed to entice her out of her self-enforced hiding in her quarters. Lennon widened the song to take in a pantheistic vision of the world's beauty, one of the few positive statements to emerge from his stay in India. (Another, a song called 'Child Of Nature', wasn't considered for this album; instead, it was rewritten three years later as 'Jealous Guy' for his *Imagine* LP, its original spirit of universal harmony replaced by fear and guilt.)

This was another of the recordings done during Ringo Starr's departure from the group: strange that The Beatles should open their album with two tracks that were both recorded by a three-man line-up.

BACK IN THE USSR

(John Lennon/Paul McCartney)
Recorded 22, 23 August 1968
For many of the 'White Album' sessions, The Beatles were able to work on separate, individual projects at the same time, and keep their four-man performances – and the resulting tension they caused – to a minimum. But on August 22 1968, when all of The Beatles assembled to record Paul McCartney's 'Back In The USSR', tempers frayed, and it was Ringo Starr – pegged by the world as the least opinionated of the group – who walked out, announcing he'd quit the band.

In his place, McCartney played drums, with a little assistance from Lennon and Harrison; and the entire song was cut without Ringo. The result was a magnificent Beach Boys pastiche, which that group's lead singer, Mike Love, later claimed to have helped write. Hunter Davies's official Beatles biography, published in 1968, offered another story.

DEAR PRUDENCE

(John Lennon/Paul McCartney)
Recorded 28, 29, 30 August 1968
Prudence Farrow, sister of the actress Mia, was the subject of this generous, warm-hearted Lennon song. It was inspired by her

GLASS ONION

(John Lennon/Paul McCartney)
Recorded 11, 12, 13, 16 September, 10 October 1968
Like 'I Am The Walrus', 'Glass Onion' was written by John Lennon as a deliberate riposte to critics and fans who thought they were discovering the Holy Grail in some of his more recherché lyrical imagery. "I wrote 'The Walrus was Paul' in that song," John explained many years later. "At that time I was still in my love cloud with Yoko, so I thought I'd just say something nice to Paul – you did a good job over these few years, holding us together. I thought, I've got Yoko, and you can have the credit."

Besides the deliberately obtuse lyrics 'Glass Onion' boasted a searing Lennon vocal, and a mournful string coda that cut against the mood of the song.

OB-LA-DI, OB-LA-DA

(John Lennon/Paul McCartney)
Recorded 3, 4, 5, 8, 9, 11, 15 July 1968
Day after day, Paul McCartney dragged The Beatles through take after take, and arrangement after arrangement, of a throwaway, mock-reggae tune about a singer and a man who "has a barrow in the marketplace". Was it worth it?

Well, the song has humour on its side, especially with the other Beatles throwing in the off-the-cuff comments that were fast becoming a trademark on their 1968 recordings. And 'Ob-La-Di, Ob-La-Da' did become a No. 1 hit for Marmalade. But rarely in The Beatles' career did they spend so much time on something so ephemeral.

WILD HONEY PIE
(John Lennon/Paul McCartney)
Recorded 20 August 1968
During the 'White Album' sessions, Paul McCartney felt comfortable enough for the first time to capture some of his one-minute

WHILE MY GUITAR GENTLY WEEPS
(George Harrison)
Recorded 5, 6 September 1968
George Harrison won such acclaim for this song that he was tempted to write a much less successful follow-up, 'This Guitar (Can't Keep From Crying)'. Ironically, the most famous guitar solo on any Beatles record was played by an outsider – Cream guitarist Eric Clapton, a close friend of Harrison's, who was invited to the session both for his musical skills and in an attempt to cool the frequently heated passions in the studio.

"I wanted to do something in music and my dad gave me a trumpet for my birthday. I went through trying to learn that but my mouth used to get too sore. Then I realised I woulnd't be able to sing if I played the trumpet, so I figured a guitar would be better." – Paul

moments of madness on tape. He recorded this strange, whimsical ditty as a one-man band, overdubbing several vocal parts and guitars, and emerging with 53 seconds of music that would never have been considered for release on any Beatles album but this one.

THE CONTINUING STORY OF BUNGALOW BILL
(John Lennon/Paul McCartney)
Recorded 8 October 1968
Anything went for this one-day session – a Spanish guitar intro borrowed from a sound effects tape, a vocal cameo from Yoko Ono, harmonies from Ringo's wife, Maureen Starkey, and mellotron from producer Chris Thomas. Lennon's lyrics told the semi-humorous story of a fellow Meditation convert, addicted to big game hunting, and everyone in the vicinity of the studio contributed to the singalong chorus.

As it was originally written, and demoed via a solo performance at Abbey Road, Harrison's song had an additional verse, which didn't survive beyond this initial (and quite magical) acoustic performance.

HAPPINESS IS A WARM GUN
(John Lennon/Paul McCartney)
Recorded 24, 25 September 1968
The song's original title – 'Happiness Is A Warm Gun In Your Hand' – left its social message perfectly clear. But besides reflecting John Lennon's moral outrage at the American firearms lobby, it also had a second function, as John explained: "It's sort of a history of rock and roll." And a third inspiration for the track was confirmed later, when he revealed that much of the most direct imagery in the song conveyed his sexual passion for Yoko Ono. Beatles and Apple Corps press officer Derek Taylor

contributed some of the song's most mysterious lines.

Musically, the track was a *tour de force*, albeit without the theatrics and orchestrations of the 'Pepper' album. It moved swiftly from a dream state to an air of menace, then a frenetic middle section, and finally a repeated four-chord chorus which somehow combined erotic fervour with an affectionate pastiche of Fifties rock'n'roll.

MARTHA MY DEAR
(John Lennon/Paul McCartney)
Recorded 4, 5 October 1968
What began as a McCartney solo piece, a deliciously romantic piano piece in his utterly distinctive style, ended up with the accompaniment augmented by a troupe of brass and string musicians. Thankfully, they didn't bury the whimsical charm of the song, whose heroine took her name from McCartney's near-legendary sheepdog.

I'M SO TIRED
(John Lennon/Paul McCartney)
Recorded 8 October 1968
Like 'Yer Blues', 'I'm So Tired' wins the Lennon prize for irony, this paean of self-doubt and boredom having been composed in the supposedly spiritual surroundings of the Maharishi Mahesh Yogi's Indian retreat. The ennui and desolation of Lennon's vocal filled in the tiny fragments of obliqueness in one of his most direct songs, and made for an eerie counterpoint to the optimistic, joyous McCartney numbers which surrounded it.

BLACKBIRD
(John Lennon/Paul McCartney)
Recorded 11 June 1968
Nature song? Love ballad? Message of support for the black power movement? McCartney's gently beautiful 'Blackbird' supported several interpretations, but required nothing more than appreciation for its flowing melody and its stark visual imagery. The recording was a solo performance, aided only by bird sounds borrowed from the EMI tape library.

Paul never wrote a simpler or more effective song.

PIGGIES
(George Harrison)
Recorded 19, 20 September, 10 October 1968
With the aid of his mother, who wrote the "damn good whacking" line, George intended 'Piggies' as humorous social satire – though its title soon meant that the counter-culture adopted it as an anti-police anthem. Continuing the animal theme of 'Blackbird', pig noises were added to the basic track (Lennon's sole contribution to the song), which was also augmented by a hefty orchestral arrangement, and a harpsichord played by the man who produced several 'White Album' sessions, Chris Thomas.

ROCKY RACCOON
(John Lennon/Paul McCartney)
Recorded 15 August 1968
Anyone scouring The Beatles' catalogue for early signs of the playfulness in which Paul McCartney indulged – some would say over-indulged — during his solo career could find plenty of evidence on the 'White Album'. With the assistance of George Martin on saloon-bar piano, the group (minus Harrison) completed this attractive but lightweight mock-Western ditty in just one session.

DON'T PASS ME BY
(Richard Starkey)
Recorded 5, 6 June, 12, 22 July 1968
After five years of trying, Ringo Starr finally got his first solo composition on a Beatles album. It turned out to be a country hoedown with playful lyrics and a generally lugubrious air, with some off-the-cuff fiddle playing by Jack Fallon, who'd met The Beatles six years earlier when he promoted one of their concerts in Stroud.

For some reason – maybe because they felt it was one of the least important songs on the album – Lennon and McCartney chose to experiment with the mixing of this track, emerging with mono and stereo versions that run at recognisably different speeds, and have variations in the instrumental overdubs.

WHY DON'T WE DO IT IN THE ROAD?
(John Lennon/Paul McCartney)
Recorded 9, 10 October 1968
John Lennon called this near-solo McCartney performance "one of his best", which was either sarcasm or showed that he always valued his partner's off-the-cuff moments more than his controlled ones. Ringo added his drums to a basic piano, guitar and vocal track that Paul had recorded without the assistance or knowledge of the other group members. Raucous and good-humoured, it was a rare moment of levity from the man increasingly left to direct the group's activities.

The song's (very) slightly risqué lyric, all two lines of it, heightened the vague air of controversy surrounding the album. McCartney was already in trouble with the press for allowing a minuscule nude picture of himself to be included on the set's free poster.

I WILL
(John Lennon/Paul McCartney)
Recorded 16, 17 September 1968
It took 67 takes for Lennon, McCartney and Starr to come up with a basic track for this gentle love song that met its composer's expectations. McCartney then added his tuneful vocal, sang his bass part rather than playing it, and still found time during the session to ad-lib a dreamy song called something like 'Can You Take Me Back', which duly found its way onto the finished album as an uncredited snippet between 'Cry Baby Cry' and 'Revolution 9'.

JULIA
(John Lennon/Paul McCartney)
Recorded 13 October 1968
It was Donovan who taught John Lennon the finger-picking style that he used on this song, as well as 1969 recordings like 'Sun King' and Yoko Ono's 'Remember Love'. For the first and last time in The Beatles' career, this was an entirely solo performance by John – dedicated both to his late mother (Julia Lennon) and to Yoko. Translated into English, her name apparently means 'Ocean child', a phrase which was incorporated into Lennon's lyric.

BIRTHDAY
(John Lennon/Paul McCartney)
Recorded 18 September 1968
Either side of repairing to McCartney's house to watch the classic rock'n'roll movie, *The Girl Can't Help It*, on TV, The Beatles recorded this riff-based rocker – one of the last genuine Lennon/McCartney collaborations. Two Beatle partners, Pattie Harrison and Yoko Ono, sang the answer vocals in the chorus, while the band rocked out as if they hadn't a care in the world. It was a rare show of old-style unity during a difficult few months of recording.

YER BLUES
(John Lennon/Paul McCartney)
Recorded 13, 14, 20 August 1968
Written from the supposed haven of the Maharishi's camp in Rishikesh, 'Yer Blues' was an anguished confession of loneliness and pain, wrapped in a deliberately self-mocking title. "There was a self-consciousness about suddenly singing blues," Lennon explained in 1970. "I was self-conscious about doing it."

With its references to Bob Dylan and rock'n'roll, 'Yer Blues' was obviously intended to be a definitive statement of Lennon's boredom with his role – definitive, that is, until the "I don't believe in Beatles" cry in 'God' on his *Plastic Ono Band* album. The song meant enough to him to be reprised both at The Rolling Stones' *Rock'N'Roll Circus* TV show in December, and at the Toronto festival the following year.

MOTHER NATURE'S SON
(John Lennon/Paul McCartney)
Recorded 9, 20 August 1968
Like 'Blackbird', 'Mother Nature's Son' was a gentle, pastoral acoustic song which captured McCartney's writing at its most inspired. Augmented by a subtle horn arrangement, it epitomised the devastating switch of moods and tempos that made this album – and indeed The Beatles' work in general – so remarkable.

EVERYBODY'S GOT SOMETHING TO HIDE EXCEPT ME AND MY MONKEY
(John Lennon/Paul McCartney)
Recorded 26, 27 June, 1, 23 July 1968
Playing with lyrical opposites, then lapsing into nonsense for the chorus, John Lennon concocted a rock'n'roll song that suggested more than it meant. Such a tongue-in-cheek number deserved an appropriate arrangement, and The Beatles set out to enjoy the process of recording it – speeding up the tape of the backing track to heighten the frantic feel, and then hurling a motley collection of screams, cries and even some singing into the fade-out.

SEXY SADIE
(John Lennon/Paul McCartney)
Recorded 13, 21 August 1968
"That was about the Maharishi," explained John in 1970, when quizzed about the identity of the mysterious Sadie. "I copped out and wouldn't write 'Maharishi, what have you done, you made a fool of everyone'. There was a big hullabaloo about him trying to rape Mia Farrow, and things like that.

So we went to see him. I was the spokesman, as usual whenever the dirty work came. I said, 'We're leaving'. He asked, 'Why?', and all that shit, and I said, 'Well, if you're so cosmic, you'll know why.'"

In the studio, Lennon briefly demonstrated the song's original obscene lyrics, which made no attempt to shield the Maharishi by the use of poetry. On the record, though, the insult was softened by the sheer beauty of the music, which hinged around McCartney's brilliant piano playing, and some acerbic singing from John. Eight bars of instrumental work were removed from the fade-out during the final mix, incidentally.

HELTER SKELTER
(John Lennon/Paul McCartney)
Recorded 9, 10 September 1968
"That came about because I read in *Melody Maker* that The Who had made some track or other that was the loudest, most raucous rock'n'roll, the dirtiest thing they've ever done," Paul McCartney explained. "I didn't know what track they were talking about but it made me think, 'Right. Got to do it.' And I totally got off on that one little sentence in the paper."

On July 18, then, The Beatles gathered at Abbey Road to match that description, and emerged with a 27-minute jam around a menacing guitar riff. Still unreleased, this live-in-the-studio recording was the heaviest track The Beatles ever made.

Seven weeks later, they tried again, this time aware that they needed to make their statement in five minutes, not 27. Having cut the basic track, they added a chaotic barrage of horns, distortion and guitar feedback, and then prepared two entirely different mixes of the song – the stereo one running almost a minute longer than the mono, which omitted Ringo's pained shout, "I've got blisters on my fingers."

A year later, Charles Manson's followers wrote the words 'Helter Skelter' in blood as they killed actress Sharon Tate and her friends in her Hollywood home. Bizarrely, John Lennon (rather than McCartney, the song's composer) was called as a witness in the trial, but refused to attend. "What's 'Helter Skelter' got to do with knifing somebody?" he complained. "I've never listened to the words properly, it was just a noise."

LONG LONG LONG
(George Harrison)
Recorded 7, 8, 9 October 1968
Without John Lennon, who as usual was mysteriously absent when a Harrison song appeared on the agenda, The Beatles managed 67 takes of this delicately lyrical number. Then they capped a low-key, almost inaudible performance with a few moments of chaos – capturing the sound of a wine bottle vibrating on top of a speaker cabinet, and matching it with a flurry of guitars, groans and drums.

REVOLUTION 1
(John Lennon/Paul McCartney)
Recorded 30, 31 May, 4, 21 June 1968
For the first and last time, The Beatles succeeded on 30 May 1968 in recording the basic backing for two different tracks at exactly the same time. How? It was quite simple. At the first session for their new album, they recorded a ten-minute rendition of John's latest song – best interpreted as an overt political statement, backing the stance of the main Communist Parties in the debates over the student riots in Paris, rather than the calls from ultra-left parties for immediate revolution. (Later, Lennon would take entirely the opposite political position.)

The first four minutes became 'Revolution 1', originally planned as a single but eventually deemed too low-key, and subsequently re-recorded in an entirely electric arrangement; the last six minutes, a cacophony of feedback and vocal improvisation, was transported to become the basis of 'Revolution 9'.

HONEY PIE
(John Lennon/Paul McCartney)
Recorded 1, 2, 4 October 1968
Not a revival of a flappers' favourite from the Twenties but a McCartney original, 'Honey Pie' must have owed something to the music of his father Jim McCartney's jazz band. Scratches from an old 78rpm record were added to one of the opening lines of the song, to boost its period flavour. George Martin scored the brass and woodwind arrangement, and that arch experimentalist, John Lennon, was quite happy to add electric guitar to a song that was the total opposite of all his contributions to the album.

SAVOY TRUFFLE
(George Harrison)
Recorded 3, 5, 11, 14 October 1968
George Harrison wrote this playful song, inspired by a close friend: "Eric Clapton had a lot of cavities in his teeth and needed dental work. He ate a lot of chocolates – he couldn't resist them. I got stuck with the two bridges for a while, and Derek Taylor wrote some of the words in the middle." Taylor therefore collected his second anonymous credit on the 'White Album', but no royalties. Harrison, meanwhile, borrowed most of the lyrics from the inside of a chocolate box, while John Lennon commented on proceedings by not turning up for any of the sessions where the song was recorded.

CRY BABY CRY
(John Lennon/Paul McCartney)
Recorded 16, 18 July 1968
Consult Hunter Davies's book once again to find John Lennon's rather apologetic description of how he wrote this song – which in one of his final interviews he denied ever having been involved with, the two days of sessions obviously struck from his mental record.

Using characters that sounded as if they'd been borrowed from a Lewis Carroll story, Lennon spent some time (but not too much) working up a song which he seems to have regarded from the start as a blatant piece of filler.

REVOLUTION 9
(John Lennon/Paul McCartney)
Recorded 30, 31 May, 4, 6, 10, 11, 20, 21 June, 16 September 1968

On the raucous collage of sounds that was the second half of the original 'Revolution 1' (see opposite), John Lennon and Yoko Ono built an aural nightmare, intended to capture the atmosphere of a violent revolution in progress. By far the most time-consuming 'White Album' track to complete, and then the most controversial when the record was released, 'Revolution 9' was John and Yoko's most successful venture into the world of sound-as-art.

The track began bizarrely enough, with a snippet of an unreleased Paul McCartney song (see 'I Will'), then an EMI test tape repeating the words "number nine" over and over again. After that, there was chaos – a cavalcade of tape loops, feedback, impromptu screams and carefully rehearsed vocal overdubs, sound effects recordings and the noise of a society disintegrating. Reportedly, Paul McCartney agreed to the inclusion of the track only with severe misgivings, which George Martin expressed more forcibly.

GOOD NIGHT
(John Lennon/Paul McCartney)
Recorded 28 June, 2, 22 July 1968

The composer of this lush and sentimental ballad was not the lush and sentimental Paul McCartney, but the acerbic and cynical John Lennon, whose contributions to the 'White Album' therefore ranged from the ultra-weird to the ultra-romantic within two consecutive tracks. Fast becoming the children's favourite of The Beatles, Ringo Starr sang this lullaby, to a purely orchestral accompaniment. None of the other three Beatles appears on the track.

YELLOW SUBMARINE

Parlophone CDP7 46445 2
Released December 1968

The decision to base a cartoon film on a fictionalised version of the 1967 Beatles, named after one of their best-loved songs and featuring characters loosely taken from several others, brought to an end a stand-off which had been threatening to become embarrassing. Ever since they'd completed *Help!* in the summer of 1965, The Beatles had owed United Artists another film. Initially, they'd swallowed their lack of enthusiasm for another comic romp, and considered various scripts submitted in late 1965 and early 1966. A year after that, Brian Epstein was still promising the outside world that the movie would shortly begin production – though no final script or concept was ever agreed.

One of Epstein's last important deals before his death was his agreement to assist with the making of *Yellow Submarine*, which would require little or no active involvement from The Beatles, bar the submission of several new songs. The group did not even have to supply the voices for their cartoon selves, actors taking over that role, and creating a minor press 'scandal' in the process. As it turned out, The Beatles were so delighted by the finished cartoon – having expected crassness and been shown something close to art – that they agreed to appear in a final real-life scene, giving their public approval to the movie.

Until then, however, their contribution had been minimal. The film company has asked for new songs but not many were forthcoming, and those that did were rejects from 1967 sessions. The balance of power in the group dictated that two of the four rejects were George Harrison compositions – one of them the most striking piece of psychedelia The Beatles ever recorded.

These four new songs were originally planned for release as an EP. This was considered unsuitable for the American market, however, and so an album was concocted, combining the new items with two old songs from the soundtrack, plus twenty minutes of George Martin's incidental music. The group presumably decided against an LP made up of all their film songs because it would have repeated too many of the numbers from the *Sgt. Pepper* and *Magical Mystery Tour* albums.

YELLOW SUBMARINE
(John Lennon/Paul McCartney)
Recorded 26 May, 1 June 1966
Unchanged from its appearance on *Revolver*, the title song from the *Yellow Submarine* cartoon was one of two songs making its second appearance on a Beatles record.

ONLY A NORTHERN SONG
(George Harrison)
Recorded 13, 14 February, 20 April 1967

"A joke relating to Liverpool, the Holy City in the North of England," is how George Harrison described this song – bizarrely never issued in 'true' stereo. The joke, incidentally, refers to Northern Songs, the company who published compositions by Lennon, McCartney and (in 1967, at least) Harrison. The lyrical *non sequiturs* and lugubrious musical backing made this one of the more unusual Beatles recordings, even by 1967 standards.

ALL TOGETHER NOW
(John Lennon/Paul McCartney)
Recorded 12 May 1967
Written with the film very much in mind, McCartney's singalong ditty became a children's favourite, completed in just over five hours of studio work. It's hard to imagine a song this slight being considered for any of the other Beatles albums.

HEY BULLDOG
(John Lennon/Paul McCartney)
Recorded 11 February 1968
"I went to see The Beatles' recording, and I said to John, 'Why do you always use that beat all the time, the same beat, why don't you do something more complex?'" Yoko Ono's question mightn't have been the most tactful way of greeting her first sight of her husband-to-be at work. On this occasion, in fact, simplicity was bliss. Gathered in the studio to shoot a promo film for the 'Lady Madonna' single, The Beatles made use of the opportunity to complete their obligations to the film company. Like 'I Am The Walrus', 'Hey Bulldog' defied detailed lyrical analysis, but its wonderfully chaotic production and raw Lennon vocal made it a minor classic. The Beatles enjoyed it, too, as a listen to the fade-out makes clear.

IT'S ALL TOO MUCH
(George Harrison)
Recorded 25, 26 May, 2 June 1967
This song, said composer George Harrison, was "written in a childlike manner from realisations that appeared during and after some LSD experiences and which were later

confirmed in meditation." It was also a wonderfully inventive piece of psychedelia, a spirit-of-'67 freak-out that won fresh acclaim from a later wave of acid-rock adventurers in the late Seventies and early Nineties. Discordant, off-beat and effortlessly brilliant, the song was (alongside 'Taxman') Harrison's finest piece of Western rock music to date. Sadly, it was edited before release, losing one verse in its reduction from eight minutes to six.

 ALL YOU NEED IS LOVE
(John Lennon/Paul McCartney)
Recorded 14, 19, 23, 24, 25 June 1967
Fanatics please note: the mix of this song included on the *Yellow Submarine* album was marginally different from the original hit single.

Remaining tracks on original album by George Martin
PEPPERLAND
George Martin
SEA OF TIME & SEA OF HOLES
George Martin
SEA OF MONSTERS
George Martin
MARCH OF THE MEANIES
George Martin
PEPPERLAND LAID WASTE
George Martin
YELLOW SUBMARINE IN PEPPERLAND
(John Lennon/Paul McCartney); arranged by George Martin

Aside from Martin's orchestral revamp of the film's title song, these attractive instrumental numbers had no connection with The Beatles. Their presence on the CD made *Yellow Submarine* the least inspiring of The Beatles' albums for all but the determined completist.

In September 1999, to coincide with the release of a remastered print of the *Yellow Submarine* film, a new *Yellow Submarine* 'songtrack' album was released. It included all Beatles songs heard in the film, without

the George Martin instrumental material.

Described not as a soundtrack but as a 'songtrack', the album features 15 fully remixed and digitally remastered tracks: 'Yellow Submarine', 'Hey Bulldog', 'Eleanor Rigby', 'Love You To', 'All Together Now', 'Lucy In The Sky With Diamonds', 'Think For Yourself', 'Sgt. Pepper's Lonely Hearts Club Band', 'With A Little Help From Myself', 'Baby You're A Rich Man', 'Only A Northern Song', 'All You Need Is Love', 'When I'm Sixty Four', 'Nowhere Man' and 'It's All Too Much'.

ABBEY ROAD

Parlophone CDP7 46446 2
Released September 1969

The Beatles finished work on the 'White Album' in October 1968. It was released in November, followed in January 1969 by the *Yellow Submarine* soundtrack LP. That month, The Beatles also recorded what eventually became the *Let It Be* LP. And three weeks after the end of the basic sessions for that record, the group began work on another new album.

Within the space of a year, then, The Beatles recorded or released around 60 new songs. So you'd expect the last of these albums to suffer in the songwriting stakes. *Abbey Road* may have its throwaways, especially in the lengthy medley on the original second side of the LP, but many fans regard it as the best album The Beatles ever made. It's also their best selling album.

That isn't a view that John Lennon would have backed, though. He regarded the album as contrived, a deliberate repair-job on The Beatles' image after the disastrous *Let It Be* sessions. Producer George Martin had a more balanced view of *Abbey Road*: "That whole album was a compromise. One side was a whole series of titles which John preferred and the other side was a programme Paul and I preferred. I had been trying to get them to think in symphonic terms and think of the entire shape of the album and getting some form to it – symphonic things like bringing songs back in counterpoint to other songs, actually shaped things. And I think if we had gone on making records, that was the way I would have done it. But we were already breaking up. *Abbey Road* was the death knell."

Martin's admission that he sided with Paul's concept for the record rather than John's is a tacit admission that the trio's working relationship had become irretrievably fragile. Lennon's response was virtually to withdraw

from the sessions. *Abbey Road* is very much a McCartney album, with strong cameos from George Harrison: Lennon's material either sat uneasily alongside the rest of the songs, or else was little more than hackwork.

And yet: The Beatles never played or sang together more brilliantly than they did on *Abbey Road*. In particular, the much-maligned Side Two medley – assembled from a collection of vignettes – is instrumentally tighter than anything they'd cut since *Revolver*. And never had The Beatles' harmony vocals been more inventive, or stunningly precise, than on this record. Countless times on the album there are moments of pure beauty, proof that if the talent is there art can sometimes force its way to the surface almost against the wishes of its creators.

 COME TOGETHER
(John Lennon/Paul McCartney)
Recorded 21, 22, 23, 25, 29, 30 July 1969
During the Lennons' Toronto bed-in in May 1969, one visitor to their humble hotel room was Timothy Leary, LSD guru and would-be liberator of the world's collective mind. Leary had decided to run for Congress, or the Senate, or anywhere that would have him, and had decided on a campaign slogan: 'Come together'. Knowing Lennon to have been a keen user of his favourite drug, Leary commissioned John to write a song of that title, which his followers could sing on the campaign trail.

Lennon did as he was asked, and came up with a banal ditty along the lines of "Come together and join the party". Then Leary went to jail. Lennon reckoned his obligations had now expired, and used the "come together" idea for himself. Instead of a political anthem, 'Come Together' became a celebration of marital sex, with verses that free-associated Chuck Berry style. (In fact, Lennon borrowed a little too blatantly from Berry's 'You Can't Catch Me', sparking a legal dispute that was still affecting his career six years later.)

John Lennon, Yoko Ono and Son Julian, December 10, 1968

In the studio, Lennon prefaced the song with a whispered refrain of "shoot" – which gained an unwelcome dose of irony 11 years later. The Beatles' version never quite caught fire, however, and Lennon remained fonder of the live remake he taped in 1972 at Madison Square Garden.

SOMETHING
(George Harrison)
Recorded 2, 5 May, 11, 16 July, 15 August 1969
What Frank Sinatra called "the greatest love song ever written", and he'd sung a few in his time, began life in 1968, when George Harrison listened to a track on one of the first batch of Apple Records LPs. The track in question was James Taylor's 'Something In The Way She Moves', and Harrison soon built a song around the phrase – little realising that it would become his best-known and most lucrative composition.

After recording a solo demo of 'Something' in February 1969, Harrison brought it to the 'Abbey Road' sessions in April. An initial attempt to cut the backing track was rejected; so the band, plus Billy Preston, regrouped early in May. At that point, the track lasted nearly eight minutes, ending in a rather low-key instrumental jam which was subsequently edited out of the mix. Sporadically over the next two months, Harrison added to the basic track, the final session featuring overdubs from 21 string players.

As he did later with 'My Sweet Lord' and 'All Things Must Pass', George had already given one of his best songs away to a friend by the time he recorded it himself. The recipient this time was Joe Cocker, though luckily for The Beatles his version appeared only after theirs. The Beatles' rendition, meanwhile, went on to become the first UK single pulled from one of their previously released albums, plus Harrison's first Beatles A-side.

The song reached a wider currency via Sinatra's regular performances. Tailoring the lyric to his own needs, Ol' Blue Eyes rewrote part of the middle section: "You stick around, Jack, she might show". Amused by this bastardisation of his work, George retained Sinatra's phrasing when he performed the song live in the early Nineties.

MAXWELL'S SILVER HAMMER
(John Lennon/Paul McCartney)
Recorded 9, 10, 11 July, 6 August 1969
To judge from the general level of enthusiasm on display when the song is performed in the *Let It Be* movie, no-one had much time for 'Maxwell's Silver Hammer' apart from its composer, Paul McCartney. A novelty song about a serial killer, it was distinguished by its blatant commercial appeal, and for its subtle use of a prototype Moog synthesiser by Paul.

OH! DARLING
(John Lennon/Paul McCartney)
Recorded 20, 26 April, 17, 18, 22, 23 July, 8, 11 August 1969
To his dying day, John Lennon resented the fact that Paul McCartney didn't ask him to sing the throat-shredding lead vocal on this Fifties-styled rocker. At session after session, in fact, McCartney would arrive early to attempt a take before his voice lost its flexibility. Eventually he nailed it, completing a performance that later inspired a 'tribute' of sorts, in the shape of 10cc's 'Oh Donna'.

OCTOPUS'S GARDEN
(Richard Starkey)
Recorded 26, 29 April, 17, 18 July 1969
As seen in the *Let It Be* movie, Ringo Starr arrived at the Apple Studios one day with the idea for a song. George Harrison turned it into one, rewriting the chord sequence, and suggesting ways in which the melody could be improved. With no egos at stake when a Ringo song was on the menu, The Beatles lent themselves whole-heartedly to the playful spirit of the song. Ringo revived memories of 'Yellow Submarine' with some suitably aquatic sound effects.

I WANT YOU (SHE'S SO HEAVY)

(John Lennon/Paul McCartney)
Recorded 22, 23 February, 18, 20 April, 8, 11, 20 August 1969

The first of the *Abbey Road* songs to be started was one of the last to be finished – and also the only Lennon composition on the album that sounded as if it came from the heart. Deliberately unpoetic, it was a simple cry of love for Yoko Ono, with a bluesy verse (based around the rhythm of the mid-Sixties Mel Torme hit, 'Coming Home Baby') locked to a relentless, multi-overdub guitar riff, concocted by Lennon and Harrison.

Besides the relentless plod of the guitar battalions, the closing minutes of the track resounded to the hiss and moan of the Moog synthesiser, adding an unearthly menace to what began as a simple song of love and lust.

HERE COMES THE SUN

(George Harrison)
Recorded 7, 8, 16 July, 6, 11, 15, 19 August 1969

Faced with a day of business meetings at Apple, George Harrison repaired to Eric Clapton's garden, where he wrote this beautiful song around some simple variations on a D-chord. Another instant classic to set alongside 'Something', it revealed Harrison as the dark horse of the group, rapidly rivalling his more prestigious bandmates. Once again, some delicate Moog touches enhanced the final mix.

BECAUSE

(John Lennon/Paul McCartney)
Recorded 1, 4, 5 August 1969

Though John Lennon later nailed this track as "a terrible arrangement", most fans regard it as one of the highlights of *Abbey Road* – both for the beauty of its lyrics (a pantheistic vision that was closer to romantic poetry than acid-inspired fantasy) and for the stunning three-part harmonies of Harrison, Lennon and McCartney. Lennon wrote the song around a piano riff he found when he asked Yoko to play Beethoven's 'Moonlight Sonata' – backwards.

YOU NEVER GIVE ME YOUR MONEY

(John Lennon/Paul McCartney)
Recorded 6 May, 1, 11, 15, 30, 31 July, 5 August 1969

"*Abbey Road* was really unfinished songs all stuck together," complained John Lennon in 1980. "Everybody praises the album so much, but none of the songs had anything to do with each other, no thread at all, only the fact that we stuck them together."
That's true, but it ignores the fact that the medley – which began with this song, and climaxed some fifteen minutes later with 'The End' – was great pop music, with a cascade of hooks, mini-choruses and themes interlocking to produce a tapestry of melody and sound.

'You Never Give Me Your Money' is the strongest of the medley songs. It began life as an ironic comment on The Beatles' business disputes, and achieved the same oblique lyrical significance as McCartney's best songs on *Pepper*. Within four minutes, it moves through five distinct sections without once appearing contrived.

SUN KING

(John Lennon/Paul McCartney)
Recorded 24, 25, 29 July 1969

'Sun King' revamped the guitar picking technique Lennon had used on 'Julia' the previous year, matched with the vocal harmonies of 'Because'. The song was a complete throwaway – most of the lyrics were mock-Spanish gobbledegook – but it *sounded* wonderful.

MEAN MR. MUSTARD

(John Lennon/Paul McCartney)
Recorded 24, 25, 29 July 1969

Originally up for consideration for the 'White Album', 'Mean Mr Mustard' was a Lennon fantasy which he'd based around a newspaper story about a notorious miser. Though it has an entirely different feel to 'Sun King', the two songs were recorded together as one musical piece, under the working title of 'Here Comes The Sun-King'.

POLYTHENE PAM
(John Lennon/Paul McCartney)
Recorded 25, 28 July 1969

Demonstrating that the medley was planned from the start, 'Polythene Pam' and 'She Came In Through The Bathroom Window' were also recorded as one. 'Polythene Pam', showing off John Lennon's best Scouser accent, was based loosely around a character he'd met in a near-orgy the previous year. It led seamlessly into...

SHE CAME IN THROUGH THE BATHROOM WINDOW
(John Lennon/Paul McCartney)
Recorded 25, 28 July 1969

Like its companion piece, 'She Came In Through The Bathroom Window' was loosely autobiographical – the spur this time being an attempted robbery at Paul McCartney's house, in which a fan had climbed in through aforesaid window in search of first-hand souvenirs. And like 'Something', a cover of this song ended up on Joe Cocker's second album, part of The Beatles' thank-you for Cocker's remarkable interpretation of 'With A Little Help From My Friends'.

GOLDEN SLUMBERS
(John Lennon/Paul McCartney)
Recorded 2, 3, 4, 30, 31 July, 15 August 1969

Thomas Dekker's 17th century lullaby took musical shape in Paul McCartney's hand, with one of those melodies that was entirely original but sounded on first hearing as if you'd known it your entire life. Once again, the song was recorded from the start as part of a medley with...

CARRY THAT WEIGHT
(John Lennon/Paul McCartney)
Recorded 2, 3, 4, 30, 31 July, 15 August 1969

Another McCartney composition, this reprised some of the lyrical and musical themes of 'You Never Give Me Your Money', and featured mass vocals from McCartney, Harrison and Starr. Lennon missed the sessions for this song, being otherwise detained in a Scottish hospital after a car crash.

THE END
(John Lennon/Paul McCartney)
Recorded 23 July, 5, 7, 8, 15, 18 August 1969

'Carry That Weight' sounds as if it had been taped at the same time as 'The End', but the latter was actually inserted over the fade-out of 'Carry That Weight' as an entirely separate recording. It features two lines of vocals, the second of which became something of a valediction to The Beatles: "And in the end, the love you make is equal to the love you take". There was Ringo's one and only drum solo on record, and a lengthy guitar section which featured interplay between Harrison, Lennon and McCartney. An orchestra was added to the final seconds of the song – all part of the extravaganza which provided a fitting finale to The Beatles' longest and most carefully structured suite of songs.

HER MAJESTY
(John Lennon/Paul McCartney)
Recorded 2 July 1969

It wasn't quite 'The End', though. At the close of a tape carrying a rough mix of the second side of the album, engineer John Kurlander inserted a brief 20-second ditty which had originally been meant to appear between 'Mean Mr Mustard' and 'Polythene Pam', until Paul McCartney decided he wanted it removed. When another engineer, Malcolm Davies, cut an acetate of the side, he assumed 'Her Majesty' was meant to be the final track. Paul liked the surprise element of including the song on the album – even though it began with the final chord of 'Mean Mr Mustard', while its own final chord was missing, hidden beneath the opening flurry of 'Polythene Pam'. Just as the chaos of 'You Know My Name (Look Up The Number)' brought The Beatles' singles career to a tongue-in-cheek close, 'Her Majesty' prevented anyone from claiming that the group's lengthy *Abbey Road* medley was a sign of pomposity.

LET IT BE

Parlophone CDP7 46447 2
Released May 1970

In November 1968, Paul McCartney finally realised that The Beatles were on the verge of internal collapse. Faced with the alternative of letting the group slip away, or fighting for their future, he made a decisive move. John Lennon and George Harrison had made their opposition to performing live with The Beatles very clear; Ringo Starr, meanwhile, was happy to go with the flow. But for one last time, McCartney persuaded the group to think again – to regain contact with their core audience by performing one, or at most two, live concerts, which would be filmed for a TV special. Maybe there'd be two TV shows in the deal, one covering the rehearsals, the other the concert. And the live performance would in turn become The Beatles' next album – a deliberate opposite to the months-long sessions for *Sgt. Pepper* and *The Beatles*.

Dates were booked at the Albert Hall, then the Roundhouse, for December; but the plans fell through. Harrison's opposition proved to be the crucial factor, but he did agree to film cameras documenting the band at work, with the possibility of a live show if the rehearsals went well enough.

So on January 2nd 1969, The Beatles assembled at Twickenham Film Studios for the first of three weeks' of fraught 'private' rehearsals. "It was a dreadful feeling in

Twickenham Studio being filmed all the time," said John Lennon after the trauma was over. "I just wanted them to go away. We'd be there at eight in the morning and you couldn't make music at that time. It was in a strange place with people filming and coloured lights."

Towards the end of the month, the venue moved to the group's own, newly-opened Apple Studios, where they were joined by Beatle-for-a-fortnight Billy Preston, whose presence helped calm the group's internal friction. There they attempted to record a 'live-in-the-studio' LP, taping hour after hour of ramshackle recordings. On January 30, they played their concert – on the roof of the Apple building, a couple of hundred feet above any possible audience. The next day, they performed several more songs live in front of the cameras, within the safety of the Apple studios. Then they dumped the tapes on engineer Glyn Johns, and told him to go away and come up with an album. Three weeks into February, they had already begun work on *Abbey Road*.

"We didn't want to know," Lennon admitted. "We just left it to Glyn and said, here, do it. It's the first time since the first album that we didn't have anything to do with it. None of us could be bothered going in. We were going to let it out with a really shitty condition, to show people what had happened to us."

Johns completed work on one version of the album, provisionally titled *Get Back*, in May; The Beatles rejected it. *Abbey Road* concentrated their attention for a while; then John Lennon told the others he was quitting the group. In January 1970, the remaining three Beatles taped one more song, and a final batch of overdubs, and Glyn Johns prepared a second *Get Back* LP. It too was turned down by all the group.

Enter legendary American producer Phil Spector, who'd been touting for work with The Beatles. In March 1970, he began an intensive week of remixing and overdubbing.

In the first week of May, the LP – retitled *Let It Be*, and packaged with a *Get Back* photo book that had been intended for the original album – was in the shops.

"When Spector came, it was 'go and do your audition'," Lennon explained. "And he worked like a pig on it. He'd always wanted to work with The Beatles and he was given the shittiest load of badly recorded shit with a lousy feeling to it ever, and he made something out of it. He did a great job. When I heard it, I didn't puke."

Paul McCartney did, though, appalled by the orchestral and choral overdubs added to his song, 'The Long And Winding Road'. Critics slated the album, and by the time the documentary film of the original sessions was released, McCartney had announced that he was leaving the group. Lennon's prior decision having been kept out of the media, he was promptly blamed for the break-up. By the end of 1970, Paul was suing the rest of the band in the High Court. As John Lennon put it, the dream was over.

TWO OF US
(John Lennon/Paul McCartney)
Recorded 31 January 1969
As the movie demonstrated, 'Two Of Us' began its life as a playful rocker, but quickly mutated into a gentle McCartney acoustic song – its title and duet format a final gesture of affection from Paul to John. The live-in-the-studio recording from January 1969 was brilliantly enhanced by Phil Spector's post-production, which gave the acoustic instruments a richness missing from any previous Beatles recording.

DIG A PONY
(John Lennon/Paul McCartney)
Recorded 30 January 1969
Edited down slightly from the rooftop recording, this was a typically obscure Lennon song, full of lines which promised much and never quite delivered. In the early years of the group, he'd concocted fictional love songs at will; in their closing months, he was equally capable of manufacturing lyrics that hinted at a spiritual depth they

didn't possess. Understandably, Lennon was sniffy about the song in later years.

ACROSS THE UNIVERSE
(John Lennon/Paul McCartney)
Recorded 4, 8 February 1968, 1 April 1970
John was anything but sniffy about 'Across The Universe', however. "It's one of the best lyrics I've written," he said proudly in 1970, "in fact it could be *the* best. It's good poetry, or whatever you call it. The ones I like are the ones that stand as words without melody." Composed in a stream-of-consciousness, early-hours lyrical torrent, it belongs in the category of poetry that describes its own creation, standing as a hymn of praise to whatever muse gave it birth. But Lennon never matched that sense of freedom in the recording studio. Originally taped in the same batch of sessions that produced 'Lady Madonna', the song was left to one side while the group decided what to do with it. First it was going to be a single, then a flipside, then an EP cut. It was revived unsuccessfully during the film sessions, but without a hint of inspiration. Finally, it was given away to the World Wildlife Fund for a charity album.

Phil Spector took the original tape, slowed it down a fraction, deleted the overdubbed bird sounds (see *Past Masters 2*), and added an orchestra and a choir. The result was one of the highlights of The Beatles' career, justification in itself for Spector's involvement in the creative process.

I ME MINE
(George Harrison)
Recorded 3 January, 1, 2 April 1970

For the last time, The Beatles gathered together in one place early in January 1970. Only one thing was wrong: The Beatles were now a three-piece, without John Lennon, who was having his hair cut and discovering the secret of how flying saucers worked in Denmark.

Cutting Harrison's tune – half waltz, half rocker – without Lennon wasn't a problem: the three other Beatles had performed it that way in the *Let It Be* movie, while John and Yoko danced around the studio floor. McCartney, Harrison and Starr ended up with a song barely 90 seconds long: Phil Spector simply copied chunks of the tape and nearly doubled its length.

DIG IT
(John Lennon/Paul McCartney/ George Harrison/Richard Starkey)
Recorded 26 January 1969

A brief extract from an improvised three-chord jam session that ran to more than 12 minutes on tape, 'Dig It' was included on the album to boost its verité credentials. The original *Get Back* LP would have included a longer chunk of the song, to no-one's great benefit. Check the hours of session tapes that have emerged from movie off-cuts, and you'll find that The Beatles were infatuated by the phrase 'dig it' in January 1969. They could have assembled a full album of their jams around the phrase, but thankfully resisted the temptation.

LET IT BE
(John Lennon/Paul McCartney)
Recorded 31 January, 30 April 1969, 4 January 1970

The Beatles' final single, and by far the strongest song débuted during the sessions, 'Let It Be' was a rare piece of spiritually-inspired writing from Paul McCartney. The 'Mother Mary' in the lyric was universally assumed to be his own mother, the late Mary McCartney, while the conciliatory tone of the song might have been an overt message of peace to the other Beatles.

Originally taped in front of the cameras in January 1969, the song was overdubbed with a lead guitar solo in April; then again with another in January 1970, at the same session in which a George Martin-scored brass section was overdubbed.

The first guitar solo appeared on the single; for this album mix, Phil Spector selected the rawer second effort, and also heightened the sound of Ringo and Paul's percussion, to the point where it threatened to become intrusive.

MAGGIE MAY
(Trad. arr. John Lennon/ Paul McCartney/George Harrison/ Richard Starkey)
Recorded 24 January 1969
Recorded between takes of 'Two Of Us', this was a 30-second, Lennon-led revival of a popular Liverpool folksong – rescued from the session tapes by George Martin and producer/engineer Glyn Johns.

I'VE GOT A FEELING
(John Lennon/Paul McCartney)
Recorded 30 January 1969
Mix an unfinished McCartney blues called 'I've Got A Feeling' with an unfinished Lennon acoustic ballad called 'Everybody Had A Hard Year', and you had one of the roughest and most impressive songs on the *Let It Be* album – taped during the Apple rooftop concert. This was the last song that Lennon and McCartney actively wrote as a songwriting partnership.

THE ONE AFTER 909
(John Lennon/Paul McCartney)
Recorded 30 January 1969
'The One After 909' joined 'What Goes On', 'When I'm Sixty-Four' and 'I'll Follow The Sun' on the list of pre-1960 Beatles songs released on official albums. Originally composed by John Lennon as an American-style rocker in 1959, the song was revived as a possible single in March 1963, though that version remains unreleased. Six years later, something reminded Lennon of the song, and he re-introduced it to the group's repertoire in time for the *Let It Be* film, and the rooftop concert at Apple in particular. Maybe not coincidentally, The Beatles sounded more relaxed playing this oldie in semi-satirical style than anywhere else in the movie.

THE LONG AND WINDING ROAD
(John Lennon/Paul McCartney)
Recorded 31 January 1969, 1 April 1970
One of the two great McCartney ballads premièred during these ill-fated sessions, 'The Long And Winding Road' began life as a gentle, piano-based performance, with mild accompaniment from the rest of The Beatles. In the hands of producer Phil Spector, however, it became a production extravaganza, with 50 musicians and vocalists overdubbed onto the basic track. McCartney hated the results, complaining that Spector had swamped his work with a Mantovani-style arrangement; Spector's defenders said that Phil had simply responded to the natural romanticism of the song. Paul also moaned about the presence of female vocalists on the track, which was somewhat ironic in view of his subsequent recording career.

FOR YOU BLUE
(George Harrison)
Recorded 25 January 1969
Harrison's slide-guitar blues – with John 'Elmore' Lennon on slide – was a slight but appealing song that fitted in well with the album's original, live-in-the-studio concept. It was one of the few tracks on the album taken from the early days of recording at Apple, rather than the rooftop concert or the subsequent 'before-the-cameras' session.

GET BACK
(John Lennon/Paul McCartney)
Recorded 27 January 1969
'Get Back' ended the *Let It Be* film, and the album, in 1970; and the same charming piece of Lennon dialogue ("I hope we passed the audition") followed it on both occasions. But the two versions of 'Get Back' were entirely different, the rooftop performance appearing in the film, while the LP ended with an Apple studios take that was recorded three days earlier. A longer version of the song had already been issued as a single in April 1969 (see *Past Masters* 2).

PART II
COMPILATION ALBUMS

Op Art bag from some Carnaby Street boutique, the album was useful to those who had worn out the grooves on their original singles, and by the inclusion of 'Bad Boy', originally released in the US on the *Beatles VI* in June 1965, which up until that point, had been unavailable in the UK.

A COLLECTION OF BEATLES OLDIES... BUT GOLDIES

Parlophone PMC 7016 (mono)/PCS 7016 (stereo)
Released December 1966
She Loves You, From Me To You, We Can Work It Out, Help!, Michelle, Yesterday, I Feel Fine, Yellow Submarine, Cant Buy Me Love, Bad Boy, Day Tripper, A Hard Days Night, Ticket To Ride, Paperback Writer, Eleanor Rigby, I Want To Hold Your Hand

The first official Beatles compilation assembled by EMI after realising their cash cow was unable (or unwilling) to deliver an album in time for the Christmas market. Packaged in a garish sleeve resembling an

THE BEATLES 1962-1966 (THE RED ALBUM)

Parlophone BEACD 2511
Released April 1973
Love Me Do, Please Please Me, From Me To You, She Loves You, I Want To Hold Your Hand, All My Loving, Can't Buy Me Love, A Hard Day's Night, And I Love Her, Eight Days A Week, I Feel Fine, Ticket To Ride, Yesterday, Help!, You've Got To Hide Your

Love away, We Can Work It Out, Day Tripper, Drive My Car Norwegian Wood (This Bird has Flown), Nowhere Man, Michelle, In My Life, Girl, Paperback Writer, Eleanor Rigby, Yellow Submarine

THE BEATLES 1967-1970 (THE BLUE ALBUM)

Parlophone BEACD 2512
April 1973
Strawberry Fields Forever, Penny Lane, Sgt. Pepper's Lonely Heart's Club Band, With A Little Help From My Friends, Lucy In The Sky With Diamonds, A Day In The Life, All You Need Is Love, I Am The Walrus, Hello Goodbye, The Fool On The Hill, Magical Mystery Tour, Lady Madonna, Hey Jude, Revolution, Back In The USSR, While My Guitar Gently Weeps, Ob-La-Di, Ob-La-Da, Get Back, Don't Let Me Down, The Ballad Of John And Yoko, Old Brown Shoe, Here Comes The Sun, Come Together, Something, Octopus's Garden, Let It Be, Across The Universe, The Long And Winding Road

These albums were originally issued to combat sales of *AlphaOmega,* two bootleg double album Beatles' 'hits' sets that were circulating widely in the USA. In a 1974 interview John revealed that the group had not been consulted as to the running order and he was appalled at the mixes which were used to create 'fake stereo' on certain tracks. Five years after their original release they were reissued on red and blue vinyl respectively. In September of 1993, after much procrastination due apparently to The Beatles' own refusal to sanction their

release, EMI finally issued these two albums on CD. Now universally known as the 'red' and 'blue' albums, their release caused no little controversy owing to Apple's insistence on their being produced as two double CDs – and priced accordingly – despite the fact that the two red albums lasted a total of only 62 minutes 46 seconds (and could therefore fit on to one CD). Critics were quick to point out that while the blue album ran over the limit for one CD (99.36), by shuffling the tracks around and deleting one from the blue album ('Octopus's Garden' perhaps?), the four CD package could easily have been issued as a two CD set at around £25 for the pair instead of around £50.

EMI – and Paul McCartney via a spokesman – defended themselves against the critics as best they could but the general tone of the press coverage was that for the first time ever, The Beatles had been guilty of short-changing their fans.

Nevertheless, the albums quickly ascended the charts and, of course, the music is wonderful.

ROCK'N'ROLL MUSIC

Parlophone PCSP 719
June 1976
Twist And Shout, I Saw Her Standing There, You Can't Do That, I Wanna Be Your Man, I Call Your Name, Boys, Long Tall Sally, Rock 'n' Roll Music, Slow Down, Kansas City/Hey, Hey, Hey, Hey, Money (That's What I Want), Bad Boy, Matchbox, Roll Over Beethoven, Dizzy Miss Lizzy, Anytime At All, Drive My Car,

Everybody's Trying To Be My Baby, The Night Before, I'm Down, Revolution, Back In The U.S.S.R., Helter Skelter, Taxman, Got To Get You Into My Life, Hey Bulldog, Birthday, Get Back

The first EMI compilation to emerge since the 'red' and 'blue' albums in 1973, *Rock'n'Roll Music* was largely the brainchild of Capitol Records in America, with certain tracks remastered by George Martin. Its arrival was prescient at a time when a second wave of Beatlemania was stirred up by EMI reissuing all 22 UK Beatles' singles (each of which charted), plus 'Yesterday' (which was not a British single at the time), the success of McCartney's Wings Over America tour and hot rumours of the "will they or won't they reform?" variety. Even the original *Beatles Book Monthly* was relaunched.

While the concept was off-kilter – The Beatles were more than *just* a rock'n'roll band – the album's four sides hung together well and provided useful ammunition against those who dismissed The Beatles as a prissy pop group. The thematic theme extended to the gatefold sleeve featuring an airbrushed collage of Fifties Americana: a Cadillac, a malt shake and Marilyn Monroe.

While successful commercially (US No. 2; UK No. 11), and to some, aesthetically, the artists themselves were less than amused. "I'd like some power over whoever is at EMI who's putting out these lousy Beatles compilations," Ringo ranted to *Melody Maker*. "They can do what they like with all our old stuff, we know that. It's theirs. But Christ, man, I was there. I played on those records and you know how much trouble we used to go to just getting the running order right... And the album covers! John rang them up and asked them if he could draw them one... John told me he was told to piss off. All of us looked at the cover (of *Rock 'n' Roll Music*) and could hardly bear to see it. It was terrible! So listen EMI, if you're reading this – please let us know what you're doing with the records we made.

We'd like it done, how do I say, nicely!"

THE BEATLES AT THE HOLLYWOOD BOWL

Parlophone EMTV 4
Released May 1977
Twist And Shout, She's A Woman, Dizzy Miss Lizzy, Ticket To Ride, Can't Buy Me Love, Things We Said Today, Roll Over Beethoven, Boys, A Hard Day's Night, Help!, All My Loving, She Loves You, Long Tall Sally

Several days after an unofficial Beatles live recording in Hamburg was released EMI countered with this scream-drenched document from The Beatles' three Hollywood Bowl concerts on August 23, 1964, and August 29 and 30, 1965.

Initially sceptical when approached by Capitol to release an album from the concerts, George Martin enthusiastically remixed the original three-track stereo tapes, in some cases – most notably 'Dizzy Miss Lizzy' - splicing together the different performances from each night.

The 1964 show (in mono) had long been a bootleg staple under such misleading titles as *Live At Shea Stadium* and was originally vetoed for release by Martin and The Beatles themselves who felt their performance had been drowned under the lung power of 17,000 hysterical fans.

Part of 'Twist And Shout' originally appeared on Capitol's *The Beatles Story* double in November 1964 while the August 30, 1965, performance of the same song was used for the soundtrack to the TV film of *The Beatles At Shea Stadium.*

Apart from that the tapes had lain gathering dust until EMI and Capitol, basking in the success of *Rock 'n' Roll Music* and The Beatles' single re-releases (see *Rock 'n' Roll Music*), made the approach to Martin. While John Lennon supposedly approved his work, the other ex-Beatles were not so keen, a factor which goes some way to explaining the album's non-appearance to date on the CD format. Bootlegs have helped to plug the gap while the original vinyl has increased in value.

before their next concoction; the bad news was they failed to heed Ringo's pleas (see opposite).

In common with its predecessor *Love Songs* was another thematically aimed double, instigated by Capitol, dressed up in a drab, oak coloured sleeve featuring Richard Avedon's well-known 1967 portrait of the four. To make sure that uninformed Wings' fans knew where their hero's roots lay Capitol's art department retouched the picture, shifting Paul to the front while a hapless Ringo diminished in prominence.

With punk rock at its apogee in the UK the album arrived like an unwanted guest but still managed to reach No. 7. Surprisingly the album fared comparatively poorly in America, stopping at 54.

LOVE SONGS

Parlophone PCSP 721
Released November 1977
Yesterday, I'll Follow The Sun, I Need You, Girl, In My Life, Words Of Love, Here, There And Everywhere, Something, And I Love Her, If I Fell, I'll Be Back, Tell Me What You See, Yes It Is, Michelle, It's Only Love, You're Going To Lose That Girl, Every Little Thing, For No One, She's Leaving Home, The Long And Winding Road, This Boy, Norwegian Wood (This Bird Has Flown), You've Got To Hide Your Love Away, I Will, P.S I Love You

Following the chart success of *Rock 'n' Roll Music* an EMI spokesman revealed that the company intended to release further Beatles compilations, although "we do not intend to saturate the record buying public." The good news was they waited nearly 18 months

EP tracks and other anomalies that weren't featured on those albums. Hardcore Beatles collectors were forced to pay out for the box to obtain this 'unique' item, carrying the rear sleeve disclaimer 'Sampler Album Not For Sale'.

Imagine their reactions when the very same record was issued separately (with new sleeve notes by *Sounds'* journalist Hugh Fielder) a year later. In America, a completely different version of *Rarities* was assembled by Capitol. The UK *Rarities* has now been rendered redundant by *Past Masters 1* and *2* (see entries for track details).

THE BEATLES BALLADS

Parlophone PCS 7214
Released October 1980
Yesterday, Norwegian Wood (This Bird Has Flown), Do You Want To Know A Secret, For No One, Michelle, Nowhere Man, You've Got To Hide Your Love Away, Across The Universe, All My Loving, Hey Jude, Something, The Fool On The Hill, Till There Was You, The Long And Winding Road, Here Comes The Sun, Blackbird, And I Love Her, She's Leaving Home, Here, There And Everywhere, Let It Be

In case you hadn't bought *Love Songs*, EMI issued this equally superfluous collection which duplicated many of the tracks anyway. How the likes of 'Nowhere Man' and 'Across The Universe' qualify as ballads defies logic. Expectant punters for *The Beatles Ragas* were left wanting.

RARITIES

Parlophone PCM 1001
Released October 1979
Across The Universe (World Wildlife Fund version), Yes It Is, This Boy, The Inner Light, I'll Get You, Thank You Girl, Komm Gib Mer Deine Hand, You Know My Name (Look Up the Number), Sie Liebt Dich, Rain, She's A Woman, Matchbox, I Call Your Name, Bad Boy, Slow Down, I'm Down, Long Tall Sally

The biggest con of all! When compiling their boxed collection of The Beatles' twelve studio albums in 1978 *Rarities* was put together as a catch-all for single B-sides,

REEL MUSIC

Parlophone PCS 7218
Released March 1982
A Hard Day's Night, I Should Have Known Better, Can't Buy Me Love, And I Love Her, Help!, You've Got To Hide Your Love Away, Ticket To Ride, Magical Mystery Tour, I Am The Walrus, Yellow Submarine, All You Need Is Love, Let It Be, Get Back, The Long And Winding Road

20 GREATEST HITS

Parlophone PCTC260
Released October 1982
Love Me Do, From Me To You, She Loves You, I Want To Hold Your Hand, Can't Buy Me Love, A Hard Day's Night, I Feel Fine, Ticket To Ride, Help!, Day Tripper, We Can Work It Out, Paperback Writer, Yellow Submarine, Eleanor Rigby, All You Need Is Love, Hello Goodbye, Lady Madonna, Hey Jude, Get Back, The Ballad Of John And Yoko

"I don't want to boast but when we were playing in Liverpool I was one of the two best drummers in town. We used to play for ten bob a night. I don't think I could ever do that again." – Ringo

Perhaps the absolute nadir of EMI's repackaging initiative, this assemblage of tracks from The Beatles' feature films was accompanied by a single – a cut-up medley, imaginatively titled 'The Beatles Movie Medley' - to capitalise on the contemporaneous success of the wretched 'Stars On 45' hit medleys - which cracked the Top 10 in Britain. The album (accompanied with a 12-page booklet of film stills and memorabilia) reached No. 19 in America.

A precursor to *1* (see entry) this TV-advertised hits collection was as uninviting a proposition as its tacky sleeve suggested. A Stalinist revision removed 'Please Please Me' from its rightful No. 1 status, 'Penny Lane' and 'Strawberry Fields Forever' were also expunged completely, while the singles trail ran out (undoubtedly because of space constrictions) at 'The Ballad Of John And Yoko'.

PAST MASTERS VOLUME 1

Parlophone CDP7 90043
Released March 8 1988

Once EMI had issued all the original UK Beatles albums on CD, they were left with several options for completing the digital transfer of the entire back catalogue. Happily, they chose the most sensible, collecting together all the leftover tracks, in (more or less) chronological order, across two CDs. Included were their non-LP singles (including the different versions of 'Love Me Do', 'Get Back' and 'Let It Be' from those on LPs), the songs from the *Long Tall Sally* EP, the two German-language tracks from 1964, the elusive 'Bad Boy' from 1965, and the 'original' mix of 'Across The Universe', previously issued only on a budget charity LP. EMI resisted the temptation to flesh out the packages with 'rarities' like mono mixes and marginally different edits that had appeared in Britain and around the world, though the specialist market would no doubt relish a CD or two of these minor delights.

LOVE ME DO
(John Lennon/Paul McCartney)
Recorded 4 September 1962
"Our greatest philosophical song," Paul McCartney called it tongue-in-cheek. But it was, in this original version with Ringo Starr on drums, The Beatles' first single, later replaced on album and 45 by the version available on the 'Please Please Me' CD.

FROM ME TO YOU
(John Lennon/Paul McCartney)
Recorded 5 March 1963
On the bus between York and Shrewsbury, on 28 February 1963, John Lennon and Paul McCartney wrote the third Beatles' single. Like many of their early songs, it was deliberately built around heavy use of personal pronouns – the idea being that their audience could easily identify with the 'me' and 'you' in the title.

The opening harmonica solo was George Martin's suggestion, and proved to be a major part of the record's appeal. Equally commercial was the simple melody line of the chorus, which leaves 'From Me To You' as one of the less durable Beatles 45s.

THANK YOU GIRL
(John Lennon/Paul McCartney)
Recorded 5, 13 March 1963
Songwriting for The Beatles in 1963 was less about self-expression than it was about a constant search for hit records. John Lennon's 'Thank You Girl' was one of the attempts that didn't quite make it, despite all the usual ingredients – his harmonica showcase, an easy-on-the-ear melody and a vocal gimmick. This time simplicity was taken a step too far, and 'Thank You Girl' wouldn't have withstood the constant airplay that every Beatles single was treated to in the Sixties.

SHE LOVES YOU
(John Lennon/Paul McCartney)
Recorded 1 July 1963
"People said at the time that this was the worst song we'd ever thought of doing," Paul McCartney mused in 1980, and the reviews of their fourth single were a trifle sniffy, suggesting that the group were struggling for new material. Instead, 'She Loves You' proved to be the anthem of Beatlemania. It's not the strongest song they recorded in 1963, or perhaps the most important (that honour must go to 'I Want To Hold Your Hand', which broke them in America), but more than anything else, it conjures up the exuberance which so entranced the nation in the latter half of 1963.

George Martin regarded the final vocal harmony as a cliché, which it may have been in classical terms, but to the pop audience it was a revelation. What sold the record, and The Beatles, though, was the sheer inane appeal of the chorus. Even now, repeat the phrase 'yeah, yeah, yeah' to almost anyone in the country, and they'll catch the reference to The Beatles.

I'LL GET YOU
(John Lennon/Paul McCartney)
Recorded 1 July 1963
Like 'Thank You Girl' this Lennon number came straight off the production line, though this time the melody line wasn't quite catchy enough for a single. Take note of the middle eight, however, where John demonstrated that he was every bit as strong a tunesmith as McCartney.

I WANT TO HOLD YOUR HAND
(John Lennon/Paul McCartney)
Recorded 17 October 1963
"We wrote that together," John admitted after The Beatles split up, in a rare nod of the head to his ex-partner. "It's a beautiful melody – the kind of song I like to sing."

And it broke The Beatles as a worldwide phenomenon, becoming their first No. 1 in America, and indeed topping the charts in almost every part of the globe. Cunningly structured, with a drop in tension in the middle section leading to the climactic "I can't hide" (memorably misheard by Bob Dylan as "I get high"), the song was the culmination of a solid year of experimentation and learning by The Beatles' creative axis.

THIS BOY
(John Lennon/Paul McCartney)
Recorded 17 October 1963
The first great three-part harmony vehicle in The Beatles' catalogue was written by John Lennon around the standard doo-wop chord changes that had fuelled hundreds of hit records in the Fifties. What made the song was not just the tightness of the harmonies, but the sheer liberation of the middle section – Lennon stretching out the final syllable over several bars. The Beatles accentuated the drama of the moment less on record than they did subsequently on stage, where it rivalled the two-heads-shaking-at-one-microphone routine for audience response. 'This Boy' made an ideal underbelly for the 'I Want To Hold Your Hand' single.

KOMM, GIB MIR DEINE HAND
(John Lennon/Paul McCartney/ Nicolas/Hellmer)
Recorded 29 January 1964
It was in Paris, bizarrely enough, that The Beatles recorded German-language renditions of their two most recent singles. Most recording stars of the time were required to re-cut their hits in European languages, but having endured the process once, The Beatles said never again.
This translation of 'I Want To Hold Your Hand' was marginally the more successful of the two tracks, using the original backing plus overdubbed handclapping.

SIE LIEBT DICH
(John Lennon/Paul McCartney/ Nicolas/Montague)
Recorded 29 January 1964
The original tape of the English 'She Loves You' had already been destroyed when this German version was required, so The Beatles had to re-record the song from the top, skipping through it with only minor attention to detail.

LONG TALL SALLY
(Richard Penniman/Enotris Johnson/Robert Blackwell)
Recorded 1 March 1964
In just one magnificent take, with no overdubs, The Beatles recorded the finest rock'n'roll performance of their career – seizing Little Richard's 1956 classic and remaking it as their own. George Harrison's solo was spot-on first time, and George Martin duplicated Richard's piano-thumping. What clinched the track, though, was Paul McCartney's throat-searing lead vocal, his finest uptempo performance ever in a recording studio. The song became the title track of (appropriately enough) the group's best-ever EP.

I CALL YOUR NAME
(John Lennon/Paul McCartney)
Recorded 1 March 1964
Already recorded by fellow Brian Epstein protégé Billy J. Kramer the previous year,

this Lennon song was forcibly reclaimed by its composer on the 'Long Tall Sally' EP. John's dogmatic vocals suggested he didn't care whether the girl in question answered his call or not, in stark contrast to Kramer's more submissive delivery. As Lennon remarked in 1980, the group approached the guitar solo as a ska band, loping slightly uncomfortably through the Jamaican rhythm before returning to more solid ground for the next verse.

SLOW DOWN
(Larry Williams)
Recorded 1, 4 June 1964
Though it didn't quite match the sheer excitement of 'Long Tall Sally', Lennon's ultra-confident handling of the Larry Williams rocker (the first of three the band recorded) ran it close. Aided by George Martin's piano, The Beatles cruised through this 12-bar, though it was the rasp in Lennon's voice that pushed it beyond the reach of their British beat group rivals.

MATCHBOX
(Carl Perkins)
Recorded 1 June 1964
The Carl Perkins songbook was raided for the first time on the final *Long Tall Sally* EP number. Ringo Starr was showcased on this rockabilly tune, based on lyrical ideas that had been circulating the blues world for decades. The song's composer was on hand to witness the recording, which (alongside the two Perkins covers on *Beatles For Sale*) kept him in royalties for decades to come.

I FEEL FINE
(John Lennon/Paul McCartney)
Recorded 18 October 1964
From the opening buzz of feedback (not a studio accident, as claimed at the time, but a conscious decision to use this electronic howl) to the cool passion of John Lennon's vocal, the group's final single of 1964 oozed quality and control. Lennon based the finger-twisting guitar riff on Bobby Parker's R&B record, 'Watch Your Step', which had been covered by The John Barry Seven as early as 1961, and was well known among British

THE BEATLES
THE MUSIC AND THE MYTH

1940

July 9
Richard Starkey (Ringo Starr)
born in Liverpool, the birthplace of
all four Beatles.

1942

June 18
James Paul McCartney born.

1940

October 9
John Winston
Lennon born.

1943

February 24
George Harrison born.

1957

July 6
John and Paul meet for the first time,
at the Woolton Parish Church Garden Fete,
held at St. Peter's Church where
The Quarrymen are performing.

October 18
Paul plays his first gig with The Quarrymen.

1960

January 17
John's friend Stuart Sutcliffe
is persuaded by John to
buy a bass guitar and join
Johnny & The Moondogs.

August 6
The Beatles invite Pete Best
to be their drummer.

1958

February 6
George joins
the Quarrymen.

1961

February 9
They play their The Cavern under
the name of The Beatles. The
club would become forever
associated with the group.

November 9
Brian Epstein see The Beatles for
the first time at the Cavern.

1962

January 1
The Beatles audition
for Decca Records but
are turned down.

1962

April 10
Stuart Sutcliffe, who had remained in
Hamburg, is rushed to hospital with a brain
haemorrhage, but dies in the ambulance.
He was 22.

1962

August 18
Ringo joins The Beatles.

August 23
John marries
Cynthia Powell.

1963

March 22
The album *Please, Please Me*
is released in the UK

1964

February 7
The Beatles fly to New York City
on Pan Am flight 101, where 3,000
fans are waiting at JFK airport.

1965

August 15
The Beatles play Shea Stadium, the
biggest rock in history at that time.

1966

January 21
George marries Pattie Boyd at the
Leatherhead & Esher Register Office, Surrey.

1964

February 11
They make their US live debut at
the Washington Coliseum,
protected by 362 police officers,

1966

August 29
The last ever
Beatles concert,
at Candlestick Park,
San Francisco.

1968

May 14
John and Paul give a press
conference at the Americana Hotel
on Central Park West to announce
the formation of Apple.

1967

June 1
*Sgt Pepper's
Lonely Hearts
Club Band* is
released.

1969

March 12
Paul and Linda
are married at
Marylebone
Register Office.

1969

August 8
The now famous photograph
of The Beatles walking across
the zebra crossing near the
Abbey Road recording studio
is taken.

1969

March 20
John and Yoko are
married in Gibraltar.

1969

September 19
During a meeting at Apple, John informs Allen Klein that he is quitting The Beatles.

September 26
Abbey Road is released.

1970

April 10
Paul effectively quits The Beatles by stating, in a press release that he does not foresee a time when he and John will become an active songwriting partnership again.

1970

April 1
Ringo becomes the last Beatle to play at a Beatles recording session, adding a drum part to 'I Me Mine'.

1970

MAY 8

Let It Be is released.

blues fans. But the smooth power of the song was Lennon's own, and hinted at The Beatles' development of the original beat-group sound which would follow in 1965.

SHE'S A WOMAN
(John Lennon/Paul McCartney)
Recorded 8 October 1964

For once on a Beatles record, Lennon sounded more sophisticated than McCartney when 'I Feel Fine' was supported by the raucous 'She's A Woman'. Little more than an R&B jam with words, the track was hastily and erratically recorded – the stabbing rhythm guitar drops out a couple of times midway through – but it triumphed on sheer willpower.

BAD BOY
(Larry Williams)
Recorded 10 May 1965

On the same day that The Beatles recorded 'Dizzy Miss Lizzy', they also cut a more obscure Larry Williams rocker, 'Bad Boy'. Once again, John Lennon was to the fore, whooping his way through the tale of a pre-juvenile delinquent (told in true American slang). The group's instrumental support wasn't quite in the same league, which is probably why this track was reserved initially for an American LP, *Beatles VI*, and appeared in Britain only on the compilation, *A Collection Of Beatles Oldies,* in December 1966.

YES IT IS
(John Lennon/Paul McCartney)
Recorded 16 February 1965

George Harrison made the most of his first tone-pedal (alias 'wah-wah') in February 1965, using it on every possible song he could. It was one of several striking factors to this 1965 B-side, a successor to 'This Boy' as a vehicle for three-part harmony. In retrospect, it might have been better if they'd junked this initial attempt at the song and spent the time on rehearsals instead, as the beauty of the melody is rather undercut by the flat vocals on several lines.

I'M DOWN
(John Lennon/Paul McCartney)
Recorded 14 June 1965

On the same day that McCartney recorded the folk-rocker 'I've Just Seen A Face' and the gentle ballad 'Yesterday', he also cut this raucous rock'n'roll song – the flipside of 'Help!' and a blatant attempt to write his own 'Long Tall Sally'. Indeed, 'I'm Down' replaced 'Long Tall Sally' as The Beatles' final song at almost every show they played in their last year as a live band. Despite having all the required ingredients, from Paul's raw vocal to George's stinging guitar solo, it never quite gelled as well as the Little Richard blueprint, and the lyrics seem rather misogynistic from the standpoint of the Ninetiess. But it's a powerful piece of work nonetheless.

PAST MASTERS VOLUME TWO

Parlophone CDP7 90044
Released March 8 1988

 DAY TRIPPER
(John Lennon/Paul McCartney)
Recorded 16 October 1965
For once, the guiding rule that you can tell which Beatle wrote a song by the identity of the lead vocalist breaks down with this song, originally issued as a double A-sided single in December 1965. 'Day Tripper' was a Lennon composition – the title apparently meant "a weekend hippie" – but it was McCartney who sang the verses, while Lennon handled the chorus. Like 'I Feel Fine' and 'Ticket To Ride', the song was built around a rock-solid guitar riff, which suggested that Lennon was responding to the inspiration of The Rolling Stones, who'd strung a series of singles around similar instrumental hook-lines since the middle of 1964.

 WE CAN WORK IT OUT
(John Lennon/Paul McCartney)
Recorded 20, 29 October 1965
Supporting 'Day Tripper' was this collaboration of two unfinished songs, taken by The Beatles themselves as revealing the diverse approaches of Lennon and McCartney to music and to life.
EMI immediately tried to push this as the A-side of the single, only for John Lennon to intervene and insist that the rockier 'Day Tripper' be given equal, if not superior,

status. Not that Lennon wanted to denigrate 'We Can Work It Out', to which he made a vital instrumental contribution on harmonium; he simply didn't wish to see the softer side of the group's music exposed at the expense of their rock'n'roll roots.

 PAPERBACK WRITER
(John Lennon/Paul McCartney)
Recorded 13, 14 April 1966
Widely greeted as a disappointment – a brash, insubstantial throwaway – at the time it was released, the first Beatles single of 1966 remains one of the jewels of The Beatles' crown, especially when coupled with its flipside, 'Rain'. It's true that Paul McCartney was writing a snapshot of fictional life rather than a confessional masterpiece or a straightforward teen romance, but the instrumental and vocal complexity of the song – plus its dazzling conceptual ambition – forced the ever-competitive Beach Boys to respond with the even more complex 'Good Vibrations'. The limits of EMI's studio technology were stretched to produce the richest, toughest sound of any Beatles record to date. Listen out for Lennon and Harrison's 'Frère Jacques' vocal refrain during the final verse, incidentally.

 RAIN
(John Lennon/Paul McCartney)
Recorded 14, 16 April 1966
Experimentation with drugs exploded John Lennon's creative potential. In place of the semi-fictional love songs that had been The Beatles' stock-in-trade, 1966 saw him introducing a series of numbers that explored the workings of the mind, and captured the hazy insight of the psychedelic experience.

'Rain' was one of the first, and perhaps the best, of his acid songs. Half dream, half nightmare in the wings, it combined the earthy, rich rock sound of its companion-piece, 'Paperback Writer', with an other-worldly lyric. The Beatles knew almost by instinct how to achieve that atmosphere in sound: they taped the backing track, complete with what Ringo regards as his best-ever drumming on record, at breakneck

speed, then slowed the tape. Lennon's vocal went through the opposite process: it was recorded on a machine running slowly, and then speeded up for the final track. The juxtaposition of speed and laziness – plus the final burst of backwards vocals, an idea claimed by both Lennon and George Martin – heightened the unearthly tension of this brilliant record.

LADY MADONNA
(John Lennon/Paul McCartney)
Recorded 3, 6 February 1968
From its piano intro (lifted almost directly from Humphrey Lyttleton's mid-Fifties British jazz classic, 'Bad Penny Blues') to its rock'n'roll horn section, 'Lady Madonna' was the first Beatles single of 1968. It made a perfect introduction to a year when Fifties rock'n'roll made a reappearance in the charts and the concert halls. The song itself was a more oblique piece of social comment than 'She's Leaving Home' the previous year, but its vague air of concern for a single mother fitted in with the contemporary trend for kitchen-sink drama in the theatre and on TV.

A bunch of Britain's top jazzmen were dragooned at short notice to play on the track, while Lennon, McCartney and Harrison faked one brass solo by blowing air through their cupped hands like children.

THE INNER LIGHT
(George Harrison)
Recorded 12 January, 6, 8 February 1968
After several commentators had accused George Harrison of 'stealing' the lyrics to this, his final Indian-flavoured Beatles song, from the teachings of the *Tao Te Ching*, George put the matter straight in his autobiography. In that book, he printed a letter from Juan Mascaró, who translated the *Tao*, and actually sent George a copy of his translation of section XLVII, inviting him to set it to music.

Harrison duly did just that, composing perhaps the most beautiful melody of any of his Sixties songs – which deserved a better fate than to languish on the flip of 'Lady Madonna'. The basic track for 'The Inner Light' was recorded at the same sessions as George's soundtrack music for the film *Wonderwall*, many thousands of miles away

from Abbey Road – at EMI's studio in Bombay, India, to be exact. Various Indian musicians provided the instrumental backing. Several other raga-styled pieces were taped at the same session, but they remain unreleased.

HEY JUDE
(John Lennon/Paul McCartney)
Recorded 31 July, 1 August 1968
A couple of verses, a middle section or two, a fade-out: you can't explain the impact of 'Hey Jude' by analysing the song. McCartney wrote the lyrics as a message of encouragement to young Julian Lennon, while his parents were in the throes of a very public separation. At times, the words veered into meaninglessness – "the movement you need is on your shoulder", indeed – and the tune was nothing complex. Neither was the production, which started simple and built towards an orchestral finale.

So why was 'Hey Jude' so important? Partly because of its length, though it was still shorter than another major 1968 hit, 'MacArthur Park' by Richard Harris. Mostly, though, 'Hey Jude' sounded like a community anthem, from the open-armed welcome of its lyrics to its instant singalong chorus. The fact that it didn't come with a controversial political message made its universal application complete.

At Trident Studios, The Beatles and a 36-piece orchestra recorded this remarkable record in two days – plus two beforehand for rehearsals. George Harrison's idea to answer McCartney's vocal lines with his electric guitar was vetoed, but John Lennon made his own distinctive contribution to the record with a four-letter word, hidden deep in the mix around the three-minute mark.

REVOLUTION
(John Lennon/Paul McCartney)
Recorded 10, 11, 12 July 1968
'Revolution 1' (see *The Beatles*) was meant to be a single, but wasn't immediate enough. So John Lennon persuaded The Beatles to try again, setting his non-committal response to the worldwide uprisings of May 1968 to a fierce electric rhythm. With fuzzy, distorted guitars and a screaming vocal, 'Revolution' cut to the bone; it remains by far the toughest rock song The Beatles ever issued on a single. But Lennon's ambitions for the track weren't quite fulfilled, because the emergence of McCartney's 'Hey Jude' a month later made it quite clear what the lead track of The Beatles' first single on the Apple label would be. Still, John did have the compensation of knowing his song was on the flipside of the best-selling Beatles 45 of all time.

GET BACK
(John Lennon/Paul McCartney)
Recorded 28 January 1969
Shortly before his death, John Lennon revealed his long-felt suspicion that this song had been triggered by Paul McCartney's feelings towards Yoko. In fact, as he knew very well, 'Get Back' began life as an ironic comment on British politics. Under its original title of 'No Pakistanis', it satirised the racist views of those who saw Commonwealth immigrants as an invasion force, swamping British culture. Trouble was, the irony was likely to be lost on anyone who wasn't pre-warned, and McCartney regretfully dropped the original lyrics. (His decision was proved right nearly 20 years later when *The Sun* newspaper got hold of a tape of 'No Pakistanis', and accused The Beatles of racism. Irony is just too complicated for some people.)

In its new form, 'Get Back' was a tight, attractive rocker with lyrics that meant nothing but sounded good – a combination Paul tried to repeat, with rather less success, on Wings' singles like 'Helen Wheels' and 'Junior's Farm'. It featured a rare guitar showcase for John Lennon, who commented wryly: "When Paul was feeling kindly he would give me a solo, and I played the solo on that." Though 'Get Back' was performed on the Apple rooftop on 30 January 1969, the single version was taped in the studio a couple of days earlier, issued as a single in April (after emergency last-minute remixes) and then chopped down for inclusion on the *Let It Be* LP in 1970.

DON'T LET ME DOWN
(John Lennon/Paul McCartney)
Recorded 28 January 1969

On the same day as 'Get Back', The Beatles recorded this gloriously spontaneous Lennon love song. For a brief moment, Lennon and McCartney were in perfect synchronisation, both of them keen to escape from the studio trickery and multi-overdubbing of recent Beatles albums. McCartney soon returned to over-production, on *Abbey Road*, but Lennon adopted the 'live-in-the-studio' approach as his watchword for the next couple of years.

THE BALLAD OF JOHN AND YOKO
(John Lennon/Paul McCartney)
Recorded 14 April 1969

"Standing in the dock at Southampton/Trying to get to Holland or France..." Songs should be like newspapers, John Lennon said in 1970, and 'The Ballad Of John And Yoko' was just that – a report from the front-line in the battle between, on the one side, the keen-to-be-married Lennons, and on the other, the forces of law and order who didn't want convicted drugs offenders staging bed-ins in their capital cities, thank you very much.

'Instant' was John Lennon's approach to art in 1969 and 1970: his dream was to write a song in the morning, record it that afternoon, mix it at night and have it in the shops by the end of the week. He finally achieved that aim with his own 'Instant Karma!' early in 1970; but 'The Ballad Of John And Yoko' ran it close, being recorded and fully mixed in less than nine hours.

Such was the haste with which the session was arranged that only Paul was able to meet the call. He played drums to John's acoustic guitar for the basic track, and the two Beatles then overdubbed two lead guitar parts (John), piano (Paul), bass (Paul), percussion (Paul and John) and finally their vocals. The first Beatles song to be mixed solely in stereo – the birth of a new era – also brought another era to an end. Though it was far from the last time Lennon and McCartney worked together in the studio, it was their last major artistic collaboration.

OLD BROWN SHOE
(George Harrison)
Recorded 16, 18 April 1969

Even when John Lennon was available to play on a Harrison song, an increasingly infrequent event by 1969, his instrumental contribution wasn't used in the final mix – his rhythm guitar losing its place to George's Hammond organ part. Otherwise, George's rocker was a four-man effort, thrown together with seemingly haphazard enthusiasm to create a suitable off-the-cuff flipside for 'The Ballad Of John And Yoko'. Harrison even allowed himself one of his loudest guitar solos on record as a rare moment of self-indulgence.

ACROSS THE UNIVERSE
(John Lennon/Paul McCartney)
Recorded 4, 8 February 1968,
2 October 1969

For a song whose creation was so painless – Lennon woke in the night with the melody in his head, and the words waiting to flow out of his mind – 'Across The Universe' proved difficult to capture on tape. Ironically, the most perfect version of the song exists only on an EMI acetate, documenting the state of progress at the end of the first day's work. At that point, the song was punctuated by eerily beautiful bursts of backwards electric guitar, which were wiped from the tape at the start of Day Two.

That second session ended with the group uncertain where to go next. They'd already broken new ground by inviting two young fans, Lizzie Bravo and Gayleen Pease, in from the Abbey Road steps to add vocal harmonies; and Lennon himself contributed an exquisitely precise lead vocal. But he was still dissatisfied with the results. Plans to issue the track as a single were dropped, and the attempt to re-cut the song during the 'Let It Be' sessions failed.

Eventually, the track was made available to the World Wildlife Fund, for a 1969 charity

LP called *No One's Gonna Change Our World*. As the lead-off track, 'Across The Universe' was overdubbed with wildlife sounds by George Martin in October 1969. Six months later, another producer, Phil Spector, prepared his own mix of the song (see *Let It Be*).

LET IT BE

(John Lennon/Paul McCartney)
Recorded 31 January, 30 April 1969, 4 January 1970
This was the George Martin mix of the song, rather than what John Lennon called the "fruity" Phil Spector mix (see *Let It Be*). Spector heightened the percussion and chose a raucous Harrison guitar solo; for the group's final UK single, George Martin made more conservative choices.

YOU KNOW MY NAME (LOOK UP THE NUMBER)

(John Lennon/Paul McCartney)
Recorded 17 May, 7, 8 June 1967, 30 April, 26 November 1969
The Beatles' career as Britain's greatest singles band ended with this off-the-wall track, issued on the flipside of 'Let It Be'.

It began life during the sessions for *Magical Mystery Tour*, with Brian Jones of The Rolling Stones playing saxophone, was left to one side for two years, then overdubbed during the recording of *Abbey Road*. Once The Beatles' split was confirmed, towards the end of 1969, Lennon decided to rescue the track, and planned to issue it as a Plastic Ono Band single, alongside another Beatles off-cut, 'What's The News Mary Jane'. That plan was stymied, and so the song ended up as a Beatles recording after all.

"It's probably my favourite Beatles track," said Paul McCartney, "just because it's so insane. It was just so hilarious to put that record together." And the humour survives, from the deliberately over-the-top repetition of the title, to the Goons-like parade of vocal imitations that Lennon and McCartney unveiled for the last three minutes of the song. More than any other Beatles recording, it captures the sheer pleasure that was their lasting legacy to the world.

PART III
NON-EMI
SESSIONS

Three sets of recordings taped before The Beatles' rise to fame were issued on a variety of official and unofficial LPs and CDs until court cases in the Nineties established their illegal nature. Their release was often surrounded by arguments over copyright, and as a result the Decca tapes recordings never included the three Lennon/McCartney composition recorded on January 1, 1962 ('Love Of The Loved', 'Like Dreamers Do' and 'Hello Little Girl'). Comprehensive collections of this material are now hard to obtain through legitimate sources, though some songs from the Tony Sheridan and Decca sessions appeared on *Anthology I*.

THE TONY SHERIDAN SESSIONS

My Bonnie *(Charles Pratt)*/Cry For A Shadow *(John Lennon/George Harrison)*/Ain't She Sweet *(Jack Yellen/Milton Ager)*/Why *(Tony Sheridan/Bill Crompton)*/Take Out Some Insurance For Me Baby (sometimes listed as If You Love Me Baby) *(Charles Singleton/Waldenese Hall)*/Sweet Georgia Brown *(Ben Bernie/Maceo Pinkard/Kenneth Casey)*/The Saints *(Traditional, arranged Tony*

Sheridan)/Nobody's Child (Mel Foree/ Cy Cohen)

The Beatles' first experience of a professional recording studio didn't turn out the way they'd imagined. Signed as backing group to London rocker Tony Sheridan during one of their first visits to Hamburg, they expected to be whisked straight to Polydor Records' German HQ for champagne and state-of-the-art technology. Instead, they wound up in a Hamburg school hall, taping eight tracks which have haunted them ever since.

The original deal, arranged by German producer and bandleader Bert Kaempfert, was for The Beatles to back Sheridan on a single, 'My Bonnie'/'The Saints'. That duly appeared as a single, credited to Tony Sheridan and The Beat Boys, in the summer of 1961. During the same sessions (or possibly as much as a year later, as the chronology of this period is still hazy), they taped six other tracks – four of them supporting Sheridan, two without his help. The latter were an instrumental, 'Cry For A Shadow', and John Lennon's first recorded lead vocal, 'Ain't She Sweet'.

These eight tracks, plus variations (there are two slightly different versions of 'My Bonnie', for instance, while Tony Sheridan re-recorded the lead vocal for 'Sweet Georgia Brown' in 1964) have appeared on countless LPs and now CDs since the mid-Sixties, often with Tony Sheridan's name relegated to the small print, and almost always alongside Sheridan recordings which have no Beatles involvement. Some companies have dared to package the tracks with a sleeve showing a photo of the group after 1962, only for Apple to intervene with a fistful of writs. In the end, the eight songs are only of minor importance, particularly the Sheridan vocals, behind which the backing is so anonymous that it could have been anyone.

THE DECCA AUDITION

Besame Mucho *(Consuelo Velasquez/Selig Shaftel)*/Hello Little Girl *(John Lennon/Paul McCartney)*/The Sheik Of Araby *(Harry Smith/Ted Snyder/Frances Wheeler)*/ September In The Rain *(Al Dubin/Harry Warren)*/Three Cool Cats *(Jerry Leiber/Mike Stoller)*/Love Of The Loved *(John Lennon/Paul Mccartney)*/Memphis, Tennessee *(Chuck Berry)*/Till There Was You *(Meredith Wilson)*/Crying, Waiting, Hoping *(Buddy Holly)*/Like Dreamers Do *(John Lennon/Paul Mccartney)*/Money *(Berry Gordy/Janie Bradford)*/Searchin' *(Jerry Leiber/Mike Stoller)*/Sure To Fall *(Carl Perkins/William Cantrell/Quinton Claunch)*/To Know Her Is To Love Her *(Phil Spector)*/Take Good Care Of My Baby *(Gerry Goffin/Carole King)*

On January 1, 1962, The Beatles celebrated New Year by recording 15 songs for Decca A&R man Mike Smith at the label's West Hampstead studios. It was their first encounter with the London record industry, and it ended in disappointment, when Decca (in the person of the much-maligned Dick Rowe, under advice from Smith) chose instead to sign another of the day's auditionees, Brian Poole & The Tremeloes, largely because they came from Dagenham rather than Liverpool and would therefore have a shorter distance to travel to recording sessions.

Listening to the contents of the tape, which first surfaced on bootleg in the late Seventies, it was easy to see why The

Beatles didn't become Decca recording artists. They sound appallingly stilted and ill-at-ease; McCartney over-sings every lead vocal, while Lennon is subdued; Pete Best's drumming is little more than basic; and only George Harrison comes through the audition with his reputation intact.

The historical value of the tape was enormous, of course. Rumour had it that Decca executives pulled it out of the vault every Christmas and drowned their sorrows while they listened to it one more time, trying to discover how they missed out on the world's best-selling pop group. Ownership of the tape was open to question, however, and in 1982 the US label Backstage Records took the plunge. With the backing of Pete Best, they issued ten of the audition tracks on an 'official' LP set. The more established Audio-Fidelity label followed suit a few months later, upping the contents to 12 songs – but omitting the three Lennon/McCartney compositions, in the hope of avoiding legal tangles. For the next few years, these 12 tracks appeared on countless LPs and CDs, before the lawyers took control. No-one still seems sure who owns the rights to the tracks, but no-one

has dared to reissue them since the late 80s, either.

LIVE AT THE STAR-CLUB, HAMBURG

I Saw Her Standing There (John Lennon/Paul Mccartney)/I'm Gonna Sit Right Down And Cry (Over You) (Joe Thomas/Howard Biggs)/Roll Over Beethoven (Chuck Berry)/The Hippy Hippy Shake (Chan Romero)/Sweet Little Sixteen (Chuck Berry)/Lend Me Your Comb (Kay Twomey/Fred Wise/Ben Weisman)/Your Feet's Too Big (Ada Benson/Fred Fisher)/Where Have You Been All My Life? (Barry Mann/Cynthia Weil)/Twist And Shout (Bert Russell/Phil Medley)/Mr. Moonlight (Roy Lee Johnson)/A Taste Of Honey (Ric Marlow/Bobby Scott)/Besame Mucho (Consuelo Velalquez/Selig Shaftel)/Reminiscing (King Curtis)/Till There Was You (Meredith Wilson)/Everybody's Trying To Be My Baby (Carl Perkins)/Kansas City; Hey Hey Hey Hey (Jerry Leiber/Mike Stoller; Richard Penniman)/Nothin' Shakin' (But The Leaves On The Tree) (Cirino Colacrai/Eddie Fontaine/Dianne Lampert/Jack Cleveland)/To Know Her Is To Love Her (Phil Spector)/Little Queenie (Chuck Berry)/Falling In Love Again (Sammy Lerner/Frederick Hollander)/Sheila (Tommy Roe)/Be-Bop-A-Lula (Gene Vincent/Tex Davis)/Hallelujah I Love Her So (Ray Charles)/Ask Me Why (John Lennon/Paul Mccartney)/Red Sails In The Sunset (Jimmy Kennedy/Will Grosz)/Matchbox (Carl Perkins)/I'm Talkin' 'Bout You (Chuck Berry)/I Wish I Could Shimmy Like My Sister Kate (Piron)/Long Tall Sally (Richard Penniman/

Enotris Johnson/Robert Blackwell)/
I Remember You *(Johnny Mercer/Victor Schertzinger)*

John Lennon: "We were performers and what we generated was fantastic. We played straight rock, and there was nobody to touch us in Britain. Brian put us in suits and all that, and we made it very, very big. But we sold out. We always missed the club dates because that's when we were playing music."

Paul McCartney: "In Hamburg, we'd work eight hours a day, while most bands never worked that hard. So we had developed our act, and by the time we came to America, we had all that worked out. When we started off in Hamburg, we had no audience, so we had to work our asses off to get people in. People would appear at the door of the club while we were on stage and there would be nobody at the tables. We used to try to get them in to sell beer. The minute we saw them, we'd just rock out, and we'd find we'd got three of them in. We were like fairground barkers. We eventually sold the club out, which is when we realised it was going to get really big."

The appearance in 1977 of 30 songs recorded during the final week of The Beatles' life as a club band in Hamburg, Germany, gave the rest of the world its first chance to hear the music behind the legend. Many people were disappointed: The Beatles sounded less like "fairground barkers" than bored, overworked money-slaves – which is exactly what they were, as they plodded through their last exhausting German shows, knowing the prospect of stardom awaited them at home in Britain.

Even under these less than promising circumstances, though, the Star-Club tapes do capture the manic humour and rock'n'roll prowess of the pre-fame Beatles. But those qualities are mostly buried in the muddiness of the sound, which is the best that can be achieved from the impromptu amateur source-tape.

That was made by Liverpudlian engineer Adrian Barber, who went on to produce the MC5 and The Velvet Underground in New York many years later. Via a series of pub encounters, the raw tape ended up with original Beatles manager Allan Williams. He offered it to Brian Epstein, who turned it down; a decade later, he played it to George and Ringo at Apple, who loved what they heard, but still didn't come up with a deal. Eventually, Williams took the tape to Lingasong Records in London, who cleaned it up and readied it for release. Apple belatedly tried to prevent the release, but failed. The tracks have since been issued on a variety of LPs and CDs, often with completely misleading credits, and their current legal status is uncertain. Strangely, the one company who had a perfect right to stop the release, but seem to have made no attempt to do, was EMI: when it was recorded, on December 31, 1962, The Beatles were under exclusive contract with its Parlophone subsidiary. Lingasong cleverly sidestepped this question by claiming that the tape pre-dated the signing of the deal, something which the evidence of the tape itself proved to be false.

PART IV
THE NINETIES

AND BEYOND

PREFACE TO PART 4

The best-selling British band in America during 1996 were The Beatles. Over a quarter of a century on from their final performance together on a windswept London rooftop, the world's most widely imitated and influential rock group were right back at the toppermost of the poppermost. The fads and fashions which had shaped and reshaped the rock landscape during the 27 years since The Beatles' split were once again swept aside by the Fabs. Newcomers like Oasis, Blur and George Michael were swiftly relegated by the global knockout delivered by the release, in quick succession, of *The Beatles At The BBC* and the six CD, three volume *Anthology* sequence.

There are an estimated 2,000 Beatle books in print, and countless newspaper and magazine articles which endlessly recycle the 20th Century's most enduring and endearing fairy tale, but here at long last was something new to get your teeth into.

Over an extraordinary seven-year recording career, The Beatles had become rock'n'roll's Neil Armstrong – from small steps to giant

leaps. From the chirpy Merseybeat beginnings of *Please Please Me* and *With The Beatles*; through the sublime song-mastery of *Help!*, *Rubber Soul* and *Revolver*; to the studio wizardry of *Sgt Pepper's Lonely Hearts Club Band* and the flawed magnificence of the 'White Album', *Abbey Road* and *Let It Be*.

Never had such a career been so thoroughly documented and carefully analysed: that historic first encounter between John Lennon and Paul McCartney at the Woolton Village Fete on July 6, 1957; the local rumours that drew Brian Epstein down the cellar steps one lunchtime; the sweaty energy of those Cavern performances; the Hamburg all-nighters; the heady burst of Beatlemania; the inevitable conquest of America; the flirtations with drugs and meditation, big business and legal minefields; and the final, unpleasant, break up. But above all, running alongside everything else, were the regular withdrawals to EMI's nondescript studios in a previously anonymous north London street where they created *Sgt Pepper* the world's greatest rock'n'roll album, the back to roots *Let It Be*, the let's-try-and-do-it-one-more-time-like-the-old-days *Abbey Road*... and in the end, 'The End'.

The divorce was messy, public, protracted and bitter. Schoolboy squabbles escalated and were trawled through the law courts, petty playground disputes built up into front-page news in which 'I left first' defiance from John was met by 'No you didn't' knee-jerk responses from Paul. Sniping on record and squabbling in print – vicious, spiteful, silly stuff (John's 'How Do You Sleep?'; Paul's letter to *Melody Maker* about the "the limping dog of a news story") – left a public once besotted by The Beatles sad and disillusioned.

The group which had defined the Sixties, spent the Seventies in dispute and bitter, open warfare. No solo career came even close to matching that of The Beatles, but then none could. The peerless timing, the fluency and inherent quality of those

12 original albums, 15 non-album singles and 13 EPs, constituted a career of quite simply matchless brilliance. By the time the Beatles began making solo records, the rock world had moved on – thanks mainly to their own pioneering work.

As Pink Floyd, Led Zeppelin, Bruce Springsteen and David Bowie upped the rock'n'roll ante, The Beatles began to seem just a little, dare one whisper it, old-fashioned? Punk's snarling shot of vitriol in the late Seventies, pushed the Liverpool quartet even further onto the sidelines ("No Elvis, Beatles or Rolling Stones in 1977" sang The Clash infamously).

The Beatles were always there though, on the sidelines or not. Their records were still heard on the radio and newspaper editors dutifully dusted down anniversaries. The Punks may not have been interested in what had gone before – Punk itself was Year Zero; but after the Molotov blaze had burned out, and particularly in the wake of John Lennon's senseless murder in December 1980, came a fresh and widespread understanding of The Beatles' position right at the heart of rock'n'roll history.

The development of new technology, the increased activities of bootleggers and the realisation that many much-touted Eighties acts (Duran Duran, Spandau Ballet) simply weren't going to stick around... all contributed to a new and lasting appreciation of, and fondness for, the Fabs' back catalogue.

EMI were never slow off the mark acknowledging their best-known and most lucrative act. For the 30th anniversary of the release of 'Love Me Do' in 1992, a British Council exhibition celebrating the group's career was seen in 56 countries, while in October the day itself was marked by the single's re-release "on Compact Disc, limited edition digipack CD, tape and 7" single".

Since 1976 when their contract with The Beatles expired, EMI had made several attempts to repackage the back-catalogue, although their hands were tied by only being able to re-shuffle existing material. The only 'new' Beatles release between *Let It Be* and *The Beatles Live At The BBC* had come in 1977 with *The Beatles At The Hollywood Bowl* which was never released on CD. At the time there was no likelihood of a Beatle reunion – although ironically the nearest the four ever got to regrouping was in 1976, when the top American TV comedy show *Saturday Night Live* offered their standard rate of $3,200 for a Beatles reunion. John happened to be watching the show in New York with Paul – at what proved to be their last ever meeting, and George and Ringo were just a phone-call away. The pair were up for the idea according to Lennon: "We nearly got a cab, but we were actually too tired."

When McCartney's Wings appeared at a Kampuchea benefit in London in 1979, it sparked off a plethora of Beatles Reunion rumours. And even after Lennon's murder in 1980, the press remained obsessed with the idea of a reunion. Promoter Sid Bernstein was forever offering a million dollars for the group to reform, as if the very idea of the four men getting back together might cure all the ills of the world.

In 1985, McCartney's closing number at Live Aid was hotly tipped to see George, Ringo and Julian Lennon sauntering on for a Fab finale. And so on into the Nineties... Following the archive releases *Live At The BBC* and *Anthology*, the media had the 'Threatles' (Paul, George and Ringo) declining an offer of $225 million for a comeback tour; while the 1996 Prince's Trust concert in Hyde Park featuring The Who, Bob Dylan, Eric Clapton and Alanis Morissette, was also attended by the usual hysterical 'Beatles To Reform' headlines.

Every solo appearance by one of the band generated another slew of rumours.

London's buses and every Beatle single was sequentially re-released. 'Love Me Do' (made available as a picture disc, complete with alternate take) got to No. 4 – 13 places higher than on its original release in 1962! But this success was not repeated, and subsequent releases resulted in gradually diminishing returns – 'Please Please Me (No.29), 'From Me To You' (No.40), 'She Loves You' (No.45)...

The closest EMI came to releasing something new was in 1985, when they had a fresh Fabs album all set to go: "At last!" boasted the cover of Parlophone LP No. 064 2402701, "a new collection of previously

"We reckoned we could make it because there were four of us. None of us would have made it alone because Paul wasn't quite strong enough, I didn't have enough girl appeal, George was too quiet and Ringo was the drummer. But we thought that everyone would be able to dig at least one of us, and that's how it turned out." – John

At Limehouse in 1985 for the taping of a Carl Perkins TV tribute the great man was joined onstage by George Harrison and Ringo Starr, and there was a start of recognition when the audience suddenly realised that 50% of the world's best-known band were up there on stage before our very eyes.

As far as EMI were concerned, any opportunity for milking the cash cow was welcome. In 1976 'Yesterday' was made available as a single for the first time in the UK, reaching No. 8 a full six years after the group had split. Even the ill-conceived 'Beatles Movie Medley' got to No. 10. But it was not until 1982 that a campaign to systematically re-promote the group's back catalogue was launched. 'It Was Twenty Years Ago Today...' was plastered all over

unreleased material". Compiled by an EMI employee, the album boasted 13 new tracks (all of which found their way onto the subsequent *Anthology* releases). But at the time none of the surviving Beatles were keen on the idea, and the beautifully packaged *Sessions*, having provided the bootleggers with a God-given window of opportunity, went back into the vaults.

During 1983, the widespread availability of compact discs provided a technological revolution the record industry had badly needed: here was the opportunity to re-sell existing product, often to the same salivating punters. It took four more years though for The Beatles' back catalogue to be transferred from the familiar black 12" vinyl albums onto shiny silver CDs.

John Lennon and Yoko Ono in Paris.
March 22, 1969

1987 was selected for the inaugural release of The Beatles' albums on CD for two reasons: it was 20 years since the release of the best-known album in rock history, *Sgt Pepper's Lonely Hearts Club Band*; and it was 25 years since the release of their first EMI single 'Love Me Do'. Given that the whole point of CDs was their enhanced technology, much was made of the decision to make the first four albums available on CD only in mono mixes.

Sticking with mono seemed to defeat the object of the new format, but George Martin was determined that the records should be heard as they were made: "I was... worried because they were perpetuating a kind of myth that had grown up that those early records were made in stereo." Given the extra space on a CD (up to an hour and a quarter of music, compared to an old vinyl album's 45 minute maximum) there was even criticism that room could have been found on the CDs for both mono and stereo mixes. But in the end the CDs were straight transfers of the familiar old vinyl originals; in George Martin's words: "I haven't changed it, because it's kind of history."

While the advent of CDs made the record industry rub its collective hands, it also helped bootleggers, and as rock's most enshrined institution, The Beatles were obviously near the top of the bootleggers' charts. The Beatles may not have had Bob Dylan's spontaneous improvisational genius in the studio or the live variety of Bruce Springsteen or Led Zeppelin, but fans were nonetheless fascinated to hear just what was left in the BBC and EMI vaults. The *Let It Be* sessions alone had generated over 30 hours of music, of which only a tiny fraction had been officially released.

Following John Lennon's murder the continuing disharmony between surviving group members came to seem even more poignant. Coming from a group (The Beatles were always a group rather than a 'band') which had preached so much about love and harmony, the internal bickerings were especially heartbreaking for fans. After all the money, fame and acclaim which had come their way in the 30 years since the group's Liverpool beginnings, it was disillusioning to see only George, Ringo and Yoko at The Beatles' 1988 induction to The Rock & Roll Hall Of Fame. Paul's absence was explained away by a fax he sent which read in part: "After 20 years, The Beatles still have some business differences which I had hoped would have been settled by now..."

Those "business differences" not only dogged the posthumous career of The Beatles after their official split in April 1970, but also prevented fans from hearing any new material. There were constant rumours: of acrimony between George and Paul, of George and Ringo's bitterness that Paul had re-negotiated a personally superior royalty rate... What finally drew the three survivors and Yoko together can only be a matter of conjecture, but the proliferation of Beatle bootlegs which flooded the market during the late Eighties may well have played a part. The quality and sheer quantity of the material was probably the prod that was needed: the superior reproduction available via CD bootlegs meant that one way or another, fans were finally getting to hear what had been denied them for nearly 30 years.

Bootleggers had long had an eye on The Beatles, but the bulk of the poorly-recorded pirate recordings emanated from the sprawling *Get Back/Let It Be* sessions of January 1969, by which time The Beatles were visibly splintering. Then late in 1988, two bootleg CDs slipped onto the market entitled *The Beatles: Ultra Rare Trax*. In the words of Clinton Heylin in *The Great White Wonders: A History Of Rock Bootlegging*: "The effect of the release of these CDs... was nothing short of cataclysmic... Hearing the second cut on Volume 1 of *Ultra Rare Trax* – the original *Please Please Me* out-take of 'One After 909' – in perfect stereo was enough to convince even the most jaundiced of Beatles fans that bootlegs had entered a new era."

The respected collectors' magazine *ICE* trumpeted: "The concept of bootleg CDs graduating from mere copies of noisy bootleg records to professional-sounding entities within themselves has exploded into reality with the arrival of (these) two new Beatles bootleg CDs of session out-takes. Sounding every bit as good – and in some cases, better – than EMI/Capitol's official Beatles CDs... A question that begs to be addressed is whether or not this is just the tip of the iceberg, a sort of 'greatest hits' harbinger of things to come..."

The release of *Ultra Rare Trax* in 1988 sent shock waves through EMI, while considerably upping the ante on rock bootlegging. It was now obvious that public fascination with all things Beatle was not going to diminish. EMI, Apple and The Beatles could no longer avoid dealing with the vexed issue of their back catalogue and recorded archives. The fans' fervour demanded that as pop hurled towards its first half century, any appreciation of pop music history must include The Beatles' music, official and unofficial. On splitting in 1970 the group had become legendary, ten years later in 1980, with the murder of John Lennon, they had moved into myth. They were, and would always remain, the boys, the men... The Beatles. But now it was time to deal with the future.

It was unquestionably time for something new.

THE BEATLES LIVE AT THE BBC

Apple 7243 8 31796 2 6
Released November 1994

"Strictly Embargoed Until 11am GMT, Friday October 28 1994: Beatles release new album..."

It was the press release that the world had been waiting over a quarter of a century to read. Despite the criticisms over their price, the Red and Blue albums had performed spectacularly well when they were released on CD the previous year, proving beyond any doubt that there was still an audience for The Beatles at the tail end of the 20th Century.

The release of *The Beatles Live At The BBC* was particularly well-timed, the climate could hardly have been more welcoming: Oasis' *Definitely Maybe*, the most keenly anticipated album by a British band in a decade, had just been released, and in interview – when they weren't mouthing off about each other – the Gallagher brothers were singing the praises of The Beatles to anyone who would listen. Noel particularly was an astute appreciator of pop history, with special reference to The Beatles' (and Oasis') role in it.

By 1994, there was a feeling that the time was right for *The Beatles Live At The BBC*. Since the advent of the compact disc and all the attendant possibilities offered by the new format, Rock culture had come increasingly to celebrate itself – and part of that appreciation was a serious rediscovery of its roots. This search for a history had seen the rise and rise of the box set.

Bob Dylan had released two highly acclaimed packages, the Led Zeppelin *Remasters* and Eric Clapton *Crossroads* had been critical and commercial successes, and the back catalogues of acts such as The Who, Elvis Costello, David Bowie and Elvis Presley had also been re-aligned and re-positioned. By 1994, only The Beatles and The Rolling Stones – whose career was split right down the middle contractually – had fought shy of a box celebrating their career. The release of *The Beatles Live At The BBC* was to be the beginning of a sequence which would put 'Beatlemania' back into the pop thesaurus – this time around wedged between The Beat and Beautiful South.

One, probably apocryphal, story has a fan asking Ringo to autograph a beautifully packaged Italian nine CD box-set of The Beatles' BBC recordings. The former drumming Beatle, impressed by the production values of the box, murmured appreciatively but confessed to remembering little about the recordings, and even less about the release of this box-set.

The artist formerly known as Richard Starkey was dismayed to discover that what he was cradling was in fact a bootleg recording, from which he would never see so much as a single lire in royalties. It was, so the story went, a phone call from the outraged Ringo to his former colleagues which finally set in motion the process that led to the official release of a double CD, double cassette and double vinyl album: *The Beatles Live At The BBC*.

That august broadcasting institution has come in for a lot of criticism from music lovers during the course of rock'n'roll's 40-year history, but it was the very nature of the BBC's innate conservatism and bureaucratic hierarchy that made possible a project like *The Beatles Live At The BBC*. Like the Civil Service, both EMI and the BBC were run on clearly delineated bureaucratic lines, which meant that documentation, studio logs and correspondence had all been kept and neatly filed away. This precise – even pedantic – eye for detail proved a Godsend for diligent chroniclers like Mark Lewisohn and Kevin Howlett, two writers who have ably documented The Beatles' work at EMI and the BBC.

Kevin Howlett had already put together two radio programmes documenting The Beatles' BBC sessions which were broadcast in 1982 and 1988, so the existence of the recordings was never in doubt. The Beatles had performed 52 sessions for the BBC between March 1962 and June 1965, during which 88 songs were taped, 36 of which had never been made available on record. But it was not just its curiosity value which made this material so fascinating, it genuinely was a vital missing link in Beatle history. These were songs the group had come fresh from performing in Liverpool and Hamburg, before the roar of the crowd completely drowned out their voices, and before they began to have confidence in their own original material.

Live At The BBC attracted some criticism for the odd bum note and muffled guitar part, but many did appreciate its historic significance, among them Peter Doggett who wrote in *Record Collector*: "Apart from the sonically challenged Hamburg tapes, *The Beatles Live At The BBC* is our only link to the music that gave Lennon, McCartney, Harrison and Starr the thrill which they inspired in millions around the world."

The music on this double CD is like a bundle of snapshots from a black and white world. This was a time before videos and pop culture, when LP records were simply vehicles to accommodate singles. It was a time when rock was pop, and The Beatles were little known outside Liverpudlian cellars.

In order to get your music heard in the early Sixties, you would pick up your equipment on Hire Purchase, play the local Conservative Club, and hope to be spotted by an A&R man from one of the two record labels (EMI and Decca) on one of their rare sorties outside London. If you got lucky, you would promote your little 6/8d, 7" single, by slogging up and down Britain's only motorway (the M1) in the back of an old Ford Transit van, living off plates of chips and pots of tea in greasy spoons and motorway service stations.

Then if you got really lucky, you might get a spot on one of the few pop programmes on BBC Radio. The Light Programme (renamed Radio 2 in 1967) was the only official forum for 'pop' back then – there was no Radio 1 as yet, and the commercial stations still lay a good decade in the future. It was against this rather austere background that, between 1962 and 1965, The Beatles made those historic recordings.

As you listen to *Live At The BBC*, it is worth recalling that these performances were recorded in the brief intervals between stints at Abbey Road, or in an odd few hours before setting off for gigs – frequently hundreds of miles away. They were never intended for posterity, but rather as spontaneous moments, snatched from the ether for the immediate delight of fans and then gone with the wind.

The BBC performances rarely attracted the same lavish attention to detail as The Beatles' Abbey Road recordings; for one thing, they were working without the benefit of George Martin, and for another, the tapings took place amidst burgeoning Beatlemania and there just wasn't time. Of course *The Beatles Live At The BBC* doesn't stack up alongside *Rubber Soul*, but it was never intended to. These were performances recorded on the run, in gaps between increasingly hysterical tour schedules and frenetic recording sessions; quick opportunities to plug a new release or blow the dust off old favourites from the Reeperbahn or Cavern Club days.

As with every other act of the period who wished to play for the BBC, The Beatles had to undergo an audition. It took place in February 1962 for a show called *Teenager's Turn*, and producer Peter Pilbeam noted: "An unusual group. Not as rocky as most, more country and western with a tendency to play music." Then Pilbeam wrote the one word for which The Beatles had waited five years: "Yes". It confirmed the group's first-ever radio session for the BBC, scheduled for March 7, 1962. It had begun.

DISC ONE

BEATLE GREETINGS

(Speech)
The soon to be Fab Four introducing themselves on a BBC magazine programme, *The Public Ear*, in November 1963. Outside in the real world, 'She Loves You' had heralded the Birth of Beatlemania. The Royal Variety Performance was around the corner. Ahead lay the unknown.

FROM US TO YOU

(Lennon/McCartney)
The Beatles adapted the chorus of their third single for the title of four programmes broadcast by the Beeb on Bank Holidays throughout late 1963 and 1964. Guests included Rolf Harris, Susan Maughan, Joe Brown and Kenny Lynch – who, strange as it may seem, was the first artist ever to cover a Lennon & McCartney composition. The BBC's Audience Research Department commented on the shows: "This was definitely family listening... I found it quite happy and melodious, with plenty of zip. I am quite a fan of The Beatles. To me they are the new 'Today', clean and wholesome and gay."

RIDING ON A BUS

(Speech)
Broadcast in late November 1964, by which time The Beatles were the four most famous people in Great Britain. These chirpy reflections on the early pressures of fame were recorded by disc jockey Brian Matthew, a 36-year-old veteran by the time he came to interview the Fabs – although as host of the Light Programme's *Saturday Club* since 1957, he had provided an entire generation with their first exposure to pop music. The Beatles enjoyed a refreshingly candid relationship with Matthew and in June 1966 guested alongside him on a special 400th edition of Saturday Club, one of their final BBC appearances as a group.

I GOT A WOMAN

(Charles)
Recorded for a 1963 edition of *Pop Go The Beatles*, the song had been a hit in 1955 for its composer Ray Charles, although The Beatles were more familiar with the version Elvis Presley had included on his first album in 1956. As with many of the BBC recordings, a raucous John Lennon vocal found him emulating Elvis, his first idol. With the added historical significance of being the

first previously unavailable Beatle release in almost 25 years, this track took the group and their fans right back to those early days as a human jukebox, when lacking sufficient confidence in their own material, they delighted instead in recreating their teenage influences and covering contemporary favourites.

TOO MUCH MONKEY BUSINESS
(Berry)

While The Rolling Stones were better known as champions of Chuck Berry's songs at the time, The Beatles were equally enamoured of the first poet of rock'n'roll. A total of nine Berry titles appear on *Live At The BBC*, making him the most represented act (followed by Carl Perkins and songs associated with Elvis Presley). Lennon clearly revels in 'Too Much Monkey Business' (from a 1963 *Pop Go The Beatles* broadcast), and its rolling litany of dissatisfaction makes it without a doubt one of Chuck's best-ever songs – a fact not lost on Bob Dylan who borrowed the structure for his 1965 electric breakthrough 'Subterranean Homesick Blues'.

KEEP YOUR HANDS OFF MY BABY
(Goffin/King)

Recorded in January 1963 for *Saturday Club*, this was an example of The Beatles covering a current chart hit – in this case, Little Eva's follow-up to 'The Locomotion'. The tinny recording quality, rather than detracting from it, actually lends a quaint period atmosphere to the song. Ironically the Gerry Goffin/Carole King songwriting partnership, one of the most successful of pre-Beatle teams, would soon find their abilities overshadowed by the all-conquering Lennon and McCartney pairing.

I'LL BE ON MY WAY
(Lennon/McCartney)

Unique for being the only previously unavailable Lennon/McCartney original in the package, this composition was singled out for criticism on the release of *Live At The*

BBC – unfairly I think. Bashed out for a Billy J. Kramer B-side, no one (including the composers) made any great claims for the song, but it does stack up favourably against many of the pair's efforts during that period. 'I'll Be On My Way' is certainly stronger than much of the filler material that padded out the first four Beatle albums; and there is an engaging, period charm to hearing Paul croon "as the moonlight turns to June light", thus only narrowly avoiding the timeless songwriting cliche of rhyming moon with June. 'Eight Days A Week' it ain't, but I'd back 'I'll Be On My Way' against 'I Don't Want To Spoil The Party' any day.

YOUNG BLOOD
(Leiber/Stoller/Pomus)

Jerry Leiber & Mike Stoller (here with a little help from that other songwriting legend Doc Pomus) were another of pop's premier partnerships, with a proven track record going right back to the birth of rock'n'roll. They had written hits for Elvis, The Drifters and, most notably, The Coasters – from whom The Beatles culled this song. The Coasters' version of 'Young Blood' had appeared on the B-side of their 1957 hit 'Scarchin'', and The Beatles performed both songs during their unsuccessful 1962 Decca audition. Interesting too, to hear just how marked George's Liverpool accent was when singing.

A SHOT OF RHYTHM & BLUES
(Thompson)

Lennon particularly was a fan of Arthur Alexander, who recorded this in 1962, the year before The Beatles covered it for *Pop Go The Beatles*. This is not a particularly outstanding version, but it does act as a valuable reminder of the group's influences at the time – they also recorded Alexander's 'Anna' which was included on their 1963 LP debut. Another Alexander original, 'You Better Move On', was recorded by The Beatles' rivals The Rolling Stones, appearing in 1964 on their first EP.

a jagged electric guitar solo, and melting harmonies clustered around a single microphone. Many Beatle fans from the Cavern days treasure among their fondest memories the group tearing up a frenzy on this R&B stormer. Coincidentally, The Beatles' first ever television appearance came in 1962 when Granada filmed them at the Cavern performing 'Some Other Guy'.

THANK YOU GIRL
(Lennon/McCartney)
This live performance of the B-side of their current single ('From Me To You'), was broadcast on Brian Matthew's programme *Easy Beat*, which in January 1960 had begun its run billed as "new on the Light on Saturday night". Curiously, the song never appeared on an album until its début on *Past Masters, Volume I*. The version here displays those inimitable Beatle harmonies: well known for sending audiences into a frenzy, but also capable – until the screams drowned them out – of being right on the button in performance. Just the sort of souvenir to give a late Nineties audience the flavour of Beatlemania.

SURE TO FALL
(IN LOVE WITH YOU)
(Perkins/Claunch/Cantrell)
George Harrison was the chief Carl Perkins fan in The Beatles – during the group's abortive 1960 tour of Scotland with Johnny Gentle, he had even re-christened himself 'Carl' in homage. Taken from Perkins' 1956 debut album, and sung here in 1963 by Paul – with a little help from his harmonising friends, this is precisely the sort of performance that makes this album priceless in terms of pop history, allowing you the rare opportunity to hear The Beatles trying out as a Country & Western outfit. The following year, two of Carl's songs were recorded for *Beatles For Sale*, while the composer looked on delightedly from the Abbey Road control room. Perkins remained a Beatle favourite right up until his death in 1998: George and Ringo appeared on the 1985 TV tribute, and Paul welcomed Carl as a special guest on his *Tug Of War* album.

SHA LA LA LA LA!
(Speech)
The BBC broadcast 15 weekly episodes of *Pop Go The Beatles* during 1963, as the country became gripped by the curious triumvirate of Profumo, Beatles and Great Train Robbers. Egged on by Beatles, host Lee Peters does a credible James Mason introduction, although in the memo suggesting the series, the ever cost-conscious BBC had noted that "it could be compered by Paul McCartney and John Lennon, this would... cut down the cost."

SOME OTHER GUY
(Leiber/Stoller/Barrett)
This minor 1962 hit for the otherwise forgotten Richie Barrett was a virtual Merseybeat anthem, recorded by The Big Three and The Searchers long before The Beatles. This is British Beat in excelsis, a pounding bass and drum foundation,

BABY, IT'S YOU
(David/Bacharach/Williams)
Even before he was hailed as the High Priest of Easy Listening, anyone with half a brain knew that Burt Bacharach was one of the supreme song-crafters in popular music. In tandem with lyricist Hal David (and here with a little help from Barney Williams),

Bacharach has created some of pure pop's most potent and poignant moments. The Beatles were familiar with this song from the American hit by The Shirelles – a group best known for 'Will You Love Me Tomorrow', Goffin & King's archetypal teenage angst ballad. Such was The Beatles' fondness for 'Baby It's You', that they recorded it again for their début album *Please Please Me*, which was released five months after this recording. The version here, from *Pop Go The Beatles*, ends on an up note rather than the more familiar fading of the LP version.

THAT'S ALL RIGHT (MAMA)
(Crudup)
Immortalised in rock'n'roll history as *the* song that in 1954 began it all, when Elvis Presley – goofing around in Memphis' Sun Studios with guitarist Scotty Moore and bassist Bill Black – inadvertently fused white country & western with black rhythm & blues. This version from the series *Pop Go The Beatles*, compered by Lee Peters and Rodney Burke, is breezily sung by Paul, with some effective guitar punctuation from George. Arthur 'Big Boy' Crudup died aged 69 in 1974.

CAROL
(Berry)
Another borrowing from the Chuck Berry songbook, 'Carol' also appeared in the repertoire of The Rolling Stones, who included it on their first album. Although The Beatles had been on a Berry jag since 1960 when they first began performing this song, this is a lacklustre Lennon performance; but then it was also a long way from being one of Chuck's best songs.

SOLDIER OF LOVE
(Cason/Moon)
Like 'A Shot Of Rhythm & Blues' this was a number made popular by Arthur Alexander, The Beatles also recorded Alexander's own composition 'Anna' and his 'Where Have You Been All My Life?' had been a feature of their 1962 Hamburg residency. Long held as one of the great lost Beatle performances, this is indeed a

Lennon tour-de-force – strident and confrontational – with those unique backing vocals from George and Paul and some rock-steady drumming from Ringo. The song was later recorded as an homage to Lennon by Marshall Crenshaw, who had played him in a touring production of the Seventies stage show Beatlemania.

A LITTLE RHYME
(Speech)
Rodney Burke prompts John into reading a schoolgirl's request for a "beaty song" during an early *Pop Go The Beatles* broadcast.

CLARABELLA
(Pingatore)
Even before Lennon & McCartney elbowed their way to the forefront of British rock'n'roll, The Beatles had an edge over their Liverpool contemporaries, marked among other things, by the group's choice of material to cover. When The Beatles did a cover it was rarely the obvious song – more likely the B-side of some obscure American

hit. And few were more obscure than this McCartney favourite, originally recorded in 1956 by The Jodimars, and an occasional feature of Beatle set lists since 1960. A blowsy Paul vocal, and some wailing Lennon harmonica get this going hard and fast.

I'M GONNA SIT RIGHT DOWN AND CRY (OVER YOU)
(Thomas/Biggs)

Another track which had featured on Elvis's first album, released back in 1956 when The Beatles were all just impressionable Liverpool teenagers. The group's ambitions were to be bigger than Cliff, and then bigger than Elvis; but they still had some way to go when they came to record this version. It was a largely unremarkable performance; but just hearing The Beatles do that sort of song in this sort of style is like travelling back in time to the heady summer of 1963, and tuning in to hear *Pop Go The Beatles* on the highly-esteemed BBC Light Programme.

CRYING, WAITING, HOPING
(Holly)

After Elvis, Chuck and Carl, the brightest light in The Beatles' rock'n'roll firmament was the Texan singer-songwriter Buddy Holly. The first time Lennon, McCartney and Harrison ever appeared together on a record they were covering a Holly song ('That'll Be The Day', in Liverpool 1958) and the result appears on *Anthology 1*. This beautiful ballad was originally cut solo by Buddy in his New York apartment only weeks before his premature death in a plane crash in February 1959. Posthumously overdubbed, Holly's plaintive original is well worth seeking out. 'Crying, Waiting, Hoping' was one of the songs The Beatles tried out at their 1962 Decca audition. This BBC version has a hesitant George vocal, but is redeemed by some of his beautiful guitar. So impressed was Paul McCartney with Buddy's songs that in later life he went out and bought the company, and now every September around the time of Holly's birthday, his company MPL celebrates Buddy Holly Week.

DEAR WACK!
(Speech)

Brian Matthew prompts John into reading a request from a listener. Interesting as an example of just how gripped by The Beatles the nation was during 1963 – regional loyalties went straight out the window, and all eyes travelled North, to Liverpool.

YOU REALLY GOT A HOLD ON ME
(Robinson)

Written by William 'Smokey' Robinson and recorded for *Saturday Club* in July 1963, this song had been an American hit for The Miracles earlier in the year, and was included on *With The Beatles*, the group's second album, in November of that year. Few would contradict Bob Dylan who called Smokey Robinson the greatest living American poet. The Beatles' love of Berry Gordy's fledgling Tamla Motown label has been well-documented, and John's handling here of a vintage Smokey song ("I don't like you, but I love you...") can only whet the appetite for others such as 'Tracks Of My Tears', 'Tears Of A Clown' and 'I Second That Emotion'. As always, part of the fascination of hearing these early performances is in realising how much George Martin brought to the production of the more familiar album versions.

TO KNOW HER IS TO LOVE HER
(Spector)

Along with George Martin, Phil Spector remains the best-known record producer in pop history, but before that he was in a group called The Teddy Bears, and this was their very first recording. Adapted by Spector as an 18 year-old from an inscription on his father's tombstone, 'To Know Her Is To Love Her' turned into a massive hit for Spector and his group in 1958. By the time The Beatles came to record this cover in the summer of 1963, Spector was already legendary for his Wall of Sound productions. John's vocal is a touch leaden on this track, but help is close at hand from Paul and

George. Ironically, seven years later Phil Spector had a hand in the break-up of The Beatles – his grafting of female voices onto Paul McCartney's 'Long And Winding Road' on *Let It Be* was considered "distasteful" by the composer. He went on to work closely with John, George and Ringo, but as late as 1997, when Spector was honoured at an awards ceremony in London, McCartney was the first on his feet – to leave!

A TASTE OF HONEY
(Marlow/Scott)
The film of Shelagh Delaney's 1960 play was described as the "adventures of a pregnant Salford teenager, her sluttish mother, black lover and homosexual friend", which made it fairly typical of the kitchen sink dramas of the period. The tune had been written by Ric Marlow and Bobby Scott for the original play, but it was the 1962 vocal version by Lenny Welch with which The Beatles were familiar. The song first entered the group's repertoire during the punishing Hamburg all-nighters, when Paul's tender rendering supplied a little light relief from the relentless rock'n'roll. His vocal here is spot-on, almost exactly matching the version which had appeared on *Please Please Me* four months before this BBC recording.

Shelagh Delaney incidentally, would later prove to be a firm favourite of Morrissey, who used her picture on the sleeves of two Smiths' releases.

LONG TALL SALLY
(Johnson/Penniman/Blackwell)
The Beatles had been performing this classic Little Richard rocker virtually since the day John met Paul back in 1957. This is where Paul lets rip, giving lie to the idea of him as the 'soft' Beatle. While McCartney's were the more melodic and durable of The Beatles' compositions, he was always equally capable of rocking out. The Beatles' studio version of this rock'n'roll classic appeared on a 1964 EP and *Past Masters, Volume I*. Significantly, 'Long Tall Sally' was the final song The Beatles played as a group at their last appearance before a

paying audience in August 1966 – a mere three years after they recorded this version for the Beeb.

I SAW HER STANDING THERE
(Lennon/McCartney)
The song on the previous track would eventually close one era of Beatle music, but this is the one that had begun it all for them. 'I Saw Her Standing There' was the opening track of their début album, which had been available for eight months by the time they came to record it again for BBC's *Easy Beat* – this time in front of a Beatle-besotted audience. Full of oomph, this McCartney rocker had been tellingly amended by Lennon (Paul's original "never been a beauty queen" changed to John's more knowing "you know what I mean"). This vivacious and energetic reading captures the full exuberance of The Beatles as a live act, before the road-weariness set in.

THE HONEYMOON SONG
(Theodorakis/Sansom)
The theme song from a botched 1959 film in which cinema maestro Michael Powell attempted to replicate the success of

The Red Shoes a decade before. Marino Marini & his Quartet had enjoyed a spell of Easy Listening chart success in the late Fifties, and by all accounts their live performances were a popular draw in Liverpool – which is where Paul first discovered the song. He remained fond of it, and six years after this BBC recording produced a version by Mary Hopkin for her 1969 album *Postcard*. This is the soft, showbiz side of The Beatles with a smooth McCartney vocal, but there is also a sense of the exotic, which must have played well in the drab grey Great Britain of the early, pre-Beatle Sixties. For the young Lennon & McCartney, rhymes such as "love is a ceiling; feelings are reeling" would presumably have seemed the acme of sophistication.

JOHNNY B. GOODE
(Berry)
By the time The Beatles came to record this classic Berry rocker in early 1964, the pressure was really on. In the few weeks between recording this Saturday Club slot on January 7, and its broadcast on February 15, The Beatles had played their first bill-topping shows in France AND conquered America. Their fondness for the eponymous, guitar-playing hero was testified by the fact that the song had featured in their stage set since the group's inception. Here, John coasts on the vocal and George plays his guitar like the "ringing of a bell".

MEMPHIS, TENNESSEE
(Berry)
Incredibly, it was not until October 1963 that this song – a double A-side with 'Let It Rock' – became Chuck Berry's first-ever British Top 10 hit. It had been around since 1959 when it was a hit in America, and Paul remembers learning it in John's bedroom at Menlove Avenue that year, recognising it as "the greatest riff ever". It wasn't just Berry's unforgettable melodies which seared themselves into the songwriting subconscious of The Beatle tunesmiths; but also his wry way with words – the ability, unique in rock'n'roll at the time, to create two minute scenarios of depth and subtlety.

LUCILLE
(Collins/Penniman)
Another wild rocker from the repertoire of Little Richard. In 1957, when the flamboyant showman first scored with the song, the teenage Paul McCartney had been captivated – he would later feature it in Wings' Kampuchea benefit concert in 1979, and in 1988 on his return to roots rock'n'roll with the album *Back In The USSR*. In his introduction, *Saturday Club* presenter Brian Matthew makes mention of The Everly Brothers who also featured on this 1963 fifth anniversary show and had, coincidentally, enjoyed a 1960 hit with the song.

CAN'T BUY ME LOVE
(Lennon/McCartney)
The Beatles' first single of 1964 – with advance orders of one million in the UK and over two million in the USA – was the one which set the seal on Beatlemania for the following two years. The group took the opportunity to plug it on an Alan Freeman-hosted *From Us To You* Easter special, which the Light Programme broadcast in March 1964. Having just finished recording it at Abbey Road, this BBC version was near enough a note-for-note replication.

FROM FLUFF TO YOU
(Speech)
DJ Alan Freeman became a part of every teenager's Sunday afternoons in 1962, when he started hosting *Pick Of The Pops* – grabbing the attention of a pop-hungry nation with the rallying cry: "Greetings pop pickers!" Freeman's frenetic run-down of the chart had gained him the nickname of 'Fluff', and he was one of the BBC's first celebrity DJs of the pop era. He knew The Beatles well, and his efforts at a straight interview with Paul ("favourite singers? Elvis, Chuck Berry, Carl Perkins, Marvin Gaye...") are interrupted by John's endeavours to alert the nation to the publication of his first book *In His Own Write*. But Fluff won't be fluffed. Not 'arf.

TILL THERE WAS YOU
(Willson)

During live performances Paul used this song, which had originally appeared in the 1957 musical *The Music Man*, to calm down hysterical fans. It was Peggy Lee's sultry 1961 version which had first appealed to him, and by the time it was broadcast on *From Us To You* in March 1964, the number was already familiar to fans, having appeared on *With The Beatles* which had been at No. 1 for 21 consecutive weeks since its release in November 1963.

DISC TWO

 ### CRINSK DEE NIGHT
(Speech)

Former actor Brian Matthew joshes with the Fabs about their film career. Common consensus is that Ringo is best actor, and group take news that they are No. 1 in Portugal without getting too ruffled.

 ### A HARD DAY'S NIGHT
(Lennon/McCartney)

Top Gear was a late night BBC Light Programme pop music show running from 10pm to midnight and hosted by Brian Matthew. The Beatles launched the show on July 16 1964, having recorded their contribution two days earlier. That first show also featured Beatle favourite Carl Perkins, Dusty Springfield and The Nashville Teens. Such was the importance of the event that The Beatles and Dusty featured on that week's cover of *Radio Times* – then Britain's biggest-selling magazine title. As their first film had just premiered, the group took this opportunity of performing the theme song, for the benefit of anyone who didn't know there was a Beatles film on release. With neither the time nor the confidence to recreate George Martin's piano solo from the disc, the producer's taped contribution is rather obviously dropped in, but otherwise the group effectively replicate the studio original.

 ### HAVE A BANANA!
(Speech)

Just to prove that he really has got The Beatles in the studio, Brian Matthew cuts the take short, but George just won't let go.

 ### I WANNA BE YOUR MAN
(Lennon/McCartney)

Equally familiar to fans of The Rolling Stones, to whom the composers donated it for their second single late in 1963 – at around the same time it appeared on *With The Beatles*. A live favourite for singer Ringo, 'I Wanna Be Your Man' was nonetheless an incongruous song for The Beatles – more raucous and loose-limbed than their pop image at the time.

 ### JUST A RUMOUR
(Speech)

George gets all coy with Alan Freeman about "da classics".

 ### ROLL OVER BEETHOVEN
(Berry)

Another Chuck Berry masterpiece, another song from *With The Beatles* – still the nation's No. 1 album when this was broadcast on Easter Monday 1964. It was John who sang the song when it first became part of The Beatles' stage show in 1961, but by the time they came to record the album George had taken over the duties, and it is his voice you hear on this *From Us To You* version. Berry's 1956 hit is a brilliant take on rock'n'roll's increasing incursion into the world of popular music: the walls of the city were well and truly shaking by the time The Beatles came to tell Tchaikovsky the news.

 ### ALL MY LOVING
(Lennon/McCartney)

Almost unbelievably, this stand-out track from *With The Beatles* was never a single. At a time when LP records were often little more than dumping grounds for A and B-sides of hit singles, The Beatles were busy fashioning albums which could stand alone as separate entities. Making a number like 'All My Loving' an LP track, when it would have made a more than convincing single, also helped to ensure that fans got excellent value for money. Many American fans had their first exposure to The Beatles with 'All My Loving', which was the first song the group performed when they made their US TV début on *The Ed Sullivan Show*, on February 9 1964. This BBC recording may lack the smooth veneer of the familiar album version, but it is cheerfully brash and invigorating – displaying again just how captivating The Beatles were at this time.

THINGS WE SAID TODAY
(Lennon/McCartney)
Again unbelievably, this McCartney classic was never issued as an A-side, though it did appear as the B-side of 'A Hard Day's Night' and on the second side of the UK soundtrack album. The introduction here, from DJ Brian Matthew, is taken from a BBC World Service programme which took performances from UK programmes and put them on transcription discs for use on the network's global outlet. These transcription discs would prove a lucrative source for bootleggers in later years. Even today, *Record Collector* magazine regularly carries

a warning that it "cannot accept any advertisements which offers... BBC Transcription Discs... (as) any items described in this manner contain unauthorised recordings of BBC broadcast material."

SHE'S A WOMAN
(Lennon/McCartney)
Familiar as the B-side of 1964's Christmas No. 1 'I Feel Fine', this staccato rocker was broadcast on *Top Gear* on November 26, 1964. Originally recorded during the *Beatles For Sale* sessions, the song wasn't included on an official album until the relatively rare *Rarities* of 1978, although ten years later it did appear again, on *Past Masters, Volume I*.

SWEET LITTLE SIXTEEN
(Berry)
This was Chuck Berry's first-ever British hit, way back in 1958. In the early years Berry's chronicle of an autograph-hungry pop fan was always a firm favourite of The Beatles' live act, and in later years John would return to the song for his 1975 album *Rock & Roll*. But in the summer of 1963, when The Beatles came to record this

version for *Pop Go The Beatles*, they had become all too familiar with the type of obsessive teenage fan detailed in the song. A storming Lennon vocal and chunky George guitar help to make this a *Live At The BBC* highlight.

1822!
(Speech)
John introduces a song on *Pop Go The Beatles* in the style of his beloved Goons.

LONESOME TEARS IN MY EYES
(J & D Burnette/Burlison/Mortimer)
This cover of a 1957 Johnny Burnette Trio single testified to The Beatles' fondness for the obscure. One of the lost names of Fifties rock'n'roll, Johnny Burnette is venerated by aficionados – the first song Led Zeppelin ever played together, for example, was Burnette's magnificent, unhinged slice of rockabilly 'The Train Kept A-Rollin''. The Beatles 'Lonesome Tears...' is a more subdued cover, although once again there is that tantalising Country tinge. Ringo is all over his kit and John is clearly enjoying the song – some have even suggested that this song provided the melodic inspiration for his 'Ballad Of John & Yoko' six years later.

NOTHIN' SHAKIN'
(Fontaine/Calacrai/Lampert/Gluck)
Eddie Fontaine originally recorded this number, although the anodyne Craig Douglas produced a British cover in 1958. The Beatles would have been familiar with Eddie Fontaine from his appearance in the classic 1956 rock'n'roll film *The Girl Can't Help It*, and the song was a regular feature of their Hamburg performances. In September 1968 while they were recording 'Birthday' for the 'White Album', the group nipped back to Paul's home from Abbey Road to watch the film's TV premiere. George Harrison particularly had a fondness for rockabilly, and his enthusiasm is apparent in this 1963 performance.

THE HIPPY HIPPY SHAKE
(Romero)
Like 'Some Other Guy' and the songs of Chuck Berry, this 1959 Chan Romero song was a firm favourite of all the Merseybeat groups, but it was The Swinging Blue Jeans who had the hit – in December 1963, five months after The Beatles recorded this for *Pop Go The Beatles*. Finally surfacing after remaining unheard for over 30 years, Paul's frothy enthusiasm and hallmark 'whoos' make this BBC take a quintessential souvenir of the Beat Boom.

GLAD ALL OVER
(Bennett/Tepper/Schroeder)
Another opportunity for George to try out a Carl Perkins song. Carl's third single, and a Beatles stage number since 1960, this shuffling rockabilly number again displayed The Beatles' penchant for the less-obvious. When The Dave Clark Five pushed 'I Want To Hold Your Hand' off the No. 1 slot in January 1964 with a completely different 'Glad All Over', it prompted the cruel cartoon "she must be really old, she remembers The Beatles"; but by April The Beatles had stormed back to No. 1 with 'Can't Buy Me Love'.

I JUST DON'T UNDERSTAND
(Wilkin/Westberry)
The Beatles were always keen to excavate obscure songs to cover, but even by their standards this one was buried deep. 'I Just Don't Understand' had reached No. 17 in August 1961, the first and only American hit for the Swedish-born singer/actress Ann-Margaret who would later star alongside Elvis Presley in *Viva Las Vegas*, and in *Tommy* with The Who. Coincidentally, harmonica on her version had been played by Delbert McLinton, the man who taught John Lennon how to play the instrument. Ann-Margaret's sultry original can now be found on Ace Records' 1997 compilation *Early Girls, Volume 2*.

SO HOW COME
(NO ONE LOVES ME)
(Bryant)
The third Everly Brothers album, released in 1961, was the source for this cover. Although written by husband and wife duo Boudleaux & Felice Bryant, who throughout the Fifties were virtually the Everlys' exclusive songwriting team, this hardly stacks up against 'Bye Bye Love' or 'Love Hurts'. Such were the pressures for new material from The Beatles in the summer of 1963, that they were forced to dig back deep into their repertoire from the previous seven years in order to meet the incessant demands of radio, TV, touring and recording commitments. The session for this edition of *Pop Go The Beatles* was recorded on the morning of July 10, 1963; in the afternoon the group hurriedly completed the following week's show and then raced back to The Winter Gardens in Margate, where they were playing two houses a night for six consecutive nights as part of the summer season.

I FEEL FINE
(Lennon/McCartney)
An opportunity for the group to promote their latest single on *Top Gear*. While the bulk of the BBC sessions reveal The Beatles' fluency at playing live, despite being away from the studio wizardry of

George Martin and Abbey Road, there were occasional fluffs. Given that 'I Feel Fine' was their most technically sophisticated single to date, this performance is a fair duplication, but the sheer pressure of their life was undoubtedly beginning to take its toll. Apart from anything else, the group's inability to hear what they were actually playing onstage due to the mounting hysteria, was becoming increasingly stressful. There were of course offstage compensations, but this was the period when The Beatles finally became trapped in the bubble of fame – and there would be no escape for the remainder of their career together.

I'M A LOSER
(Lennon/McCartney)
Eventually they all lost out to 'I Feel Fine', but for a while this song (along with 'No Reply' and 'Eight Days A Week') was under consideration as a single. This *Top Gear* appearance gave a taster of tracks from the forthcoming *Beatles For Sale* album. As well as a pronounced Country feel, there is now clear evidence of Lennon coming under the influence of Bob Dylan and beginning to display traces of autobiography in his lyrics, it was all a long way from the bubbly Beatle image of the previous year.

EVERYBODY'S TRYING TO BE MY BABY
(Perkins)

Another favourite from Carl Perkins; another track from their current album. The group had performed the same song on *Pop Go The Beatles* nearly a year and a half before this *Top Gear* recording; and a studio version had provided the baffling conclusion to *Beatles For Sale* – which inevitably became the Christmas No. 1, knocking *A Hard Day's Night* off the top. This is an unremarkable performance, hardly elevating The Beatles above contemporaries like The Searchers or Gerry & The Pacemakers.

ROCK & ROLL MUSIC
(Berry)

An American Top Ten hit for Chuck in 1957. The Beatles were familiar with the song from 1959 on, and when they were looking for material to pad out *Beatles For Sale*, this one-take wonder did the trick. The Saturday Club performance here has Lennon at his rockin' best on what was already a rock'n'roll anthem. The mention of "backbeat" in the song's chorus would later provide the title for 1993's Stuart Sutcliffe biopic.

TICKET TO RIDE
(Lennon/McCartney)

A fluent re-recording of their current single, which marked a definite progression from 'I Feel Fine'. It had been six months since The Beatles last recorded a session for the BBC, and as the title suggests, *The Beatles Invite You To Take A Ticket To Ride* was little more than a shameless plug for their new single, album and film (*Help!*). The show was broadcast on June 6 1965, the Whit Monday Bank Holiday, and it proved to be the final Beatle programme of this nature. Fond as they were of the Beeb – and of the opportunity to actually hear what they were playing – by mid-1965 The Beatles were Members of the British Empire, film stars and Britain's most valuable export; there just wasn't time for everything.

DIZZY MISS LIZZY
(Williams)

The Beatles had already recorded two Larry Williams songs ('Slow Down' and 'Bad Boy') by the time John came roaring through this rough-edged rocker. After years of poorly-recorded bootlegs and desperate attempts to imagine those marathon sets in the cellars of Liverpool and Hamburg, The Beatles Live At The BBC finally gave fans a small taste of the sheer power of The Beatles tearing through a live show.

MEDLEY: KANSAS CITY /HEY! HEY! HEY! HEY!
(Leiber/Stoller)(Penniman)

This short medley from a 1963 *Pop Go The Beatles* would later grace *Beatles For Sale*, while Leiber & Stoller's 1952 original went on to become one of rock'n'roll's first, and greatest, geographical landmarks. It was Little Richard who first welded it onto his own song, and The Beatles, who supported him in Hamburg and Liverpool before they broke big, were mightily impressed.

SET FIRE TO THAT LOT!
(Speech)

Rodney Burke banters with Beatles; Ringo says "hello kiddies".

MATCHBOX
(Perkins)

This time it's Ringo who gets a go at a Carl Perkins number. The original was released in 1957, and the song found a place in The Beatles' stage show soon after. On record, it featured on the *Long Tall Sally* EP and later on *Past Masters, Volume I*. Significantly, George and Ringo's appearance at 1985's TV tribute to Carl Perkins marked the first time the two Beatles had played together in front of a UK audience since 1966.

I FORGOT TO REMEMBER TO FORGET
(Kesler/Feathers)

George gets to croon like the King on this cover, featured on the second *From Us To You* show of 1964. The song was originally

a double A-sided August 1955 release – with 'Mystery Train' – for Elvis Presley. It was to be Elvis' final release on Sun Records and also, in November, his first for RCA. Significantly, the majority of the Presley songs The Beatles cover here are from the Sun era: "Elvis died when he joined the Army," Lennon was famously quoted as saying many years later.

LOVE THOSE GOON SHOWS!

(Speech)
John really did – the influence of Spike Milligan on his prose is self-evident; and Lennon made a rare appearance in his critic's hat when he reviewed the first collection of Goon Show Scripts for the *New York Times* in 1973.

I GOT TO FIND MY BABY

(Berry)
This 1963 *Pop Go The Beatles* session finds John playing harp on the group's cover of an obscure 1960 Chuck Berry original. Berry in his turn had been inspired by a 1954 recording of harmonica ace Little Walter; but harp-playing aside, there is little of any lasting value in this performance.

OOH! MY SOUL

(Penniman)
A frenzied performance from *Pop Go The Beatles*. Little Richard's 1958 hit had made its mark on 16-year-old Paul McCartney, who later made sure that it was one of four Little Richard songs The Beatles performed during their BBC career. Listening to McCartney's manic reading, you begin to comprehend the impact The Beatles made when they burst onto the national scene during 1963. After half a decade of polite pop, The Beatles made it all more... exciting.

OOH! MY ARMS

(Speech)
Corny link wherein BBC announcer pretends to have flown in on his arms, prompting much Beatle giggling.

DON'T EVER CHANGE

(Goffin/King)
The period bordered by Elvis entering the Army and the emergence of The Beatles, is often characterised as pop's wilderness years, but there were highlights: the pop singles of Ricky Nelson, Del Shannon and Roy Orbison; Phil Spector's 'Wall Of Sound'; Berry Gordy's Motown label; the early work of Bob Dylan; and the songs

HONEY DON'T

(Perkins)

This was the B-side of 'Blue Suede Shoes' – and it was typical that The Beatles chose the lesser-known song to perform. Whenever Ringo performed live he would always find space for this Carl Perkins song which he first performed on *Beatles For Sale*. Prior to the group's success, John had always taken the lead vocal on the song, and this 1963 performance from *Pop Go The Beatles* provides a unique souvenir of the way things once were.

LOVE ME DO

(Lennon/McCartney)

The Beatles Live At The BBC concludes aptly with a performance of the group's first-ever single. This is a cockier, looser version than on the single and album-track; Ringo's drumming is right on the mark, and Paul's singing really swings. The nine months between the release of 'Love Me Do' and this performance on *Pop Go The Beatles*, had seen the group's world turned upside down: From being an obscure provincial novelty who scraped to a desultory No. 17 with this song, The Beatles had become established as an all-powerful entertainment phenomenon with their very own radio series. But although they may have sensed it, none of those at the epicentre – The Beatles themselves, Brian Epstein or George Martin – could envisage the scale of success they would experience over the next three years until they ceased performing during 1966. Their first single, performed confidently here for their first radio series, brings to an end Phase One of The Beatles' career.

of Gerry Goffin and Carole King... 'Don't Ever Change' had been a big hit for The Crickets in June 1962, and was enjoying a minor revival when The Beatles came to record this 1963 version on which George tackles the vocal confidently, with bravura backing. Although they were still well-known from their work with Beatle idol Buddy Holly, The Crickets struggled to sustain a career in the mellower pop scene of the early Sixties. In later years, Paul McCartney would become close to The Crickets when he launched Buddy Holly Week in 1976.

SLOW DOWN

(Williams)

Another cover from the 1963 series of *Pop Go The Beatles*, this time featuring some distinctive bass from McCartney and crashing drums from Ringo. The song, which had originally appeared as the B-side of Larry Williams' own 'Dizzy Miss Lizzy', became such a Merseybeat favourite that Gerry & The Pacemakers included it on their début album the same year as this Beatles broadcast; but it would be another year before it appeared on a Beatles record – on the *Long Tall Sally* EP.

While listening to *The Beatles Live At The BBC* on your shiny new Compact Disc played on your state of the art sound system, it is worth remembering that these songs were intended to be heard only once. They were recorded hurriedly, to be broadcast over the airwaves and then forgotten. There was never a thought that they might be dusted down, cleaned up, and repackaged for repeated listening.

Back in those antediluvian times, aside from records and draining live performances, radio broadcasts were the only method a group had of communicating with their fans. By and large television turned a blind eye to pop music, and even on radio the sniffy BBC rationed its broadcasting of pop music as cautiously as someone dispensing spirits to an alcoholic.

The Beatles Invite You To Take A Ticket To Ride in 1965 was the final time the group went to a BBC studio specifically to record songs for later broadcast. Of course there had been little necessity for The Beatles to bother going back to the BBC since the end of 1963, but it provided them with a useful opportunity to acquaint fans with their new music, and to remind themselves of the music that had so inspired them over the preceding decade. But by the middle of 1965, with *Rubber Soul* on the horizon and the group increasingly flexing their creative muscles at Abbey Road, the appeal of going to the Beeb and attempting to re-record their increasingly complex musical efforts on mono tape, with one eye always on the BBC clock, held little real appeal.

When The Beatles had begun going along to Broadcasting House in 1963, to appear on *Saturday Club*, *Easy Beat* and *Swinging*

Sound '63, they were only too happy to be there. But 1965 was the year of Bob Dylan's electric *Bringing It All Back Home*, Donovan's 'Universal Soldier', The Byrds' 'Mr Tambourine Man', The Rolling Stones' 'Satisfaction'... And suddenly breezy Merseybeat seemed like ancient history, and the idea of The Beatles sharing a bill with The Bachelors was preposterous.

During the remaining five years of their existence as a group, The Beatles would make odd individual appearances on the Beeb – particularly in shows featuring old mates like Brian Matthew and Alan Freeman from the days when they were starting out, or newer Radio 1 DJs with whom they felt an empathy, like Kenny Everett or John Peel. As late as March 1970, when The Beatles were effectively over as a group, George Harrison was still telling Radio 1's Johnny Moran: "I certainly don't want to see the end of The Beatles."

In December 1994, the media revelled in the new outburst of Beatlemania which greeted the release of *Live At The BBC*. It was just as if the Fab Four had never gone away. A crowd of 200 queued outside Tower Records in Piccadilly Circus and, as Big Ben struck midnight, 33 year-old Steve Bennett became the first member of the public in a quarter of a century to buy an album of new Beatles material.

Demand for the package far outstripped EMI's ability to manufacture *The Beatles Live At The BBC*. 'Beatlemania Puts EMI At Full Stretch' ran the headline in trade paper *Music Week* the week after the album's release; and the report carried on: "The major was able to satisfy only 50% of retail demand, with re-orders adding up to 350,000 units by Monday". The record sold an incredible 180,000 copies in four days to reach No. 1, but it held the top slot for only a week, soon being replaced by *The Best of The Beautiful South* which went on to become the UK's No. 1 album for Christmas 1994. In other countries around the world *The Beatles Live At The BBC* reached No. 1 only in Canada and France, although it did go gold and platinum in most territories.

Sensitive to the criticism which had attended the CD release of the Red and Blue albums, EMI were ecstatic at the response to *The Beatles Live At The BBC* – it all boded well for their decision to go ahead and release what became the *Anthology* sequence the following year.

Further testing the water, a press release dated February 28, 1995, announced the release of "a new Beatles single on Monday March 20". On its release, 'Baby It's You' from *Live At The BBC*, reached No. 7 in the UK. Three further previously unreleased tracks were dug out of the BBC's vaults as an extra incentive to purchasers:

I'LL FOLLOW THE SUN
(Lennon/McCartney)
This version of a track from *Beatles For Sale*, came from the group's second appearance on Brian Matthew's *Top Gear*, broadcast on November 26, 1964. Even before they were The Beatles, The Quarry Men had tried out this early Paul McCartney composition, but 'I'll Follow The Sun' was uncharacteristic of the mid-Sixties period, owing more to the folk-induced, acoustic leanings of *Help!* and *Rubber Soul* the following year.

DEVIL IN HER HEART
(Drapkin)
Recorded for *Pop Go The Beatles* in the summer of 1963, this track – plucked from a single by an obscure all-girl group called The Donays – later appeared on the group's second album *With The Beatles*. This take was recorded on 16 July 1963, a day about which Beatle authority Mark Lewisohn wrote: "Justifiably, The Beatles' February 11, 1963 recording session has gone down in popular music history, the group taping all ten new tracks for their début album in one day. But on this day, 16 July, in less time, the group actually taped 18 new tracks, with only one repetition, and considerable on-mike conversation too. A remarkable feat."

BOYS
(Dixon/Farrell)
Originally the B-side of The Shirelles' biggest hit (the Goffin/King masterpiece 'Will You Love Me Tomorrow') this Ringo favourite had found its way onto the debut Beatles album *Please Please Me*, which was released three months before this radio session. The version here was recorded for *Pop Go The Beatles* at the BBC's Maida Vale Studios, only a stone's throw from EMI's base at Abbey Road where the launch party for *The Beatles Live At The BBC* would be held in 1994.

The success of *The Beatles Live At The BBC* – with an estimated global sale of over six million double CD packages – was to open the floodgates. A double CD of the best of Led Zeppelin's BBC sessions was released in 1997, and there are plans for similar Beeb-related collections from Marc Bolan, David Bowie, Pink Floyd and the Rolling Stones in the foreseeable future.

The Beatles too, retained a real fondness for the BBC. Interviewed in 1980 by Radio 1's Andy Peebles, John Lennon demonstrated an astonishing recall of the group's early Beeb sessions, and took the opportunity of attacking Prime Minister Margaret Thatcher's plans to cut back on BBC World Service funding as "the greatest disservice to peace, love and understanding."

For years, 'What's The New Mary Jane' had been rumoured as a *Sgt Pepper* out-take, worthy of mention in the same breath as 'A Day In The Life'. While the worldwide network of dedicated Beatles fans had a fairly good idea what had been buried away, they were also prepared for some real surprises – whether from the individual collections of Lennon, McCartney, Harrison and Starr, or the corporate vaults of Apple and EMI.

Among the treasures were known to be early versions, original demos, live performances, out-takes and radically different spins on familiar Beatle songs. The full scale of The Beatles' achievements at Abbey Road had been made public in 1988 with the publication of Mark Lewisohn's exhaustively researched book, *The Complete Beatles Recording Sessions*; while 1985's bootleg album *Sessions* had confirmed the innate brilliance of the group with revealing gems like McCartney's demo of 'Come And Get It', George's acoustic 'While My Guitar Gently Weeps', and the original 'One After 909'.

It was at long last time to bow to the inevitable. And so, in the wake of the successful release of *Live At The BBC*, EMI braced itself for what would prove to be the most ambitious and keenly awaited series of archive releases in the history of popular music.

After decades of delay, the promise that new Beatle recordings were about to made available made front-page news around the world. Now it was known that the vaults were to be opened, the major preoccupation of the media and the question which obsessed fans was: what would actually be on the archive releases?

Hottest tip for opening track was a four-minute snatch of John Lennon performing with the Quarry Men on July 6, 1957 – the day Lennon first met Paul McCartney and consequently Year Zero of Beatle history. A tape recorded by Bob Molyneux at the Woolton Village Fete on that historic summer day had come up for auction at Sotheby's in

ANTHOLOGY 1

Apple 7243 8 34445 2 5
Released November 1995

Such is the value placed on The Beatles' music, that the master tapes stored at Abbey Road are protected by alarms linked directly to St John's Wood Police Station. Over the years, pressure had been growing for EMI and the surviving Beatles to let the world hear what we knew was in those vaults.

The Beatles' *Anthology* was the most keenly-anticipated archive release in the 40-year history of rock'n'roll. For over a quarter of a century, the fabled Fab Four fought shy of having their discarded linen aired in public.

September 1994. The 30-second soundbite of John Lennon singing 'Putting On The Style', which was all that was offered for public consumption, sounded just as you'd expect: like an inebriated teenager tearing through Lonnie Donegan's current hit. Except that it was, undeniably, John Lennon. EMI purchased the tape for £78,500, and many reasoned that it would provide an apt opening for the forthcoming Beatles retrospective. But to date it remains locked in the company's archives.

Six months before the release of *Anthology*, news of another tape recording provided more Beatle headlines. Recorded in 1959 on a tape recorder Paul McCartney borrowed from one Charles Hodgson, the tape is believed to contain Lennon & McCartney performing 'Hello Little Girl' and 'Hallelujah, I Love Her So' in the front room of the McCartney family home at 20 Forthlin Road.

Then, as the release of *Anthology* approached, news broke that Paul, George and Ringo had got together in a studio again to record a Lennon demo. The sense of excitement was palpable. But there was also a degree of nervous trepidation: The Beatles were, after all, the yardstick by which all other rock'n'roll contenders had been measured. Their career arc – from the naive enthusiasm of 1962's 'Love Me Do' to the accomplished sophistication of *Sgt Pepper* in a mere five years – was seen as a template against which all progress points in pop could be measured. Any band who stuck around for longer than the 15 minutes of fame allotted by Andy Warhol, was inevitably hailed as "the new Beatles".

The reunification of The Beatles on disc after such a long absence inevitably begged the question: would they have got back together had John not been murdered? It is, of course, impossible to know, but given the climate of the times, with rock's increasingly retrospective nature bringing about reunions of Led Zeppelin, The Eagles, The Who and Fleetwood Mac; with huge one-off made-for-TV events like Live Aid and the Nelson

Mandela tributes; with the atmosphere ripe for reunion and reconciliation; it is hard to believe that the four Beatles could have avoided for ever the temptation to get back.

Finally, on November 20, 1995, all rumours were brushed aside, and there it was – the first album of new Beatles material since the release of *Let It Be* on May 8, 1970. The opening track was another astonishing first: the Woolton tape was conspicuous by its absence, but in its place was the first song the group had recorded together since 1969. So much had whipped across the pop landscape in the ensuing 25 years that it had seemed impossible that this release could live up to the ridiculously high expectations; but it became apparent now, that even in their absence The Beatles had cast a very long shadow.

It was suggested that making available material never intended for release may reveal The Beatles as idols with feet of clay; that the archive recordings might actually impair our enjoyment of music which had formed the soundtrack to our lives; even that *Anthology* could completely undermine the greatest body of work in rock.

Then there was the vexed question of the new Beatles' single 'Free As A Bird'. This was a real bone of contention: even diehard fans who had waited their whole adult lives for the official mining of the EMI/Apple archives, began to ask what the survivors were doing tampering with the past. There was a feeling that by sanctioning the release of *Anthology* and 'Free As A Bird' the remaining three Beatles were finally confronting and coming to terms with their own legacy; but was it really wise to start playing around with the most perfectly formed body of work in pop history?

Cynics suggested that *Anthology* was Paul's attempt to juggle with history, by showing that it was he, not John, who had steered The Beatles on their historic course; that George was in trouble following the collapse of Handmade Films; that Ringo simply needed the money... But it was hard to believe that money was at the root of it all. Even prior to the release of the first *Anthology* in September 1995, The Beatles – with an estimated income of $130 million for the year – were still the third biggest showbusiness earners in America, behind Oprah Winfrey and Steven Spielberg.

The UK premiere of 'Free As A Bird' was broadcast on ITV at 8.30 p.m. on the night of Monday November 20, 1995. It was an extraordinary night for couch-potatoes everywhere: barely an hour later on BBC1, Diana Princess of Wales appeared on Panorama speaking frankly and openly about the breakdown of her marriage to Prince Charles.

The Beatles' avowed intent was to return to the toppermost of the poppermost. But they were denied a Christmas No. 1 by Michael Jackson and his seasonal 'Earth Song'. Ironically it was Jackson who had purchased Northern Songs – the company which owned the rights to the Lennon & McCartney back catalogue. A further irony was to be found in the title of the Oasis single which was dipping down the charts while 'Free As A Bird' edged up. The Beatle-obsessed Mancs'

'Wonderwall' took its the title from a 1968 George Harrison soundtrack – significantly the first time that one of The Beatles had gone off alone and made a solo recording.

With the memory of the *Live At The BBC* frenzy fresh in their minds, key retailers opened at midnight in an attempt to satisfy the *Anthology* demand. But once again market forces dominated, and The Beatles were denied the No. 1 UK album slot by Robson & Jerome, a pair of singing TV soldiers whose eponymous début shifted 213,000 that week compared to *Anthology's* 125,000 – though presumably there was some consolation to be had in the fact that both albums contained versions of Lennon & McCartney's 'This Boy'. And the Fabs' enduring influence didn't stop there, *Music Week's* Alan Jones sleuthed out a number of other Lennon & McCartney songs in the charts that week – on albums by Michael Jackson, Shirley Bassey, Foster & Allen, Chris De Burgh and James Last.

In a retrospective appraisal of the period's sales, *Music Week* found Robson & Jerome at No. 1, The Beatles at No. 9, with Oasis, Simply Red, Queen, Pulp, Madonna, Michael Jackson and Elton John in-between.

Anthology may not have been the all-conquering, knock-out blow which had been anticipated, but it was by no means a failure financially. Artistic success, as always, was another matter...

DISC ONE

FREE AS A BIRD

(Lennon/McCartney/Harrison/Starr)
The idea of marrying the three surviving Beatles with the voice of the late John Lennon came from George Harrison (the same George Harrison who had cautioned in 1989: "You can't have a Beatles reunion as long as John Lennon remains dead"). But in the wake of Roy Orbison's death in 1988, Harrison and the other surviving Traveling Wilburys (Bob Dylan, Tom Petty and Jeff Lynne) were reluctant to call it a day and so, looking for a replacement, they looked to Elvis Aaron Presley: "We talked to the estate," Harrison told Dave Marsh, "they loved the idea of Elvis being in the Wilburys, so they gave us the rights to a song... but we never did it because I thought it seemed a bit too gimmicky. I was talking to Yoko, however, and telling her this idea and she said 'I think I've got a tape of John'...".

Working from a piano demo Lennon recorded at the Dakota building during his years of house-husbandry, the three surviving Beatles co-opted George's fellow Wilbury Jeff Lynne to try and rekindle the old Beatle magic. Opinion remains sharply divided as to their success: too many felt it sounded like Lynne's Electric Light Orchestra rather than the fabulous Beatles, while others (Mark Lewisohn, Derek Taylor, Neil Aspinall) pronounced it "wonderful".

Leaving aside the aesthetics and even the questionable ethics of tinkering with a Lennon demo without his permission, it did seem rather inappropriate to treat 'Free As A Bird' as a new Beatles single, as if this was the natural follow-up to 'Let It Be' – which for twenty-five years had been unchallenged

as the final single issued by The Beatles as a group. Whatever it was, 'Free As A Bird' definitely wasn't a Beatle single to be classed alongside 'Can't Buy Me Love' or 'Hello Goodbye'. It was merely a curio, a grafted-on afterthought, with no right to be included in that phenomenal, unparalleled seven year run between 1962 and 1970.

There was something rather distasteful about the way that, having finally consented to look back over their shoulder, the surviving trio determined not only that 'Free As A Bird' was a Beatle single, but that as a Beatle single it should be the Christmas No. 1. There was a distinct loss of dignity in that unhealthy race to get back to the top – as if the past two and a half decades and John Lennon's brutal murder had counted for nothing.

There were other ways to handle the release of 'Free As A Bird'. It could have been released just as a charity single and left off *Anthology*, with all proceeds going to War Child – the Bosnian aid charity which had impeccable rock links, or even to an organisation concerned with gun control – which besides being an appropriate acknowledgement of Lennon's murder, would have been very prescient given the March 1996 massacre at Dunblane. The other alternative would have been to include 'Free As A Bird' as the final track on *Anthology III* with a disclaimer saying in effect: "Look, we know this isn't The Beatles. But with all the new technology available, we thought you would be interested in how we (with a little help from our old friend George Martin and our new chum Jeff Lynne) tackled recording with John again. We like the results, hope you do too. Love, The Beatles."

But in the end, after a media hype which made the Millennium Dome look like a well-kept secret, 'Free As A Bird' was made the opening track of *Anthology I*. Technologically, it was miraculous: John's original 1977-ish mono home demo was boomed and boosted into 48-track state-of-the-art Nineties technology, and enriched by guitars, drums, double-tracked piano, bass, drums and, crucially, backing vocals from McCartney, Harrison and Starr.

It was in fact Ringo's drums that were the star of the show; crashing and continent-splitting, they took you right back to the thunderous skin-work on 'Rain'. Paul was as ever gracious about the new treatment of John's song: "We took the attitude that John had gone on holiday saying 'I finished all the tracks except this one, but I leave it to you guys to finish it off'." There were even some nice little Beatle-style homages, including the use of a ukulele at the end – both John and George were George Formby fans, and John's mother Julia had played the instrument.

WE WERE FOUR GUYS...
(Speech)
Taken from John's lengthy and iconoclastic interview with Jann Wenner. When it first appeared in *Rolling Stone* in 1970, this was the first real indication of just how bitter a split had taken hold of The Beatles – who the world had still perceived as being together.

THAT'LL BE THE DAY
(Allison/Holly/Petty)
In hindsight, it is significant that the first time Paul McCartney, George Harrison and John Lennon got together on disc they covered a Buddy Holly song. When the three embryonic Beatles got together in the back room of a Liverpool electrical shop in the summer of 1958, The Beatles were still The Quarry Men and Buddy Holly was still alive and well. They pooled their pocket money to pay Percy Phillips to record two songs (this track and the next) on a Shellac disc, aided and abetted by drummer Colin Hanton and pianist John Lowe.

'That'll Be The Day' had been a UK No. 1 in September 1957 and Paul went to see Buddy perform during his only British tour in March the following year; he was particularly impressed by the simplicity and strength of Holly's three-chord appeal. For John, what stood out was Holly's willingness to wear his glasses onstage – something the short-sighted and vain Lennon refused to do. This was the very first song that John ever learned to play on the guitar.

Buddy's death in February 1959, six months after this recording ("the day the music died" Don McLean called it in 'American Pie'), was the first of a major rock'n'roll star – whose young audiences still thought them immortal. The song's title came from John Wayne's catch phrase in John Ford's classic 1956 Western *The Searchers* – a film which had also supplied some Liverpool contemporaries of The Beatles with a name for their group.

IN SPITE OF ALL THE DANGER
(McCartney/Harrison)
The other side of that first 1958 acetate. The quality is exactly as you'd expect from a primitive 40-year-old recording, but then this hadn't been offered up as a 'new Beatle song' it was simply a fascinating glimpse of history – you wouldn't expect a first sketch by William Blake to have the depth and maturity of a completed painting, but it would still be of interest. This is the only Paul and George collaboration from their 40-odd years as colleagues.

In 1986 McCartney told me: "Our first song was modelled on an Elvis song, 'Trying To Get To You', which I heard at scout camp!... We went to a place called Phillips... just a little feller with his tape recorder in his back room. It was like the dentist's! You paid £5, and there's your acetate. There were five of us, who paid £1 each, and we'd each have it for a week to play to our parents and friends, and John Lowe was the last to have it. We went off to get famous, but sometimes I wondered what happened to it. I read in the *Radio Times* recently that the 'proud owner' of the first Beatles single was John Lowe, and I thought hold on a minute, we each had a pound of that!" Paul did eventually get the acetate back, although it ended up costing a tad more than his original investment.

SOMETIMES I'D BORROW...
(Speech)

Paul recalling the very first sessions the nascent Beatles attempted together. They were believed to have been recorded by his brother Mike on a reel-to-reel tape recorder, and over the years, began appearing on bootlegs. It raised an interesting legal question as to copyright. As one ardent Beatle fan put it to me: "recorded in somebody's front room! Five years before they singed to EMI!" But the position is apparently that, in the absence of a contract or assignation of rights, the performers on any recording can legally object to the performance being issued without their agreement.

HALLELUJAH, I LOVE HER SO
(Charles)

This was the first official release of material from the tapes recorded at the McCartney home, 20 Forthlin Road. In 1995 the Liverpool house was purchased by the National Trust, who described it as "unquestionably of historic interest. The music that took shape here touched the lives of millions of people all over the world."

Although composer Ray Charles had recorded the song in 1956, it was memorably rocked up by Eddie Cochran just prior to his death in 1960. Cochran was another Fifties star with a strong influence on the early Beatles, who included four original Cochran songs in their stage set: 'Three Steps To Heaven', 'Twenty Flight Rock', 'I Remember' and 'C'mon Everybody'. Following in the footsteps of Buddy Holly and Little Richard, Eddie Cochran also planned to play a concert in Liverpool, but he was prevented by his untimely death in a road crash near Bristol just a few weeks before the scheduled appearance.

YOU'LL BE MINE
(McCartney/Lennon)

Although the quality of these home recordings is undeniably poor, there is a real frisson in hearing the Boys Who Would Be Beatles cut their teeth. This song in the style of many Fifties popular music hits – sincerely sung, with an even more sincere spoken middle-eight – is here hijacked by the teenage John Lennon with some nonsense about toast and National Health eyeballs.

CAYENNE

(McCartney)
The precocious Paul McCartney began writing songs as a teenager and, in homage to the huge popularity of The Shadows, soon after he turned his hand to this jaunty instrumental. Around this time he also wrote 'Catcall' which Chris Barber recorded in 1957. In his authorised biography McCartney recalled that John also had a fondness for instrumentals and could do "a mean Harry Lime Theme".

FIRST OF ALL...

(Speech)
Paul in 1962, recalling 'My Bonnie' in Hamburg the year before, and proudly announcing that it had got to "No. 5 in the German hit parade".

MY BONNIE

(Trad. arr. Sheridan)
Although widely accepted as the first Beatles single, this rock'n'roll version of the traditional lament was actually released under the name Tony Sheridan And The Beat Brothers. But you can already hear that unmistakable Beatle harmonising behind Sheridan's Elvis style vocal. This was the song which inspired Raymond Jones to walk into Brian Epstein's record store on the afternoon of Saturday October 28, 1961, and ask the smartly-dressed owner if he had a copy of 'My Bonnie' by The Beatles – thus altering forever, in his own unknowing way, the course of history. That simple enquiry was the first Brian Epstein knew of the group's existence; less than a fortnight later he would walk down the stairs of the Cavern Club to witness the group whose destiny would be inextricably linked with his own for the remaining six years of his life.

The real gap in this *Anthology* release is an example of The Beatles as a live attraction at the Star Club or the Cavern. Tapes are believed to exist, and the technology which rendered the McCartney home tapes into CD quality could presumably have been applied just as easily to live recordings from 1961 or 1962. In the event, this rocked-up version of the popular singalong, recorded in a Hamburg schoolroom in June 1961, will have to suffice. In addition to the distinction of being The Beatles' first single, 'My Bonnie' actually became a minor hit when it was re-released in 1963 at the height of Beatlemania.

Tony Sheridan was a fascinating character who had been Cliff Richard's first choice as guitarist for his backing group The Shadows, but he eventually lost out to Hank Marvin and then just a few years later he missed the opportunity to be a Beatle. Remarkably though, the Irish-born singer displayed precious little bitterness about his multiple lost opportunities.

AIN'T SHE SWEET

(Ager/Yellen)
As well as backing Tony Sheridan on a handful of numbers at that June 1961 Hamburg session (Ray Charles' 'What'd I Say', Dion's 'Ruby Baby', Lonnie Donegan's 'Nobody's Child', the all-purpose 'When The Saints Go Marching In', as well as the three included here), The Beatles were allowed to shine on two tracks of their own (this track and the next). Modelled on Gene Vincent's 1956 version, 'Ain't She Sweet' was a staple of The Beatles' 1961 Hamburg set and here features a distinctive Lennon vocal. Strange to think that within two years that voice would be recognised worldwide. In 1964 when 'Ain't She Sweet' was released in America in an attempt to capitalise on all things Beatle, it reached No. 19 on the US chart.

CRY FOR A SHADOW

(Harrison/Lennon)
The only George and John collaboration ever attempted, this instrumental was another deliberate homage to the all-powerful Shadows, who by 1961 had grown from being Cliff's backing group to stars in their own right.

of Liverpool stars including Gerry & The Pacemakers, Billy J. Kramer and Cilla Black. But at the time of his death in 1967 Brian's exclusive contract with The Beatles was about to expire, causing him great concern.

SEARCHIN'
(Leiber/Stoller)
True to his word, Brian Epstein set about unleashing The Beatles on the world. Eventually, utilising every contact he could muster, and at a 200 mile remove from London, he secured an audition for the group at Decca's Hampstead Studios, on January 1, 1962. After a seven-hour drive by roadie Neil Aspinall, the group nervously spent the day running through a make-or-break audition. Among the 15 songs taped was a cover of this classic, which in 1957 had given The Coasters their first-ever hit. Other songs cut at the Decca audition included Chuck Berry's 'Memphis, Tennessee', Buddy Holly's 'Crying, Waiting, Hoping', Bobby Vee's 'Take Good Care Of My Baby' and Dinah Washington's contemporary hit 'September In The Rain'. The intention was to convey The Beatles' versatility, but what actually comes across listening to these Decca audition numbers is a complete lack of focus.

BRIAN WAS A BEAUTIFUL GUY...
(Speech)
Lennon in an uncharacteristically fond reminiscence of Brian Epstein, recorded for Radio 1 in 1971. In the past Lennon had been harsh about Epstein's decision to put The Beatles into suits, had slagged him off for his homosexuality and criticised the career decisions he had made on behalf of the group. But here, barely four years after Epstein's death, John speaks fondly of the group's mentor.

THREE COOL CATS
(Leiber/Stoller)
This had also been a hit for The Coasters. But the novelty number which had sounded cool in 1958 when delivered by an American close-harmony quartet, sounded extremely dubious when performed by 19 year-old Liverpudlian George Harrison. Matters weren't helped by Lennon's corny "come with me to the Casbah" interjections. Listening to bootlegs of the Beatles' complete Decca auditions, it comes as no real surprise that A&R man Dick Rowe turned them down and plumped instead for Brian Poole & The Tremeloes. There is little here to suggest the astonishing depth and development which lay just around the corner.

I SECURED THEM...
(Speech)
By the time The Beatles conquered America in 1964, everything attached to their name was potentially marketable. Spin-offs such as Brian Epstein's autobiography *A Cellarful Of Noise* and George Martin's album *Off The Beatle Track* met with considerable success, and this short excerpt came from a planned album release of Brian Epstein's life and Beatle times, which was never made. Epstein did have some success in his own right, presenting the US TV show Hullabaloo and bringing his Midas touch to bear on a stable

THE SHEIK OF ARABY
(Smith/Wheeler/Webster)
The choice of material for the audition was weighted towards the kind of showbiz favourites that Brian Epstein felt would appeal to the Decca management. 'The Sheik Of Araby' was a 20-year-old novelty song, although Joe Brown had already reworked it into the rock'n'roll style by the time the Fabs came to Decca. The Beatles "not arf" refrain was added as an homage to DJ Alan Freeman's catch-phrase.

LIKE DREAMERS DO
(Lennon/McCartney)
One of Paul McCartney's first-ever compositions, which he sings here in a cloying, crooning fashion. This was included in the audition as further proof of the versatility which Brian Epstein considered an essential part of the group's appeal. At the time though it was not customary for singers or groups to provide their own material – that task still fell to the shadowy inhabitants of Tin Pan Alley; and as the system had worked well in the past, there seemed little reason to change it now. In 1964 The Applejacks climbed aboard the Fabs bandwagon and recorded this as the follow-up to their big hit 'Tell Me When'; the move paid off when the Midas touch which clung to all things Beatle ensured that it reached No.20.

HELLO LITTLE GIRL
(Lennon/McCartney)
Within 36 hours of singing this at their unsuccessful Decca audition, The Beatles were back on stage performing at the Cavern. But the song made good in later years, when it became the first hit for those other Brian Epstein proteges, The Fourmost, in 1963. Just before his untimely death John Lennon looked back on his enormous song catalogue and recalled this as "actually my first song...", adding that it was based on something his mother Julia used to sing ('It's De-Lovely...').

WELL, THE RECORDING TEST
(Speech)
Brian Epstein's apparently sanguine reflections on his failure to secure The Beatles a recording contract; although we know now that he was bitterly disappointed and close to panic. At the time there were only really two possible outlets for The Beatles – Decca and EMI – both of which had now rejected the group.

However a chink in the EMI armour appeared when George Martin, then in charge of the group's novelty Parlophone label, agreed to audition The Beatles. The following two tracks were cut at Abbey Road on June 6, 1962 – the first of many under Martin's watchful eye. Eighteen years before, to the very day, the world had been liberated from the Nazi yoke by the Allied invasion of Europe. June 6, 1962 saw the beginnings of liberation of another kind.

BESAME MUCHO
(Velazquez/Skylar)
McCartney in particular was unhappy that showbiz chestnuts like 'Besame Mucho' were selected for inclusion on *Anthology*. He felt that it displayed an

ersatz showbiz slickness which was not truly reflective of him or The Beatles. But, as they say, "Cha-cha boom!" Again plucked again from the repertoire of The Coasters, 'Besame Mucho' had been a firm live favourite of The Beatles for a couple of years by the time they tried it out for George Martin.

LOVE ME DO
(Lennon/McCartney)
Unlike their audition for Decca five months earlier, The Beatles' Parlophone audition centred on Lennon & McCartney originals. 'Ask Me Why' and 'PS I Love You' were also routined during the three hour session, but this hesitant version of the song that would become their first self-penned single is of particular interest.

Besides being the first ever Lennon & McCartney song to be recorded at Abbey Road – the studios which would act as The Beatles' base of operations for the next seven years - this was the only EMI recording to feature Pete Best. Between The Beatles' Parlophone audition and their first sessions for the label, Best was replaced by Ringo Starr. Best's drumming here is noticeably pedestrian, and by the time The Beatles returned to Abbey Road in September 1962 to record this for real, he had become a footnote in Fab history. It would be over three decades before he received a penny, or a credit, for his work with The Beatles. Best was clearly delighted in 1995, when the release of *Anthology* restored his place in Beatle history: "Lots of people have laid claim to being the fifth Beatle. I was the fourth, and now I'm getting the credit for it."

HOW DO YOU DO IT
(Murray)
Uncertain that any of the Lennon & McCartney originals were strong enough, George Martin (with the eager collusion of Brian Epstein) tried to foist a Tin Pan Alley effort by Mitch Murray onto The Beatles for their Parlophone début. In 1998 Martin reflected: "In those days, performing songwriters were not the norm. When the Beatles came along the stuff they offered me

was not very good at all. 'Love Me Do' was the best thing I could find, and I knew it wasn't a big hit. 'P.S. I Love You', 'One After 909', not the greatest of epoch-making songs were they?"

Keen not to offend him, The Beatles did record 'How Do You Do It' for George Martin, but not until they had re-arranged Murray's demo into a more 'beat' version. Even so, little real commitment found its way into the performance. Within a year the song was picked up by The Beatles' Liverpool contemporaries Gerry & The Pacemakers, who immediately took it to No. 1. But this is a rare and fascinating glimpse of what should have been The Beatles' first Parlophone single.

PLEASE PLEASE ME
(Lennon/McCartney)
'Love Me Do' had scraped to No. 17 just before Christmas 1962, but it was not until their second Parlophone single 'Please Please Me' reached No.2, at the beginning of 1963, that the world changed for ever. This version was recorded in September 1962, a week after the desultory 'How Do You Do It', and featured session drummer Andy White who was filling in at George Martin's request. Written at his Aunt Mimi's home in Menlove Avenue, Lennon remembered it as: "My attempt at writing a Roy Orbison song...". This early version, long believed lost, lacks the single's hallmark harmonica. Unfortunately another take of 'Please Please Me' from the same session – a slower version more in the style of Roy Orbison – is long gone.

ONE AFTER 909
(Lennon/McCartney)
Critics of *Anthology* singled out the way this song was sequenced as evidence of tampering with history. Of course, some people want Takes 1-100 of everything The Beatles ever recorded at Abbey Road, which is obviously unfeasible. In shaping the *Anthology* releases nips and tucks were made in an attempt to convey the way The Beatles' music evolved and was shaped.

Before these releases, the only way you could glimpse inside the group's hermetic bubble at Abbey Road, was to read about it in Mark Lewisohn's book. Now, with *Anthology*, you could actually hear the development.

Because of its 1970 inclusion on the group's final album *Let It Be*, this is the best known of all the pre-Beatle Lennon & McCartney songs. Lennon held that it was "resurrected... probably for lack of material"; but taking into account that by then the group was visibly splintering, it seems possible that it was dusted down in a tongue-in-cheek effort to recreate the past. Here, 'One After 909' is a prime slice of chirpy, cheeky Merseybeat. Take 1 breaks down for Paul's lack of a plectrum; Take 4 falls victim to John's mis-timing, and the final complete edit is made up of three separate takes, put together by George Martin 30 years after the actual session.

LEND ME YOUR COMB
(Twomey/Wise/Weisman)
In July 1963 this 1956 Carl Perkins B-side, long a feature of The Beatles' live repertoire, found its way onto the airwaves. *Pop Go The Beatles* was the first BBC radio series devoted to a single pop group and there were fifteen half-hour episodes to fill. The pressure was clearly on, and the group

became adept at bolstering their BBC broadcasts by pillaging their live sets of the preceding six years. This was recorded at the BBC's Maida Vale Studios just along from Abbey Road, and was one of six songs recorded for the fifth edition of the programme – four of which had already appeared on 1994's *The Beatles Live At The BBC*. Paul patently has fun singing, and the others pitch in with vigour.

I'LL GET YOU
(Lennon/McCartney)
The B-side of that all-conquering fanfare for Beatlemania 'She Loves You'. The version here is a live take from the group's first appearance on *Sunday Night At The London Palladium*. Britain's most popular light entertainment TV show, this was the apogee of showbiz institutions – a prime example of the sort of cozy all-round family entertainment that The Beatles would inadvertently destroy once and for all.

News of the hysteria which greeted the group every time they broke cover was soon hitting the front pages. But what is remarkable about this performance is that despite the transparent hysteria, 'I'll Get You' still retains the howl of the Cavern. Appearing on the show alongside The Beatles, this Sunday night long ago, was Des O'Connor who five years previously had compered Buddy Holly's only UK tour.

WE WERE PERFORMERS...
(Speech)
Talking to *Rolling Stone*'s Jann Wenner, John Lennon reflected bitterly on The Beatles' decline as a live act. He was speaking in 1970 about events only seven years before, but it sounds like a whole weary lifetime ago.

I SAW HER STANDING THERE
(Lennon/McCartney)
Enshrined as the opening track on the first Beatles LP, this track always acted as a fiery onstage rocker. The version here, together with the remaining four songs on this CD,

were culled from a vibrant live performance recorded for Swedish radio in October 1963, just as The Beatles were breaking big at home. (See also chapter on *The Beatles Live At The BBC*.)

FROM ME TO YOU
(Lennon/McCartney)
This was the group's third single and their first UK No. 1. Lennon later remembered the writing of the song – while on tour with Helen Shapiro – as a real collaboration ("singing into each other's noses"). Besides being a nice souvenir of The Beatles' first visit abroad as a successful showbusiness export, you can actually hear the crackle and sizzle in their performance, making this one of the few audible souvenirs of Beatlemania. There is an enthusiasm to these performances which would soon become blunted by the insanity of performing live to hysterical audiences who couldn't hear a note of what they played.

MONEY (THAT'S WHAT I WANT)
(Gordy/Bradford)
This would be the concluding track on The Beatles' second album, but that was still four weeks away when they came to perform this version in Sweden. A hit in 1960 for Barrett Strong, this had been written by Berry Gordy, founder of the Motown empire and one of the few men who could look upon The Beatles as a creative equal. The Beatles had long championed 'the sound of young America', recognising instinctively the value of the production-line pop Gordy was producing in Detroit.

Flattered, Gordy returned the compliment: "We are very honoured The Beatles should have said what they did. They're creating the same type of music as we are and we're part of the same stream." Lennon particularly was fascinated by the sound the Motown studios consistently produced. In 1966, at a party to welcome the Four Tops to Brian Epstein's Saville Theatre, Lennon was overheard shouting across the room to the Four Tops' Larry Payton: "Tell me something man, when

you cats go into the studio, what does the drummer beat on to get that backbeat? You use a bloody TREE or something?"

YOU REALLY GOT A HOLD ON ME
(Robinson)
More Motown magic courtesy of Smokey Robinson, as pointed out by Lennon in his introduction for the benefit of the Swedish audience. (See also chapter on *The Beatles Live At The BBC*.)

ROLL OVER BEETHOVEN
(Berry)
Long a live Beatle favourite, this Swedish concert version rocks and rolls with enough vigour to awaken even the dead deaf German composer. (See also chapter on *The Beatles Live At The BBC*.)

DISC TWO

SHE LOVES YOU
(Lennon/McCartney)
Beatlemania got well and truly underway with the release of this, the fourth Beatles single, which had enjoyed a pretty much uninterrupted run at No. 1 since August. The announcement that the group

would appear at the 1963 *Royal Variety Show* – in the august company of Marlene Dietrich, Steptoe & Son and Pinky & Perky – set the seal on a triumphant year. Their appearance on November 4 was broadcast a week later, and for the fourth consecutive time *The Royal Variety Show* was the most-watched TV programme of the year, with an audience of nearly ten and a half million. The Beatles' performance of their anthem before a formally dressed audience saw them adopted by the establishment: within a week, everyone from newspaper leader writers to peers of the realm, was going "yeah, yeah, yeah".

TILL THERE WAS YOU
(Willson)
Taken from their second album *With The Beatles* – which in an example of chilling synchronicity was released the same day as President Kennedy was assassinated and Dr Who made his TV début. Paul's introduction to the song on *The Royal Variety Show* referred to "our favourite American group, Sophie Tucker", which drew a laugh from those familiar with the amply proportioned singer. This performance of 'Till There Was You' was a deliberate attempt to win over the older viewers – and by the end of the broadcast The Beatles really did appeal to everyone from eight to 80.

TWIST AND SHOUT
(Russell/Medley)
This was the group's standard set-closer in live performances that year, but the version captured here is particularly evocative for a whole generation with flickering monochrome memories of John Lennon standing cheekily at the microphone and asking the well-heeled crowed to "rattle their jewellery". It was just a joke, but the taunt of the Angry Young Man soon came to be seen as prescient when the ossified establishment was swept aside by the Government-toppling revelations of the Profumo Affair.

'Twist And Shout' was a collaboration between Bert Berns and Phil Medley, but the shadowy Berns decided for reasons best known to himself to take a pseudonym. He later went on to write a number of R&B and pop standards – 'Cry Baby', 'Here Comes The Night', 'Piece Of My Heart' and 'Everybody Needs Somebody To Love' among others. For Brian Epstein, for the moment, The Beatles at *The Royal Variety Show* was the pinnacle of his ambition.

THIS BOY
(Lennon/McCartney)
This version of the B-side of their current single was recorded a month after *The Royal Variety Show* for ITV's *Morecambe & Wise Show*. It demonstrates again that the group's harmonic abilities were still strong when they weren't subsumed by the screams which would mar their gigs during the next three years and ultimately force their withdrawal as a performing unit.

I WANT TO HOLD YOUR HAND
(Lennon/McCartney)
This is another track from the group's *Morecambe & Wise Show* appearance. No opportunity was missed to promote the current single – although it had entered the charts at No. 1 with advance orders of half a million, and was already set to become the year's second best-selling single (after 'She Loves You'). Even The Beatles struggled to find outlets to promote material, national television and radio wasn't really geared to outlets for pop groups, and Brian Epstein welcomed the opportunity for "the boys" to appear alongside the nation's favourite entertainers.

BOYS, WHAT I WAS THINKING...
(Speech)
Ernie Wise, he of the "short, fat hairy legs", coerces the group into a song. Interruptions from Eric Morecambe were frequent – though it was not until the Seventies, when the duo held sway over the nation's hearts, that Eric's interruptions and put-downs of Andre Previn, Des O'Connor, Glenda Jackson and Shirley Bassey became national

treasures. This time around, clad in Beatle wig and "yeah, yeah, yeah"-ing for all he's worth, Eric joshes with John before the Fab Six launch into "one that your dad will remember..."

MOONLIGHT BAY
(Madden/Wenrich)
A showbiz standard from the Forties which features The Beatles crooning as Eric does his Beatle impressions.

CAN'T BUY ME LOVE
(Lennon/McCartney)
One of *Anthology*'s most revealing fly-on-the-wall tracks demonstrates how a familiar Beatle song took shape. For over 30 years the single of 'Can't Buy Me Love' was as familiar as your bedroom wallpaper, until this harder edged version came along. This version is Take 2 with guitar overdubbed from Take 1, both were recorded in a Paris studio while The Beatles were appearing at the Olympia. The same session had already resulted in German-language versions of 'I Want To Hold Your Hand' and 'She Loves You'. Around this time there was a brief vogue for foreign language versions of hit records by British bands, but in the wake of The Beatles' all-conquering popularity, pop soon became a universal language and translations were no longer necessary.

This track demonstrates once again The Beatles' ability to hit a take bang-on first time round. Also of historic interest are the backing vocals from George and John which had disappeared on the subsequent single, and Paul's committed vocal – though he's not a hundred percent on the actual lyrics.

ALL MY LOVING
(Lennon/McCartney)
Familiar from *With The Beatles* (which in America was released with an altered track listing as Meet The Beatles), this was the song that first alerted America to The Beatles. Introduced by Ed Sullivan ("old Stone face") to banshee-wails from the audience, this is The Beatles caught in the act of making their American breakthrough.

The extent to which the outburst of American Beatlemania in February 1964 was rigged will probably never be known. But what is certain, is that in the aftermath of the Kennedy assassination three months before, The Beatles provided some much-needed light relief.

On Sunday February 9, 1964, an estimated 75% of the American television audience tuned in to The Ed Sullivan Show to watch the group perform this Beatle classic, which remarkably was never released as a single. McCartney remembers writing it "on a tour bus going to a gig, and so I started with the words. I had in mind a little Country & Western song... I remember working the tune out to it on the piano. It was a good show song, it worked well live."

YOU CAN'T DO THAT
(Lennon/McCartney)
By the end of February 1964 the pressure was *really* on. Having returned from their début American appearances, the group now had to write, and record, all the original songs for their first feature film, which was due to be filmed prior to their UK tour in June. The genesis of this Lennon composition, which was eventually excised from the film of *A Hard Day's Night*, lay in the soul music he loved. But the sound of the session is dominated by the 12-string guitar George had recently acquired in America – long before they were popularised by The Byrds. Take 9 was used as the B-side of 'Can't Buy Me Love' and it is interesting to compare that finished release with this – Take 6 – which is still a work in progress. The alternate takes on *Anthology* were never likely to better, or replace the album originals; but these out-takes do offer a fascinating glimpse of just how George Martin and The Beatles groped toward the familiar finished product.

AND I LOVE HER
(Lennon/McCartney)
Long hailed as one of Paul McCartney's first, and best, ballads; this run-through is Take 2, a rougher version than the

familiar, lush track which graced the soundtrack of *A Hard Day's Night*. With the slightly altered tempo, and Paul's vocal uncertainty, there is a real intimacy in hearing The Beatles move towards closure. Given the limited technology available, The Beatles were always keen to try and nail definitive versions of their songs as soon as possible. With a minimum of three non-album singles, two LPs, one American and one UK tour, not to mention the odd feature film, all to be crammed into every 12 month period; there simply wasn't the time to experiment.

A HARD DAY'S NIGHT
(Lennon/McCartney)
Hot from filming, the group adjourned to Abbey Road where they ran through a rudimentary version of the song which would give them the title for their film. This is Take 1 – just a run through to familiarise the group with the song and allow George Martin to see and hear what tinkering was necessary, but Paul's resonant bass playing is quite outstanding. Noticeably absent is the striking G suspended 4th chord played out on George's 12-string Rickenbacker, which ensured that the start of the familiar single and soundtrack version became one of the most immediately recognisable openings ever.

I WANNA BE YOUR MAN
(Lennon/McCartney)
Doubly familiar from having recently been a hit for The Rolling Stones, The Beatles take no prisoners on this all-out attack on their own song. (See also chapter on *The Beatles Live At The BBC*.)

This track and the following three were recorded for a 1964 TV special *Around The Beatles*. Filmed while the Fabs were concluding *A Hard Day's Night*, the show was directed by Jack Good, famous for the vintage Fifties TV pop shows *Six-Five Special* and *Oh Boy!* As well as providing a taste of The Beatles' stage show at the time, the programme had the group performing Shakespearean sketches.

LONG TALL SALLY
(Penniman)
Long a staple of The Beatles live sets, Paul loved letting rip on this Little Richard rocker. (See also chapter on *The Beatles Live At The BBC*.)

BOYS
(Dixon/Farrell)
This exuberant rocker provided Ringo with his obligatory solo on *Please Please Me*, as well as his token live vocal of the period.

SHOUT
(Isley)
This 1959 hit by The Isley Brothers was later famously covered by Lulu. But in the hands of The Beatles it becomes a raucous rock'n'roll soul workout with, uniquely, each of the four taking a vocal line. The group's musical contributions for *Around The Beatles* were recorded at the IBC studios, near Broadcasting House on Portland Place.

I'LL BE BACK

(Lennon/McCartney)
Originally released as the concluding track on *A Hard Day's Night*, this fascinating version of a Lennon song displays how quickly The Beatles could develop an idea: John's vocal cracks, the waltz tempo is dropped, and the song soon settles into its more familiar 4/4 Beatle time. But it would take a further 13 takes before the group were entirely satisfied. This is precisely the sort of studio observation which makes the *Anthology* releases so compelling.

YOU KNOW WHAT TO DO

(Harrison)
Although the songs of Lennon & McCartney were clearly the foundation of The Beatles' enduring brilliance, it would be a mistake to overlook the contribution made by George Harrison. As a songwriter George was destined to remain forever in the shadow of his peers, but as a musician he was always an integral part of the equation.

A tentative Harrison effort ('Don't Bother Me') had graced *With The Beatles*, but his second song 'You Know What To Do' would remain unissued for over 30 years until the release of *Anthology*. While far from being a Beatle classic, 'You Know What To Do' could have sat happily enough alongside the breezy Britpop of that period, and would have made a welcome addition to any Beatle album prior to *Help!* With double-tracked harmonies, amplified guitar and thudding drums supplied by the other Beatles, the song would not have seemed out of place on *Beatles For Sale* and could surely have provided one of Brian Epstein's other proteges with a minor hit.

NO REPLY

(Lennon/McCartney)
It wound up as the opening track on *Beatles For Sale* in December 1964, but in June this Lennon demo was dashed off quickly for Epstein singer Tommy Quickly, though in the event it was never released. John is in a hurry, Paul spars, but the song's vivacity is apparent, and playing a skeleton

like this back to back with the far more familiar album cut is one of the delights of *Anthology*. Lennon intended the song as his take on 'Silhouettes' – a Herman's Hermits hit of the time – "I had that image of walking down the street and seeing her silhouette in the window, and not answering the phone."

MR MOONLIGHT

(Johnson)
Lennon was familiar with the original Dr Feelgood version of this song, which he had worked into The Beatles' repertoire in 1962. Although used to operating under intense pressure, even the songwriting factory of Lennon & McCartney had begun to falter by the time of their fourth album; and consequently 6 of the 14 songs on *Beatles For Sale* were cover versions. The presence of an exotic George guitar solo, which predates Paul's Hammond organ on the finished album version, is the most marked difference on this take.

LEAVE MY KITTEN ALONE

(John/Turner/McDougal)
One of the undoubted highlights of the first *Anthology* album was this previously unreleased cover of Little Willie John's 1959 hit which John loved. Taped late at night, at Abbey Road in August 1964, the number ran to five takes of which this is the fifth and final. A searing Lennon vocal puts this right up there with 'Twist And Shout' and 'Money', and the track could easily have been used to conclude *Beatles For Sale*. To finally hear it in pristine stereo, over 30 years on, is a rare delight. Elvis Costello – who went on to collaborate with Paul McCartney – featured this widely bootlegged song on his 1995 album of covers *Kojak Variety*.

NO REPLY

(Lennon/McCartney)
Take 8 of this song appeared on *Beatles For Sale*. This bluesier version, introduced by long-time engineer Norman Smith, is Take 2 – but it falls apart under Lennon's laughter even though, to his evident delight, The Beatles are well on the way to nailing it down.

EIGHT DAYS A WEEK

(Lennon/McCartney)
The finished version of this song on *Beatles For Sale* – which was considered as a single prior to 'I Feel Fine' – was assembled from three separate takes. The version here, made up of the unused parts of the same three takes, has a notably different ending and features Paul's jocular criticism of his writing partner ("you daft get").
But such tinkering incensed hardcore fans who would have preferred to hear all three takes in their entirety. They particularly resented the segueing of disparate takes in order to create the illusion of a seamless whole, although in fact, this was the only way to effectively demonstrate the way the group operated in the studio.

'Eight Days A Week' displays the kind of acoustic experimentation which The Beatles would develop further on the following year's *Help!*. Paul later remembered inspiration for the song coming from a comment his chauffeur made after they had driven down to visit Lennon in Weybridge: "Neither of us had heard the expression before, so we had that chauffeur to credit for that... we just knocked it off together, just filling in from the title."

KANSAS CITY /HEY HEY HEY HEY!

(Leiber/Stoller/Penniman)
It only took two takes to get this right: Take 1 appeared on *Beatles For Sale*, and this is Take 2. Fascinating as it is to hear the way a Beatle song was developed at Abbey Road, the inclusion of a barely discernible alternate take such as this, was the sort of padding which did weaken the *Anthology* releases. In light of what we now know about The Beatles' later career, it is ironic to read the late Derek Taylor's sleeve notes on the original *Beatles For Sale* album, where he boasts of the "straightforward 1964 disc-making. Quite the best of its kind in the world. There is little or nothing on the album which cannot be reproduced on stage, which is, as students and critics of pop-music know, not always the case."

News that the three surviving Beatles were back together at Abbey Road with George Martin, Geoff Emerick and Jeff Lynne piecing together the official *Anthology* releases, resulted in press hysteria. Even the normally staid 204-year-old *Observer* predicted on its front page that "Four boys... will shake the world (again)". There had been rumours for many years, but in 1989, with all the legal acrimony finally out the way, Apple's Neil

Aspinall persuaded all concerned that the time was right.

When I interviewed George Harrison in 1992, he conceded that there were plans for an official video history of The Beatles: "We had to come up with a different angle, and the angle is: what was it really like? We were there at the epicentre, and now we're finding home movies and old footage... A couple of weeks ago, the director had 45 minutes of footage already – and Pete Best hadn't even joined the group yet!"

As late as 1993, George Martin was still dismissing the rumours of new Beatles releases with "it's all junk, couldn't possibly release it." But things change. Within a year George Martin was back at Abbey Road, persuading EMI to re-build part of their legendary No 2 Studio in order to precisely replicate the original studio atmospherics, they even agreed to resuscitate the old equipment on which he had recorded rock'n'roll's most crucial legacy: "I said... look, you've got a vintage producer and a vintage engineer, so you're going to need some vintage equipment to go with it."

Advertisements for Anthology in the trade press featured a picture of the familiar Ludwig bass drum complete with The Beatles' logo above the tag line: "You Haven't HEARD Everything Yet." There was an incredible orgy of all-things Beatles: *Mojo* magazine, under the headline 'They're Back', had four separate covers for issue No 24 – their Beatles *Anthology* edition – each featuring a different Beatle. *Record Collector*, even more arcanely, devoted two pages just to the promotional items which accompanied *Anthology 1*, noting wryly that even the Parlophone press office couldn't lay its hands on a 'Free As A Bird' promo CD, copies of which were already changing hands for £150.

With the news that the opening track on the first Anthology, 'Free As A Bird', would also be made available as a single, there was further press speculation as to whether,

a quarter of a century on, we would once again have a Beatles single at No 1 for Christmas – just like in the old days.

FREE AS A BIRD
(Lennon/McCartney/Harrison/Starr)
See left.

I SAW HER STANDING THERE
(Lennon/McCartney)
This is Take 9 which provided Paul's count-in on the finished version of the song that opened The Beatles' debut album. The rest of the album version was Take 1, and apart from the count-in, the take here has never been heard before. (See also chapter on *The Beatles Live At The BBC*.)

THIS BOY
(Lennon/McCartney)
An opportunity to eavesdrop at Abbey Road on the evening of October 17, 1963, as The Beatles muddle through Takes 10 and 11 of the B-side for 'I Want To Hold Your Hand'. George Martin urges them on from the control room, but the harmonies fall apart. This was also notable for being the first time The Beatles had got to play around with EMI's freshly-installed 4-track system – a facility which at long last opened up the brave new world of overdubbing, it would never again be necessary to go through take after take until they achieved a single perfect performance.

CHRISTMAS TIME (IS HERE AGAIN)
(Lennon/McCartney/Harrison/Starr)
The Beatles had pioneered the use of flexi-discs to keep their fans happy at Christmas. I remember the early ones being little more than: "Hi, this is George, thanks for all the birthday cards..." and perhaps Paul pleading with the fans to stop throwing jelly babies. But by 1967, things had obviously got weirder and The Beatles' Christmas Records were fast turning into psychedelic pantomimes. This hypnotic harmonising riff from '67, with Ringo helpfully pointing out that "O-U-T spells out", concludes with some

Lennon gibberish in the style of William McGonagall recorded the previous year. The Beatles' Christmas Records were great fun, and in 1970 they were collected together on an Apple album *From Us To You*.

Embargoed until 4 a.m. on November 20, 1995, on its release 'Free As A Bird' achieved a record-breaking 699 plays on UK radio stations within the first six days, becoming London's Capital Radio's most aired song ever. EMI's Malcolm Hill likened the servicing of the single to "an army manoeuvre".

The 'Free As A Bird' video was a feast of fun for Fab Fans, crammed with over 80 Beatle-related visual references – including Mother Mary, Dr Robert, egg men, walruses and newspaper taxis – but the single was beaten to the Christmas No 1 slot by Michael Jackson. Leading up to Christmas 1995, *Anthology 1* shifted over a million copies, but after just a month it too had dipped out of the Top 10 albums.

Neil Aspinall warned that there would be no further releases after the *Anthology* series: "After this, the cupboard is bare. There is no remaining new material." But *Anthology* was criticised in the main not for what it contained, but for what had been left off: Paul's 'You Just Don't Understand' from the 1960 Liverpool front room tape (which is also strongly rumoured to contain a version of 'When I'm 64'); The Beatles live at the Cavern; 'Love Of The Loved' from the Decca audition... These kind of omissions make me think that we might well see more 'new' Beatle material to take us into the next century.

ANTHOLOGY 2

Apple 7243 8 34448 2 3
Released March 1996

While diehard Beatle fans had welcomed its release with open arms, *Anthology* 1 had failed to capture the imagination of a larger cross-section of the Nineties audience. To record-buyers who had grown up accustomed to the luxury of digital, 96-track, compact disc technology, hearing rough-edged performances recorded on scratchy old shellac in 1958 lacked a certain something.

There was a feeling that however historically fascinating the teenage home recordings of Lennon, McCartney and Harrison were, what was really required was some more flesh on the bones. And here it was. *Anthology 2* covered the Glory Years, the period when the lovable mop-tops went from just plain Fab to being undeniably strange and God-like.

This second double-CD release covered the transitional years of 1965 to 1968, when The Beatles had progressed from simply bashing out hit after hit, and together with George Martin had, apparently effortlessly, expanded forever the horizons of popular music. Derek Taylor called these "the years of dash and daring". Weary of touring, The Beatles were cloistered together in Abbey Road, where they could flex, nip and tuck to their hearts content. It was up to George Martin to translate the Beatle version of what Bob Dylan had called "the sounds inside my

book. There had even been an opportunity to hear snatches of the magic on poorly recorded bootlegs. But here, finally, the world could be privy to the creation of the most influential body of work in rock'n'roll history. The words 'bated' and 'breath' hung in the air as *Anthology 2* finally made it out of myth and into the shops.

While the album would never replace existing copies of *Rubber Soul, Revolver* or *Sgt Pepper*, *Anthology 2* was a unique opportunity to eavesdrop, and to marvel at the group's astonishing rate of progress. It now seems hard to believe, almost inconceivable, that there were a mere five years between The Beatles first entering Abbey Road and the release of *Sgt Pepper*.

mind", and translate it he did. Hidebound by EMI's refusal to invest in the future, Martin laboured away for years on the same four-track equipment, but that was not enough to stop the Cinerama imaginations of The Beatles moving ever onwards and upwards. Their fantastic journey culminated in 1967 with the release of *Sgt Pepper* – still held by many to be the greatest album ever in the history of rock'n'roll. And crucially among the tracks to be found on *Anthology 2* are some early sketches of many of that album's most magical moments.

Anthology 2 is, largely, The Studio Years. Safe from the screaming hordes, The Beatles at last found the time to lavish care and attention on their records, comfortable in the knowledge that they would never be called upon to replicate those increasingly complex and ambitious sounds in live performance. During the incredibly creative period bookended by *Revolver* and *Magical Mystery Tour*, The Beatles – with a little help from their friend in the control room – completely redefined rock'n'roll.

That sense of adventure, of experimentation, of daring, made *Anthology 2* the most keenly anticipated of all The Beatles' archive releases. Many had already been tantalised by Mark Lewisohn's diligent account of The Beatles' recording techniques in his 1988

DISC ONE

REAL LOVE
(Lennon)

The single follow-up to 'Free As A Bird', 'Real Love' peaked at No. 4 in the UK and dipped out of the Top 10 completely after a fortnight. Controversy raged when Radio 1 refused to playlist the single ("Beatles Banned By Beeb!" ran the headlines), effectively banishing the song from its airwaves. The BBC's belligerent stance even raised questions in Parliament, when Conservative MP Harry Greenway railed against Radio 1's censorship, and announced his intention of tabling a Commons question asking John Major's government to intervene and require the station to play the song.

'Real Love' began life as a Lennon demo, recorded at his apartment in New York's Dakota building late in 1977. Yoko had already included it on the soundtrack of the 1988 film *Imagine*, but by anyone's standards 'Real Love' was hardly vintage Beatles. It sounded like the sort of song Lennon used to bash out by number during his post-Beatle career. Or as someone once commented: "It sounds like a song from one of those really dodgy Lennon solo albums done by Wings!"

For all his posthumous reputation as the "hard man" of The Beatles, 'Real Love' amply confirmed Lennon's soft as marshmallow side. In its own right, and as a single, it was an interesting contribution to The Beatles' discography; but its placing as the lead track on *Anthology 2* jarred.

YES IT IS
(Lennon/McCartney)
The first archive track takes us back to 1965, when this was issued in its finished form as the B-side to 'Ticket To Ride'. A John song which, as Mark Lewisohn notes, took a mere five hours from start to finish, this version is a combination of Take 2 – which breaks down, together with sections from Take 14 which highlight George's guitar and The Beatles' beguiling three-part harmonies. Lennon's vocal is undeniably weak, but it was only ever intended as a guide vocal, to help steer the rest of the group through the new song.

I'M DOWN
(Lennon/McCartney)
A timely reminder that Paul McCartney could rock out with the best of them. Fascinating to learn that this McCartney composition – a raucous Little Richard-influenced rocker – was recorded in June 1965 on the same day as 'Yesterday'.

This is Take 1: a live run through and the first time the group ever attempted the song at Abbey Road. Incredible to think that in the time it takes today's bands to get their limos parked, The Beatles had this song bang to rights. Paul ends by calling this "plastic soul" which, nipped and tucked a bit, became the title of The Beatles sixth album.

YOU'VE GOT TO HIDE YOUR LOVE AWAY
(Lennon/McCartney)
Another fascinating work-in-progress. John is quick to riff on "Paul's broken a glass…", then keenly inquires "are you ready… Macca?" Recorded for the *Help!* album, this Lennon composition displays the strong influence Bob Dylan was having on his songwriting at the time. The Beatles envied Dylan his artistic freedom and admired his refusal to compromise, while Dylan rather envied their commercial success.

This version of the Beatle favourite is notable for the absence of the familiar over-dubbed flute. The contribution from flautist John Scott on the finished version marked the first time any non-Beatle musician, apart from George Martin, had appeared on a Beatle record. This was the most folky song The Beatles had yet recorded, so it should come as no surprise that it was later covered by Brian Epstein's folk group The Silkie.

IF YOU'VE GOT TROUBLE
(Lennon/McCartney)
Since 'Boys' on 1963's *Please Please Me*, every Beatle album had found room for a Ringo vocal. On 'Boys', Ringo had encouraged Harrison's solo with a confident "alright George"; but here there is an air of desperation as the singing drummer enjoins "Rock on… anybody!" Knocked off by John and Paul as a quick token song for Ringo, 'If You've Got Trouble' was binned for 30 odd years, and it remains an undistinguished Beatle original. In the end the track was not used on *Help!* and Ringo wisely plumped instead for a cover of Buck Owens' 'Act Naturally' ("They're gonna put me in the movies…") for his contribution.

THAT MEANS A LOT

(Lennon/McCartney)

Another production-line Lennon & McCartney original, this eventually went to P.J. Proby who had appeared alongside The Beatles on their 1964 TV spectacular. But The Beatles' Midas touch was by no means infallible, and the song did little to further Proby's faltering career, scraping only to No 30 on the UK singles chart.

This Beatles demo of the song features a strong McCartney vocal, and with a little imagination and a few George Martin flourishes 'That Means A Lot' could have sat happily on side two of *Help!*. Where the *Anthology* releases really scored was in allowing this sort of discarded stuff to be heard. In pop terms, the material The Beatles left off albums was frequently better than what their contemporaries included.

YESTERDAY

(Lennon/McCartney)

The real joy of *Anthology 2* came in hearing something like this: the very first time that Paul McCartney attempted to record what was to become the most-covered song in the history of recorded music. 'Yesterday' had begun life unpromisingly as 'Scrambled Eggs' in the attic bedroom of Jane Asher's house on Wimpole Street. This tentative first run-through is the only other studio take of 'Yesterday' and has Paul running through some chord changes, blissfully unaware that he is routining a song which will live for as long as there is electricity to play it on. There is something immensely touching and poignant in hearing McCartney tackle the song. He knows how good it is, but now you can really revel in his freshness and zeal for the song which would, inevitably, define and shadow him over the ensuing years.

IT'S ONLY LOVE

(Lennon/McCartney)

Familiar as one of the Beatle gems tucked away on the second side of *Help!*, this is Take 2 of a song John later came to

regard as "abysmal". His vocal here is hesitant, and the song lacks George's hallmark lead guitar break. Recorded at Abbey Road during a lull in the making of their second film, this was another predominantly acoustic number which finds Lennon firmly under Dylan's shadow.

I FEEL FINE

(Lennon/McCartney)

This August 1965 appearance on the Sunday night programme *Blackpool Night Out* was one of The Beatles' increasingly rare TV appearances. Such was their pre-eminence that this sort of thing had now become a chore, but on the evidence of the following four tracks they still bothered to make show. This time out, they were promoting their current single and their new film *Help!* Although 'I Feel Fine' was one of the weakest Beatle singles, and in spite of their increasing reliance on the facilities of Abbey Road, the group could still cut it as a live act – as the applause on this live version testifies.

TICKET TO RIDE

(Lennon/McCartney)

In 1960 Lennon & McCartney had appeared as 'The Nerk Twins' at a pub in Caversham run by Paul's cousins the Robbins. The couple's subsequent move to run a pub at Ryde, on the Isle of Wight, was part of the inspiration for the punning title of this number. Lennon had a particular fondness for the song, and its staccato stop-start rhythm remains intriguing.

YESTERDAY

(Lennon/McCartney)

Even his fellow Beatles knew that Paul was onto something with this song. Mockingly introduced by George in the style of Hughie Green's dread *Opportunity Knocks* talent show, a solo Paul McCartney accompanied only by his acoustic guitar and a pre-recorded tape of three violins manages to still even the frenzy which normally greeted every onstage utterance.

HELP!

(Lennon/McCartney)

'Help!' was already No 1 as The Beatles played this set in Blackpool, but there was no sense in missing an opportunity to plug the product. Fans who grew up during the Beatle Years marked the passage of the seasons by the new Beatle single being No 1, summer and winter; while Christmas meant a new album too. Here in live performance, The Beatles lend a distinctive punk energy to this Lennon *cri-de-couer*.

EVERYBODY'S TRYING TO BE MY BABY

(Perkins)

The concluding track of *Beatles For Sale* was dusted down for this landmark appearance at New York's Shea Stadium. Cut from the subsequent TV broadcast, its appearance on *Anthology* marked the first time the song had been heard since that blustery day in August 1965 when The Beatles broke all box-office records with this historic appearance. But, historic though it was, this sort of material sat far more happily in the television *Anthology* than on disc.

NORWEGIAN WOOD (THIS BIRD HAS FLOWN)

(Lennon/McCartney)

Take 1 of what many regard as the finest song, on what will soon be championed as The Beatles' finest album. Rock critics have already worked backwards from *Sgt Pepper* to *Revolver*, and they should reach *Rubber Soul* before long. 'Norwegian Wood' is another song fashioned by Lennon under the shadow of Dylan. Primarily acoustic, this oblique commentary on a relationship in turn inspired Dylan's own '4th Time Around' which appeared on the following year's *Blonde On Blonde*. The distinctive sound of 'Norwegian Wood' is that of the sitar, which George had mastered between takes on the set of *Help!*, and even on this earliest version the sitar is already in evidence. Lennon's sardonic vocals, the then-trendy imagery of the ubiquitous Scandinavian pine, the world-weary lyrics... all combine to make this an instant Beatles classic.

I'M LOOKING THROUGH YOU

(Lennon/McCartney)

Further evidence of the high position *Rubber Soul* should hold in The Beatles' pantheon. This mid-paced McCartney song still needed some work on it, but this early version already displays the song's inherent strengths, although as the differences are really quite marginal I would question the value of its inclusion on *Anthology*. On October 24, 1965, The Beatles spent the whole day fashioning this version, but they would return to it on two further occasions before they completed the version which was heard on *Rubber Soul* when it was released in time for Christmas 1965.

12-BAR ORIGINAL

(Lennon/McCartney/Harrison/Starr)

Lengthy blues-based jams – as delivered by Cream, Hendrix and Ten Years After – would not be widely popular for a further two years. Recorded during the *Rubber Soul* sessions, this instrumental was never a serious contender for the album, but it does display a rare example of Beatle self-indulgence. Edited down from a sprawling six minute take, the version here shows the group paying homage to George's instrumental expertise. 'Flying', the only official Beatle instrumental, was released two years after this jam, which remained unissued in any form until premiered here.

TOMORROW NEVER KNOWS

(Lennon/McCartney)

If ever proof was needed about just how much George Martin brought to The Beatles, this is it. For this track was endlessly reworked and it was Martin's multi-tracking magic that clarified and made tangible the sound John Lennon heard in his head and wanted on disc. Nineteen sixty six was a crucial year in Beatle history, the year they gave up performing for good and focused all their creative energies on recording at Abbey Road.

George Martin suggests *Rubber Soul* as the first time the group attempted to fashion an album's worth of material rather than just a collection of A and B-sides; but *Revolver* was the album which saw the group finally bid adieu to the mop tops. Significantly, although it was the first track to be recorded for the album, 'Tomorrow Never Knows' became the apocalyptic final track on *Revolver*, as well as the song that first signposted *Sgt Pepper*. Take 1, issued here for the first time, demonstrates the foundation on which George Martin built. As so often on this collection, one is also struck by the frequently overlooked contribution of Ringo's drumming. His unfaltering thunderous power, which underpins much of The Beatles' magic, has rarely been better demonstrated than on this basic take; and the track in its entirety is a testament to the merit of the whole *Anthology* sequence.

GOT TO GET YOU INTO MY LIFE
(Lennon/McCartney)
One of the real revelations on this second batch of out-takes is the extent to which Paul's Motown-influenced rocker changed during the recording process. This Take 5 is a markedly different version of the song, with an altered tempo, more pronounced organ, and slightly different backing vocals. The

Beatles were always reluctant to leave anything alone, and despite this being near definitive, they couldn't resist returning to the song and adding the sounds and harmonies which would make the finished version so memorable.

AND YOUR BIRD CAN SING
(Lennon/McCartney)
Another of those great 'lost' Beatles songs. 'And Your Bird Can Sing' has too often been overlooked in appreciations of *Revolver*, but Paul Weller recognised the quality of the song and had The Jam record it 14 years later. By the time The Beatles came to record this Lennon original in April 1966, they truly had seen all seven wonders, and were well on their way to hearing "every sound there is". This second take of the song is recognisably similar in form to the finished version which would appear on the album when it was released in August 1966; but something causes a breakdown in communications at Abbey Road, and the singers dissolve into giggles.

TAXMAN
(Harrison)
Paul Weller again. That Jam man knew a good riff when he heard one, and he utilised George's opening to this track on

Revolver for his own 'Start' in 1980. Soon to be perceived as the most spiritual Beatle, George's lyrics for this song leave little doubt about just how worldly wise he could be. The tax regime of Harold Wilson's Labour government was taking something like 19/6d out of every £1 The Beatles earned, which prompted George's heartfelt comments here. There are noticeable differences between this track and the version which opened *Revolver* – the staccato ending and the "anybody got a bit of money?" refrain instead of the more familiar "Mr Wilson" and "Mr Heath". George's guitar still scorches though.

ELEANOR RIGBY
(Lennon/McCartney)
Just the sort of dead wood which got *Anthology* a bad name. This instrumental backing track for what was to become one of Paul's best-known songs can add little to our appreciation; at best it offers an opportunity to appreciate George Martin's skilful arrangement, at worst it's just Beatle karaoke.

I'M ONLY SLEEPING
(Lennon/McCartney)
What makes this noticeably different from the familiar *Revolver* track is the presence of a vibraphone on this rehearsal. You can just imagine The Beatles playing around with the unfamiliar instrument like a child's new toy, and then drifting reluctantly back to work. This first take has yet to develop the familiar dreamy, druggy miasma, but it still makes for another fascinating fly-on-the-wall moment from Abbey Road.

ROCK AND ROLL MUSIC
(Berry)
In June 1966, with *Revolver* completed, The Beatles immediately undertook a brief tour of Germany and Japan. This track and the following one, are versions of familiar Beatle material recorded live at Tokyo's Budokan Hall. Long regarded as sacred, there were vehement protests about the site being tainted by anything so

profane as a pop performance, and there were even fears of assassination attempts during the group's performance. Interesting as the performance is, perhaps this and the other live material on *Anthology* would have been better put together on a Beatles *Live Over The Years* CD.

Recently released Foreign Office documents received around the time of this tour from Charge d'affaires Dudley Cheke (our man in Tokyo) suggested that it would benefit trade between the two countries if Carnaby Street could cash in on the gear worn by the "agreeable, talented and quick-witted young musicians". Cheke also reported on how he had been able to "harvest goodwill" by securing tickets to The Beatles' shows for Japanese dignitaries, although there had apparently also been complaints from some quarters that two guineas was a lot to pay for a concert that lasted only 30 minutes.

SHE'S A WOMAN
(Lennon/McCartney)
A throat-lashing concert favourite coming from the end of the group's era as live performers. (See also chapter on *The Beatles Live At The BBC*.)

Of course, the perfect conclusion to this first half of the *Anthology 2* package would have been 'Long Tall Sally' from the August 29, 1966 Beatle performance at Candlestick Park, San Francisco. It would prove to be the final song in The Beatles' final appearance as a group before a paying audience. Three decades later, to the day, Beatle tribute band The Mop Tops paid homage by playing at Candlestick Park to an audience of 16,000. In 1966, there must already have been something in the air, because The Beatles asked press officer Tony Barrow to tape the show for them. However, such were the limitations of the technology available that his portable cassette player could only accommodate a 30-minute tape, and it had run out during the group's final song!

DISC TWO

STRAWBERRY FIELDS FOREVER
(Lennon/McCartney)

With EMI panicking about the prospect of Christmas without a Beatles LP, *A Collection Of Beatles Oldies... But Goldies!* was prepared for release on December 9, 1966. It effectively marked the end of a phenomenal three-year burst during which The Beatles emerged from the relative anonymity of Liverpool cellars to become the most famous people in the whole world. A fortnight before the release of *Oldies... But Goldies!* The Beatles reconvened at Abbey Road to commence recording their eighth proper album.

Exhausted by the rigours of incessant touring and recording, the group had been apart since the completion of their American tour in August 1966. Apart, but not idle – John had been filming *How I Won The War* in Germany and Spain; Paul had begun scoring the film *The Family Way*; George was in India studying the sitar; and Ringo was at home in Weybridge playing pool. It was during the long delays in filming on location that John began this fragmentary, hallucinatory recollection of life in Liverpool, long ago, before the world went mad.

The three versions of 'Strawberry Fields Forever' here demonstrate the genesis of what is probably John's best-known song. At home in Weybridge Lennon mutters "I cannae do it..." as he grapples, finger-picking, alone with his guitar. Intimate and priceless. Ensconced at Abbey Road, George Martin and The Beatles enter the Twilight Zone. This is *Anthology* at its best – giving us the priceless opportunity to hear Take 1 of the most lavishly produced Beatle song ever.

It is revealing and rewarding to follow the group as they grope their way towards realising their dreams. The third version here is the first opportunity to hear how George Martin juggled the different tempi of the various versions. Take 7 and Take 26 have all

manner of unfamiliar sounds – some cataclysmic drumming ("calm down Ringo," smiles John) and vocal extemporising. Recorded just prior to Christmas 1966, you can clearly hear Lennon saying "cranberry sauce", which survived buried in the mix on the released version of 'Strawberry Fields Forever'. For years, Beatle conspiracy theorists were convinced this was John saying "I buried Paul".

PENNY LANE
(Lennon/McCartney)

Written around the same time as 'Strawberry Fields Forever', Paul's 'answer song' was an adolescent memory of a location familiar to both as boys: "John and I would often meet at Penny Lane... There was a barber shop called Bioletti's, with head shots of the haircuts you can have in the window, and I just took it all and arted it up a little bit..."

This version of 'Penny Lane' compiled from a number of takes, demonstrates just how the song was altered and modified in production. Remixed in 1995 by George Martin to highlight the various ingredients – instrumental solos, McCartney's reduced vocal, the wayward ending – it really does help to clarify the incredibly complex layering of this much-loved song.

A DAY IN THE LIFE

(Lennon/McCartney)

Another composite – this time of the end-of-the-world conclusion to *Sgt Pepper* – revealing just how The Beatles and George Martin did it. It is a rewarding journey, and one which more than justifies the controversial technique of combining various takes. Like film-making and war, recording consists of brief bursts of tremendous excitement punctuated by long periods of boredom. The pick'n'mix patchwork approach of *Anthology* offers the opportunity to savour some of that excitement without the tedium of having to sit through take after take after take.

ONLY A NORTHERN SONG

(Harrison)

Intriguing to imagine this slotted in to the first side of *Sgt Pepper*. But in the event George's wistful song didn't appear until two years later when, with a few lyrical variants, it was used to bolster the soundtrack for the *Yellow Submarine* cartoon. This is a combination of various takes and reductions which were bounced between tracks. A fascinating stereo battle between Ringo's drums on the left, and a 'Lucy In The Sky...' type organ on the right is clear here.

"It [meditation] helps you find fulfilment in life, helps you live life to the full. Young people are searching for a bit of peace inside themselves." – George

Of all The Beatles' songs to date, 'A Day In The Life' was the most ambitious, and it acted as a suitable crescendo to the album that would alter the world on its release in June 1967. Here a relaxed (stoned?) Lennon goes "sugar plum fairy...", then it's off into the unknown: burly Beatles roadie Mal Evans counts to 24, Paul fluffs bridge ("Oh shit...") and the orchestral climax is clearer.

GOOD MORNING, GOOD MORNING

(Lennon/McCartney)

"A throwaway, a piece of garbage..." according to the composer, and indeed it was one of the less distinguished tracks on *Sgt Pepper*. This take, number 8, is more driving than the final incarnation – funky bass and astonishing drumming are to the fore, and the song had not yet disappeared under George Martin's enthusiastic production flourishes and sound effects layering.

BEING FOR THE BENEFIT OF MR KITE

(Lennon/McCartney)

Takes 1, 2 and 7 demonstrate just how a song was built during the *Sgt Pepper* sessions. Despite the assembled production expertise – and for all Lennon's wish to put everything but the kitchen sink into his songs – sometimes less really is more. The most revealing moments on *Anthology 2* are those basic master tracks which demonstrate how the early takes were used as foundations for what followed, and the way they were built into the versions familiar to everyone who has owned the best-known (and for many, simply the best) rock album ever. These 'Mr Kite' out-takes are worth it just for the banter, as when Paul chides John: "try and sing it as if you know about the show...".

LUCY IN THE SKY WITH DIAMONDS
(Lennon/McCartney)

Like unravelling a great tapestry, *Anthology* allows you the opportunity to examine this well known and much loved material stitch by stitch. Here John's vocal is ragged, but almost all the vital ingredients are in place; what it lacks is the beautiful kaleidoscope of sound which George Martin later weaved into place around John's far-away voice and hallucinatory lyrics.

WITHIN YOU, WITHOUT YOU
(Harrison)

This is another of those karaoke fillers. While the *Sgt Pepper* version of the song had a nice love-is-all-around vibe, with the vocals removed the instrumental track struggles to stand in isolation. George was never a prolific composer, and for as long as The Beatles were recording together he had to battle against the might of McCartney and Lennon to get his songs placed. This was equally true when it came to the release of the *Anthology* sequence: logistically and numerically, George was always going to be outnumbered by John and Paul. There were even rumours that the *Anthology* releases had been held up specifically because of disagreements over the question of balance – allegedly resulting in this track replacing McCartney's avant-garde 'Carnival Of Light'.

SGT PEPPER'S LONELY HEARTS CLUB BAND (REPRISE)
(Lennon/McCartney)

It was apparently Neil Aspinall's idea to reprise the album's title track, a decision which helped foster the illusion of *Sgt Pepper* as a concept album. The finished track was cut in one 12-hour session, and this is Paul's guide vocal, played out hard and fast, over a raunchy backing track (Take 5), punched out before he split to the States.

Hearing a song with which you have become so familiar, in such a markedly different version, is at first disconcerting. None of the *Anthology* takes are markedly 'better' than the official releases which have formed the soundtrack of our lives for nearly 40 years. But while it is unlikely that anyone would prefer any of the *Anthology* versions to the finished album tracks, isn't this FUN?

YOU KNOW MY NAME (LOOK UP THE NUMBER)
(Lennon/McCartney)

I once asked Paul McCartney what his favourite Beatle song was. I was expecting 'Yesterday', 'Eleanor Rigby', or perhaps 'Here, There & Everywhere'... but this is the one he said he had the fondest memories of recording. Officially released as the B-side of the six million selling 'Let It Be' single, 'You Know My Name...' remains the most obscure official Beatles release.

This master recording includes an extended ska section (popular in 1969 when the final session was completed) which was excised from the official release. A fun song, this was The Beatles letting their hair down and having fun – mocking the showbusiness superficiality (John's manifestly false MC; Paul's schmaltzy crooner) which they had already done so much to destroy.

I AM THE WALRUS
(Lennon/McCartney)

Although by now they were off the touring circuit, 1967 was another hectic year for The Beatles. The death of Brian Epstein had seen Paul McCartney take charge of the group's direction, and in the vacuum following the release of *Sgt Pepper*, he had decided to send the group off an a *Magical Mystery Tour*. This was George Martin's reference recording of the show's most ambitious song. It is quite disorientating to listen to this version which lacks all the familiar references ("Are you sir?" etc) of the finished track. Martin went off with this take (No 16) and wrote the arrangement which would expand and illuminate Lennon's challenging but disturbing creation.

THE FOOL ON THE HILL
(Lennon/McCartney)
A beautiful vignette from Abbey Road, as Paul demos one of his contributions to the *Magical Mystery Tour*. Seated solo at the piano, the composer unveils this most poignant composition. Part of the charm of this particular performance lies in the freshness with which Paul approaches it – busking the words and letting imagination fill in the familiar gaps.

YOUR MOTHER SHOULD KNOW
(Lennon/McCartney)
Another *Magical Mystery Tour* highlight courtesy of Paul McCartney. This was a basic master of Take 27, onto which further George Martin ornamentations would later be added to enhance and improve. "Was that alright?" asks the composer. Hearing these songs sequenced, you are reminded of the awesome scope of The Beatles' material at this time – from John's weird 'Walrus' to Paul's cosy 'Mother'.

THE FOOL ON THE HILL
(Lennon/McCartney)
In the space of three weeks, Paul and George Martin had developed the demo. This is Take 4, which had already grown into the shape familiar from *Magical Mystery Tour*. Paul later claimed that the song was vaguely inspired by the Maharishi, but that it was also recalled by Paul's memory of reading about an Italian hermit in the Second World War. The dream-like atmosphere of the completed track is already clearly in evidence.

HELLO, GOODBYE
(Lennon/McCartney)
One of the great overlooked Beatles singles, which is not surprising when you consider that it followed 'Penny Lane' and 'All You Need Is Love' – all in the same year! But there is something wise and all-embracing in its philosophy of the time (Paul: "It's just a song of duality, with me advocating the more positive 'You say goodbye, I say hello. You say stop, I say go'.")

Lennon had been pitching for his 'I Am The Walrus' to be the single's A-side, but commercial considerations dictated that McCartney's sure-fire winner was chosen instead. George Martin had plenty of opportunity to overdub, but this Take 16 offers the rudimentary version of the single, and a rewarding opportunity to isolate and dissect the brilliant constituents which went to make up a Beatle classic.

LADY MADONNA
(Lennon/McCartney)
Another McCartney victory. 'Lady Madonna' was The Beatles 'as nature intended', a more rock'n'rolling outfit than the bunch of hairy weirdos on *Sgt Pepper*. Taking its opening riff from Humphrey Lyttleton's 'Bad Penny Blues', this working version (Takes 3 and 4) demonstrates the rootsier, Fifties sounding, piano-heavy Fats Domino style, that The Beatles were attempting to replicate. But the most marked difference from the released single is the absence of harmonies and massed use of brass. The group's first single of 1968 was seen as a wilful step back from the florid excesses of *Sgt Pepper*, and I remember that even the trade ads of the time made much of the group's 'get back' approach.

ACROSS THE UNIVERSE

(Lennon/McCartney)

While Paul was ahead in the battle for A-side supremacy, John was no slouch. This is Take 2, recorded one Sunday at Abbey Road; and untroubled by overdubs or effects, this is Lennon in the raw, a flawed but revealing note on which to end Anthology 2.

As with the first Anthology, a 'new' Beatles song was released as a single to coincide with the second album. And as with the first, 'Real Love' was not triumphantly successful – peaking at No. 4 on the UK charts on its release in March 1996. The 13 minute CD single was bolstered by three further "exclusive, unreleased" tracks.

REAL LOVE

(Lennon)

See above.

BABY'S IN BLACK

(Lennon/McCartney)

There were compensations to being a Beatle: thousands and thousands of pubescent girls squealing with delight at your every move was one. Here is a sliver of Beatlemania, taken from the very height of that hysteria: The Beatles live at the Hollywood Bowl in August 1965. In unison, they stroll quite successfully through this waltz ("for all of you over 10") from *Beatles For Sale*.

YELLOW SUBMARINE

(Lennon/McCartney)

A never before heard spoken-word intro by Ringo is the most distinctive difference on this new take of a familiar song from *Revolver*; though the actual words – "From Land O'Groats to John O'Green..." – have a distinct Lennon ring. The beginnings of the song first came to Paul as he was drifting off to sleep in his attic room at Jane Asher's Wimpole Street home; Donovan later supplied the "sky of blue and sea of green..." lines. Some of the weird sound effects are more obviously marked on this new version.

HERE, THERE & EVERYWHERE

(Lennon/McCartney)

Begun by Paul while he was waiting at Kenwood, Lennon's house in Weybridge, for John to wake up; even the notoriously

John Lennon and Yoko Ono leaving court,
October 19, 1968

hard-to-please Lennon called it "one of his favourite Beatle songs". This alternate version is more fragile and straightforward than the *Revolver* version. The bulk of the song is the June 1966 Take 7, with extra Beatle harmonies from the same sessions overdubbed and remixed by George Martin in 1995.

Anthology 2 went straight into the UK and US album charts at No. 1 on its release in March 1995. Within six months of their release, the first two volumes of *Anthology* had sold over 13 million copies. *Anthology 2* also gave The Beatles their 17th No. 1 album in America – an unequalled record. But what was even more astonishing was the revelation that 41% of purchasers were teenagers, proving once and for all that The Beatles really could span the generation gap.

Writing in *Mojo*, Mark Ellen nailed the overall feeling of those who had grown up with the original releases and were now luxuriating in

something new: "It's chilling how familiar these songs have become. They're one of the few constant ingredients of the last 30 years. You've heard them a million times and they were always the same. Until now. There's an awkward period when the out-takes seem disorientating or just plain wrong. It's like coming home and finding the wallpaper's changed or someone's mucked about with the furniture... You know it all, the absent vocals, the missing guitar, the hole where a cymbal crash ought to be. It's appalling really. What have we done with our lives?"

Aside from the sheer quality of the music, and the golden opportunity for life-long fans to eavesdrop, the timing of the *Anthology* releases had been exactly right. Paul Weller and Oasis in particular had been singing The Beatles' praises, and now here they were with some new material. An estimated 400 million people worldwide watched the *Anthology* documentaries on television. And it seemed like they had never been away...

Maybe it was simply that by losing yourself in a welter of Beatle nostalgia you could, just for a couple of hours, forget about AIDS, crack and Bosnia. Or maybe, re-living your past courtesy of *Anthology*, it was as if neither Lennon nor Martin Luther King had ever been shot. Here was the world when it was young, and we were too young to notice.

But the success of The Beatles' *Anthology* releases was more than mere nostalgia. Finally we could begin to understand the way the group had crafted their music, to comprehend how they weaved that incomparable magic. And for the first time, we were actually able to be here, there and everywhere while they did it.

ANTHOLOGY 3

Apple 7243 8 34451 2 7
Released October 1996

Like children let loose in a sweetshop, The Beatles tried everything – sex, drugs, rock, roll, mysticism and meditation. They acted as the litmus paper of the era, the sounding board of the Sixties. And still today they remain at the heart of the 20th century's most abiding and enduring fairy tale – the story of four lads from Liverpool who took on the world, and won.

By the beginning of 1968, when *Anthology 3* opens, the group had renounced drugs and were already fully immersed in the introspective meditation offered by the Maharishi Mahesh Yogi. In February 1968, all four Beatles flew out to study with the Maharishi in India, but it was to degenerate swiftly into a year of further confusion and dubious hairstyles.

The Apple business, eventual disillusionment with the Maharishi, John's divorce, drug busts... all would take their toll on The Beatles' creativity. But despite the sudden death of Brian Epstein in 1967, and for all the superficial dallying, The Beatles remained for the time being a recording unit.

Following the psychedelic, music-hall mayhem and mysticism of *Sgt Pepper*, there was an understandable desire within The Beatles to try something (less) different. This desire to recapture something of the frivolity

and immediacy of the Fifties was apparent when they came to record 'Lady Madonna'. But what remains most remarkable about The Beatles is their prolificity; throughout their seven years of unparalleled fame, no matter what bugged them about the world, or about each other, they would always reconvene at Abbey Road to make music.

The third and final Anthology chronicles the period bordered by the 'White Album' and *Abbey Road*. This was a time when, despite all the internal dissent and bickering, The Beatles achieved a level of fecundity which even they had never approached before. George Martin has gone on record as preferring *Abbey Road* to *Sgt Pepper*, and if you can manage to shut your mind to what we now know of the internal bickering (Paul vs George, John vs Paul...), if you just relax and listen to the music... he might just have a point.

Unlike its predecessors, *Anthology 3* did not have a single to accompany its release, although Paul, George and Ringo were believed to have completed work on a third Lennon demo 'Grow Old With Me'. But the relative failure of 'Free As A Bird' and 'Real Love' (neither of which had reached No. 1 in the UK or America) made the survivors happy to rest on their laurels this time round. There are still a number of unreleased Lennon demos from the period 1975-1980, which Yoko is believed to be retaining for a possible future project – which may or may not include Paul, George and Ringo reworking them.

After the joys and delights of the first two volumes, there was not the same keen sense of anticipation prior to the release of *Volume 3*; but when it was released, and people actually got to hear the music, there were many who thought it the best of the bunch.

In Beatle history, the years between 1968 and 1970 are convoluted, frustrating, and inspiring – all in equal measure. The *Sgt Pepper* versus *Revolver* debate continues to rage, and a great deal of fond nostalgia surrounds *Help!*; but increasingly I find myself coming round to the idea of the 'White Album' – excluding 'Revolution # 9' – as perhaps *the* Beatles' album. Here was an awesome scope and sweep, a real versatility, and variety which remains unequalled in rock'n'roll. While there is a case to be made for the 'White Album' as three and a half solo albums struggling to get out, the fact is that – thanks to the unfaltering quality threshold of George Martin and The Beatles – it holds together really well as a testament to the group's instinctive genius.

In May 1968, inspired by the time they spent in India, The Beatles grouped together at George Harrison's home in Esher and demoed much of the material they had written there, this would later constitute the bulk of the 'White Album'. The majority of the material on the first CD of *Anthology 3* will be recognisable as songs from the 'White Album', while the second CD attempts to coalesce the sprawling sessions which would eventually be distilled into Let It Be and Abbey Road.

Following the release of the 'White Album' in December 1968 the group's priority was another new-phase Beatles album, but they were also under pressure to deliver the third, and final, film for which they were contracted to United Artists. The possibility of a Western (*A Talent For Loving*) was quickly rejected, and Lennon's enthusiasm for a film version of Tolkien's *Lord Of The Rings* soon got ground down in a legal quagmire. Before his death, Brian Epstein had expressed interest in controversial playwright Joe Orton writing something for the boys, but *Up Against It* wasn't what he'd expected; Epstein panicked at the script (which included "sex, scandal and four-letter words"), and the script was swiftly dropped. It was eventually produced by BBC Radio 3 in September 1997 on the 30th anniversary of Orton's death, starring Blur's Damon Albarn, and Leo McKern who coincidentally had starred alongside The Beatles in *Help!*

As had so often happened during their years together, a number of different factors worked in combination to finally lead The Beatles down a particular road. The group's desire to 'get back' owed much to George's infatuation with The Band. The legendary five-piece outfit which backed Bob Dylan during his controversial 1966 world tour, had hunkered down with Bob in the basement of their house called 'Big Pink' in a little artistic hamlet called Woodstock throughout 1967; and in 1968 they released their debut album *Music From Big Pink*. Like Eric Clapton and many others, George was enchanted by the rootsy authenticity of The Band – a grittiness which he felt could well be beneficial to The Beatles.

Around this time, John was become increasingly enchanted by Yoko Ono, and was finding his day job with The Beatles more and more at odds with his own artistic vision. For the first time in a decade, he began to envisage a life away from the group he had founded.

Paul McCartney on the other hand had come to believe that the one thing which might keep The Beatles together was if he could once again get them working as a live band – but obviously not amidst the football stadium frenzy of Beatlemania. In an effort to reclaim their turf and get the group to re-group, McCartney convinced himself that if The Beatles were to turn up unannounced and start playing, it would rekindle the feeling of unity that had kept them buoyant for over a decade. Unfortunately though, the plan to return to the road met with little favour from John or George. As a stopgap measure The Beatles agreed to be filmed rehearsing in January 1969, which would provide United Artists with their third film, as well as offering the group the opportunity to routine some new material.

It was against this troubled background that The Beatles spent much of 1968 and 1969 – the period covered by this final Anthology release. It was hard now to believe that it had once all seemed so easy.

DISC ONE

A BEGINNING
(George Martin)
Intended simply as an instrumental preface to Ringo's 'Don't Pass Me By', this was a disappointingly subdued opening to *Anthology 3*.

HAPPINESS IS A WARM GUN
(Lennon/McCartney)
This – the first track from the Esher demos – finds John besotted by his new love, Yoko Ono, and attempting to inject that love into a new song. Working with only an acoustic guitar, John juggled a couple of fragments he had worked up in India ('I Need A Fix' and 'Mother Superior Jumped The Gun') into something else. This kind of demo material provided a necessary fix for the fans: the recorded versions of Beatle songs had become so familiar, that to hear them working up material like this was almost like hearing the song for the first time – a truly enriching experience.

HELTER SKELTER
(Lennon/McCartney)
This was to become the most ill-fated of all Beatle songs when it came out on the 'White Album'. An American called Charles Manson heard the song and became convinced that it was The Beatles' call to arms – totally unaware that in Britain 'Helter Skelter' was the name for an innocent fairground ride. Many years later, U2's Bono would introduce their cover of the song by saying "This is a song Charles Manson stole from The Beatles, and we're stealing it back!"

For 30 years, Beatle fans had been obsessing about the full 12-minute version of this McCartney rocker. The *Anthology* version is Take 2 – the legendary long version – but "respectfully pruned" to a more manageable four and a half minutes. Played live by all four Beatles, on two guitars, bass and drums, you get the picture: a slow, lumbering McCartney song, moody and sombre. Although it lacks the polish later supplied by George Martin, this was nonetheless a necessary adjunct to any Beatles collection.

MEAN MR MUSTARD
(Lennon/McCartney)
Intended for the 'White Album', but held over until Abbey Road, this Lennon throwaway ("another piece of garbage") makes a nice double-tracked demo souvenir.

POLYTHENE PAM
(Lennon/McCartney)
Ditto. The composer recalled a character from a Channel Islands orgy, and as was his wont, stuck her in a song. A few minor lyrical differences distinguish this Esher demo from the Abbey Road version.

GLASS ONION
(Lennon/McCartney)
With a good deal more merit than many which emerged from the Esher sessions, this song finds John having fun with the notions of identity in Beatle myth. This version lacks most of the self-referential

and forks, but this still rates as one of Harrison's best ever Beatle songs; caustic and wry, this is a charming home demo.

HONEY PIE
(Lennon/McCartney)
Retaining the fresh charm and vivacity of the familiar album version, this is a throwaway fun piece, and Paul's demo here conveys a genuine joy and light-heartedness – you can just hear him imagining the sort of arrangement he'd like to swathe the song in. It was a time when rock music was extending its solos and and beginning to take itself terribly seriously. To hear The Beatles singing tongue-in-cheek about Thirties screen sirens was an iconoclastic delight.

DON'T PASS ME BY
(Starkey)
For over five years, whenever he was asked about his own songwriting, Ringo always cited 'Don't Pass Me By' as his work in progress. This version of the song, barely different to that which appeared six months later on the 'White Album', is presumably included so that Richard Starkey's Eaton Music can lay claim to a share of the songwriting royalties.

OB-LA-DI, OB-LA-DA
(Lennon/McCartney)
A McCartney effort through and through, and one which he would haul The Beatles through again and again, earning the loathing of Lennon in particular. The composer though had different memories: "John was late for the session, but when he arrived he bounced in, apologising, in a very good mood. He sat down at the piano and played the blue-beat style intro... He and I worked hard on the vocals, and I remember the two of us in the studio having a whale of a time."

That blue-beat version is the one you can hear on this previously unissued early take of the song which later appeared on the 'White Album'. Written by Paul while staying with the Maharishi in India, the song was inspired by

details familiar from the 'White Album', and is filled instead with Lennon lyric-filling nonsense.

JUNK
(McCartney)
Edged off the 'White Album', this one had to wait until 1970, when a slot was found for it on Paul's début solo album. The weaving, disjointed McCartney solo effort here provides just a tantalising framework, and one can only speculate as to how George Martin and the other Beatles would have enhanced it.

PIGGIES
(Harrison)
This cautionary tale is a timely relic of the period. 1968 was a year of turmoil: the year piggies like Mayor Daley's cops staved in the heads of youthful protestors at the Chicago Democratic Convention; the year Russian tanks crushed Czechoslovakian dissent; the year of street fighting men. John claims to have supplied George with the line about the piggies eating bacon with knives

a catch-phrase of conga player Jimmy Scott. Intended as a parody of reggae music which was popular in the UK charts at the time, the song became a Christmas 1968 No 1 for Marmalade.

GOOD NIGHT
(Lennon/McCartney)
This was the Lennon song which concluded the 'White Album', following his cacophonic 'Revolution #9'. This is an early take of Ringo's vocal, sung against George Martin's familiar lush orchestration which was recorded later, and superimposed on Take 34 for *Anthology*.

CRY BABY CRY
(Lennon/McCartney)
A pleasant and enlightening early take of the track which, along with Lennon's 'Good Night' and 'Revolution #9', brought the 'White Album' to a close. Although rather predictably Lennon later dismissed the song as a filler, it actually stands up rather well as a piece of Lewis Carroll-inspired whimsy. What makes this Anthology version so illuminating is to hear how quickly and surely John's Beatle partners lock into the Lennon groove.

BLACKBIRD
(Lennon/McCartney)
The version of 'Blackbird' which appeared on the 'White Album' centres on Paul solo with acoustic guitar, but George Martin emboldened the basic track by double-tracking the guitar and, famously, by superimposing a blackbird's song. This *Anthology* version has none of the embellishments, just Paul McCartney, guitar and vocal, solo and alone. He had begun the song on his farm in Scotland, and still counts it one of his own favourite songs of the Beatle era.

SEXY SADIE
(Lennon/McCartney)
A flawed but nonetheless rewarding early version of another track from 'the White Album'. This is a slower, far less 'produced' version of Lennon's dig at the

Maharishi. By all accounts, there is a libellous version of the song locked away in EMI's vaults, which apparently features Lennon making ribald and obscene comments about his former guru. But at George Harrison's suggestion he altered the title from 'Maharishi' to the less accusatory 'Sexy Sadie'. In the authorised biography, *Many Years From Now*, McCartney dismisses the suggestion that the Maharishi attempted to rape one of his adoring female followers saying, "It was Magic Alex who made the original accusation and I think that it was completely untrue."

WHILE MY GUITAR GENTLY WEEPS
(Harrison)
One of the undisputed finds of the whole *Anthology* series was this solo acoustic demo from George. Later made famous by having the weeping guitar played by Eric Clapton on the 'White Album' version, this is the song as it was originally conceived – including an extra verse which George cut from later versions. Sounding world-weary and wise, omniscient and overwhelmed, the Quiet One here delivers a spellbinding solo performance of this fragile masterpiece.

HEY JUDE
(Lennon/McCartney)
Jolly banter between John and Paul leads into this stripped-down and shorter version of The Beatles' first single on Apple. A virtual anthem during 1968, the single was renowned for its previously unthinkable seven-minute length, as well as the you-can-all-join-in chorus. This equally impactful version is a basic take of Paul's piano and impassioned vocal, plus bass, guitar and drums from the other Beatles. As with many *Anthology* tracks, this isn't a 'better' version of 'Hey Jude', rather an opportunity to appreciate a familiar painting in a refreshingly different frame.

NOT GUILTY
(Harrison)
The Beatles set a new record for perseverance with this George Harrison

composition – it was the first time they had taken over 100 takes to get a song right – and after all that they still never released it! A solo version of 'Not Guilty' did eventually appear on the 1979 album George Harrison, but this *Anthology* version marks the first appearance ever of a Beatles' take on the song. This was Take 99 of the full band version intended for the 'White Album', and it includes an absolutely blistering George solo. The song's absence from the 'White Album' seems baffling, for while nowhere near as strong as 'Piggies' or 'While My guitar Gently Weeps', it's certainly a good deal more substantial than 'Savoy Truffle'.

MOTHER NATURE'S SON
(Lennon/McCartney)
Fostered by Paul McCartney's love of the great outdoors, but more specifically inspired by a lecture about nature he heard whilst with the Maharishi in India. Deftly picked, the version here puts the song more into the territory of 'Blackbird' – with McCartney accompanied only by his own acoustic guitar, rather than the eloquent brass with which George Martin would later overlay the 'White Album''s version. Slight but charming, it displays McCartney's consummate skills at the time of its recording. He later conceded that John had helped with the lyrics.

GLASS ONION
(Lennon/McCartney)
Four months on from the solo demo cut at George Harrison's Esher home, this has developed into a recognisable version of the song which would grace the 'White Album'. All the ingredients – and more – are here. Lennon in rare good humour punctures a few Beatle myths ("the walrus was Paul"), and with George Martin absent, he and Yoko feel free to add sound effects (smashing crockery and TV soccer commentator Kenneth Wolstenhome screaming "It's a goal!"). Given Lennon's determination to develop the free-form anarchy of 'Revolution #9' on the 'White Album', it seems odd that he should later concede to George Martin's suggestion to

replace the sound effects with a more ornate string arrangement – but concede he did.

ROCKY RACOON
(Lennon/McCartney)
One of the few 'funny' songs to stay with you long after you first hear it. A tongue-in-cheek take on every Wild West cliché, this early version has all the inherent humour and much Beatle chuckling, especially when McCartney fluffs the lyric ("sminking of gin?"). The song was begun and ended in one single eight-hour session. Paul was always fond of this "quirky... talking blues", and this *Anthology* take has a little preamble from Macca about Bob Dylan's home state of Minnesota. Dylan liked the style of 'Rocky Racoon' and almost certainly had it in mind in 1974 when he recorded 'Lily, Rosemary & The Jack Of Hearts'.

WHAT'S THE NEW MARY JANE
(Lennon/McCartney)
For over a quarter of a century, this was *the* fabled lost Beatle classic. The rumour mill was set in motion by the title (a contemporary euphemism for marijuana, m'lud), and gathered steam with the story that it had been deliberately left off *Sgt Pepper*. In fact it was recorded for the 'White Album' and then wisely excluded – a stoned piece of gibberish which made 'You Know My Name...' sound like a Mozart symphony. John and George were the only Beatles present for this session in August 1968. John revels in the sound effects, but the nonsense lyrics ("he cookie such groovy spaghetti") suggest the sort of substance abuse which would have caused George Martin to raise a paternal eyebrow.

'What's The New Mary Jane' signalled the sort of direction John and Yoko envisaged for the Plastic Ono Band, but also saw The Beatles journeying down such fruitless byways as 'Revolution #9' – which David Bowie perversely but predictably chose as his all-time favourite Beatles song. There is way too much of nothing here, and 'What's The New Mary Jane' now seems destined to be

remembered as one of the bitterest disappointments of *Anthology 3*.

STEP INSIDE LOVE
(Lennon/McCartney)
While Brian Epstein's protege Cilla Black seemed content with a career which took her closer and closer to the heart of showbusiness, she remained in close contact with The Beatles even when they were at their most wayward. Having agreed to let Cilla have a new song for the theme of her BBC television series, Paul interrupted recording his 'I Will' for the 'White Album' to demonstrate the song to his fellow Beatles. But though effective, his demo breaks down, and soon McCartney is switching tempo and on into a little throwaway inspired by an ad-lib from Lennon...

LOS PARANOIAS
(Lennon/McCartney/Harrison/Starr)
Nonsense lyrics ("just enjoy us, los paranoias") played out against a throbbing Latin beat. Beatle tongues clearly in Beatle cheeks. Then back to work.

I'M SO TIRED
(Lennon/McCartney)
Dragged reluctantly into the modern age, EMI finally installed eight-track machines at Abbey Road, although much of the work on the 'White Album' had already been accomplished using four-track. This *Anthology* version of one of Lennon's best songs from the 1968 double album is an amalgam of Takes 3, 6 and 9. It retains Lennon's best-ever rhyme ("cigarette" and "stupid get"), but there are enough differences to make it of interest – it is noticeably looser and sloppier than the familiar official take, and there is an especially venomous Lennon vocal.

I WILL
(Lennon/McCartney)
Take 1 (the master wouldn't come until Take 67) of what Paul has called "one of my favourite melodies that I've written. You just occasionally get lucky with a melody and it becomes rather complete, and I think this is one of them; quite a complete tune." That feeling of completeness is confirmed by this really together first take; another of those seemingly effortless McCartney efforts which *Anthology* traces back to source.

WHY DON'T WE DO IT IN THE ROAD
(Lennon/McCartney)
I remember that on the release of the 'White Album' there was much adverse comment

about the inclusion of this song – it seemed such a frivolous, insubstantial fragment to include on a Beatles album. These were still seen as pulpits from which great statements should be made, not repositories for trivial three-line throwaways. But like all things, indignation must pass, and 'Why Don't We Do It In The Road' can now be seen as a precursor of the sort of track McCartney would try out on his first two solo albums in an attempt to take the pressure off and puncture the Beatle myth.

This was another India song: "a primitive statement to do with sex or to do with freedom really. I like it, it's just so outrageous that I like it... Good vocal, though I say it myself." This solo version is the nearest the world would ever get to hearing the song as Paul McCartney conjured it, one balmy evening in Rishikesh.

JULIA
(Lennon/McCartney)
This beautiful song evoking the spirit of John's late mother was the final number to be recorded for inclusion on the 'White Album'. It was also to be Lennon's first, and only, solo recording while still a member of The Beatles. Only three takes were ever attempted, with Take 3 selected as the master. This is the largely instrumental second take, with John receiving a few words of encouragement from his friend in the control room.

A couple of weeks of sequencing and mixing, and the 'White Album' was ready for release in time for Christmas 1968. Every Christmas for five years there had been a Beatles album in the shops, it was as much a part of the seasonal holiday as the Queen's Broadcast. But the tension which had arisen following the death of Brian Epstein, the increasingly out-of-control Apple organisation, and the introduction of Yoko Ono into The Beatles' inner circle could no longer be ignored. For many the 'White Album' was when the rot set in; certainly by the time it was released, The Beatles as a group had barely a calendar year left to run.

DISC TWO

I'VE GOT A FEELING
(Lennon/McCartney)
The sprawling sessions for an album to be called *Get Back* – which later became *Let It Be* – were said to show The Beatles "as nature intended". While the rest of the rock'n'roll firmament went further and further out (Iron Butterfly's *In-A-Gadda-La-Vida* and Jimi Hendrix's *Electric Ladyland*), The Beatles followed Bob Dylan down into the basement, or in their case, down the stairs at Apple's Central London offices.

Lennon called the plan for the official follow-up to the 'White Album': "The Beatles with their pants down" – the intention was to be iconoclastic, but there were those who considered the results to be un-produced, un-supervised and... unremarkable! The group spent the first fortnight of 1969 diligently clocking in at Twickenham Film Studios, but in the subsequent film of *Let It Be* they could be seen slowly unravelling. Disillusioned with the film-making process, The Beatles regrouped at Savile Row, from where the first nine tracks on this second CD emanated.

Despite their avowed intent to get back, The Beatles were tempted by Apple's Magic Alex who promised them the opportunity to work on a 72-track system he had invented –

a significant advance on EMI's primitive 8-track. Needless to say though, like so many of the Apple schemes, it was no more than a pipe-dream. As well as the personal problems facing The Beatles at the time, many of the sessions were dogged by technical faults, exacerbating the difficulties which plagued The Beatles (and particularly the fastidious George Martin) during the Apple recordings. This *Anthology* version of 'I've Got A Feeling' is the first fruit from those 1969 Apple sessions to be made officially available.

Even as The Beatles crumbled, Lennon and McCartney still continued to collaborate: Paul remembers John coming round to his Cavendish Avenue home (near Abbey Road) with a song 'Everybody Had A Good Time', which the two inserted into Paul's half-finished 'I've Got A Feeling', just as they had done on 'A Day In The Life' two years before. This Apple take of 'I've Got A Feeling' falls apart at the end, due to John's self-confessed cock-up, but it provides ample example of how quickly The Beatles had accepted pianist Billy Preston into their ranks. And despite what we now know of the growing tension, there is still evident good humour between Lennon and McCartney in this work-out.

SHE CAME IN THROUGH THE BATHROOM WINDOW

(Lennon/McCartney)
For years, it was impossible to document precisely what had been recorded for which album during the final year of The Beatles' career together. It wasn't until years after its release, for example, that I learned *Abbey Road* had actually been recorded *after* the group's last released album *Let It Be*. This song, run through at Apple, was intended for the *Get Back/Let It Be* album but appeared instead as part of the medley on Side 2 of *Abbey Road*, though this is a slower effort than the album version. This Anthology take was a rehearsal which allows us the opportunity to hear Paul relaying to the group how he wanted his song to sound.

DIG A PONY

(Lennon/McCartney)
The sprawling and oddly unfocussed nature of the January 1969 sessions is demonstrated on this out-take of a Lennon song which wound up on *Let It Be*. A hollow piece of philosophising it may be, but it is nonetheless intriguing to hear the studio banter, particularly the reference to 'Ricky & The Red Streaks' – one of the pseudonyms Paul favoured for The Beatles' return to live work – Linda McCartney would later release a single as 'Suzy & The Red Streaks'.

TWO OF US

(Lennon/McCartney)
Although written for and about Linda, I always associate this opening track of *Let It Be* with John and Paul – perhaps because in the film they share a microphone to sing this poignant song about "memories, longer than the road that stretches out ahead..." Another of those great 'lost' Beatle songs, 'Two Of Us' is a driving folk-rock song in the style of The Everly Brothers – prompting Paul's "Take it, Phil" comment on this rehearsal from the second day of recording at Savile Row.

FOR YOU BLUE

(Harrison)
George's homage to the blues boom prevalent in the late Sixties – which was also the subject of parodies by The Bonzo Dog Band and Liverpool Scene. This is a full four-man performance of the 12-bar song which later appeared on *Let It Be*, though the version here features a more pronounced piano contribution from Paul. There is also much fun to be had as John grapples with the intricacies of mastering the slide guitar.

TEDDY BOY

(McCartney)
A rather slight McCartney solo effort, routined in the Savile Row basement for consideration by the others. There can't have been much enthusiasm, as it was nixed for both *Abbey Road* and *Let It Be*, and

didn't make its official debut until Paul's 1970 solo debut *McCartney*. The song was inspired by Paul's teenage memories of Brylcreemed rockers in Fifties Liverpool, but this run-through lacks any real nostalgic appeal – although there are some nice little barn-dance contributions from John who dosi-does with the best of them.

needed opportunity to blow the dust off. However The Drifters' 'Save The Last Dance For Me' did make it as far as the short-list for the aborted *Get Back* album. At the time, the monthly magazine *The Beatles Book* reported that there was "enough material for a special rock'n'roll LP – including famous American rock hits like 'Shake, Rattle & Roll' and 'Blue Suede Shoes'."

"The bigger we got the more unreality we had to face; the more we were expected to do until, when you didn't sort of shake hands wioth a Mayor's wife, she would start abusing you and screaming and saying: 'How dare they?'" - John

MEDLEY: RIP IT UP
(Blackwell/Marascalco);
SHAKE, RATTLE & ROLL
(Calhoun);
BLUE SUEDE SHOES
(Perkins)

With the tapes constantly rolling as The Beatles groped for that elusive something which would provide them with the thread for a whole album, much of every working day was spent jamming. Their repertoire was already enormous, having been swollen by those eight-hour sets in Hamburg and honed at The Cavern, but now they were also picking up on the latest sounds by The Band, Bob Dylan and Tamla Motown; as a result the *Let It Be* rehearsals were a pot pourri of everything from half-remembered lines (or even titles) to complete performances.

These three rock'n'roll classics came hot from the Fifties, but were still fresh in The Beatles' minds. All four had a fondness for the Fifties – and in 1968 when the Buddy Holly catalogue was finally made available on album, four complete sets were delivered to Apple. This January 26 medley, including covers of songs popularised by Little Richard, Bill Haley, Elvis and Carl Perkins, was never intended for release, it was just a much-

THE LONG AND WINDING ROAD
(Lennon/McCartney)

Possibly the biggest bone of contention in all Paul McCartney's years with The Beatles was what Phil Spector did to this ballad. Spector's decision to graft a massive orchestral backing and a choir of female singers onto Paul's song irked the composer, who considered it "distasteful" to have a girls' choir on a Beatles' recording. The decision had been taken by Allen Klein, who was now in control of The Beatles' financial management, and this was actually one of the issues which McCartney raised in court when he was trying to separate himself from The Beatles in 1970.

In hindsight and with full knowledge of all the ensuing bitterness, it is therefore doubly fascinating to hear this unsullied pre-Spector version of one of McCartney's all-time classic ballads. Inspired by the route leading to his Scottish home, 'The Long And Winding Road' is undeniably stronger in this stripped-down version, catching the full intended impact of that atmospheric moment. By his own admission McCartney was not always an inspired lyricist, but these are among his most haunting and affecting words on record. The revelations of a track like this really do make *Anthology* an invaluable appendix to the Beatle canon.

OH DARLING
(Lennon/McCartney)
An uncharacteristically raucous McCartney song of the *Let It Be* period. This track gives offers an opportunity to eavesdrop as Paul demonstrates the song to his fellow Beatles at Apple. But John's delight at the news of Yoko's divorce soon takes priority, and Lennon takes the song somewhere else. Meanwhile, Billy Preston, whom The Beatles had first met in Hamburg, contributes some atmospheric electric piano. Eleven years later Lennon would concede: "That's a great song of Paul's that he didn't sing too well. I always thought I could have sung it better. It was more my style than his." There may be a grain of truth in that, but Paul too could rock when required (cf: 'She's A Woman', 'I'm Down', 'Helter Skelter').

ALL THINGS MUST PASS
(Harrison)
Familiar as the title of George's first proper solo album, this take comes from the *Let It Be* sessions. This solo version recorded on Harrison's 26th birthday, with a second guitar overdubbed, presages all the charm of the later version – but with the additional intimacy of a recently written song. Of all *Anthology*'s many delights, a number of the most pleasant surprises lie in discovering afresh George Harrison's songs. The Lennon and McCartney numbers are already so familiar, but a track like this, recorded at the height of the bad feeling and business wrangling, can now be appreciated as an isle of tranquillity amidst a sea of turmoil.

MAILMAN, BRING ME NO MORE BLUES
(Roberts/Katz/Clayton)
Typical of the January jams is this slow cover of a Buddy Holly album track, on which John clearly enjoys trying to emulate Holly's hiccupping vocal style. One of the best and most cohesive of songs from these sessions, it proves that if all else had failed, The Beatles would have made a decent tribute band.

The figure of 30 hours of unreleased material from these aborted *Let It Be* sessions has been mooted, and an 11 album *Get Back* bootleg box set is in circulation. But although it is tantalising to read that The Beatles recorded Eddie Cochran's 'Somethin' Else' and 'C'Mon Everybody', 'Michael Row The Boat Ashore', 'House Of The Rising Sun', 'Blowin' In The Wind', 'It's Only Make Believe' or 'All Along The Watchtower' – few of these made it much beyond the group repeating the title. Then, like the Eloi in H.G.Wells' *The Time Machine*, quoted in Michael Braun's book *Love Me Do*, they lose interest, and "like children, they would soon stop examining... and wander away after some other toy."

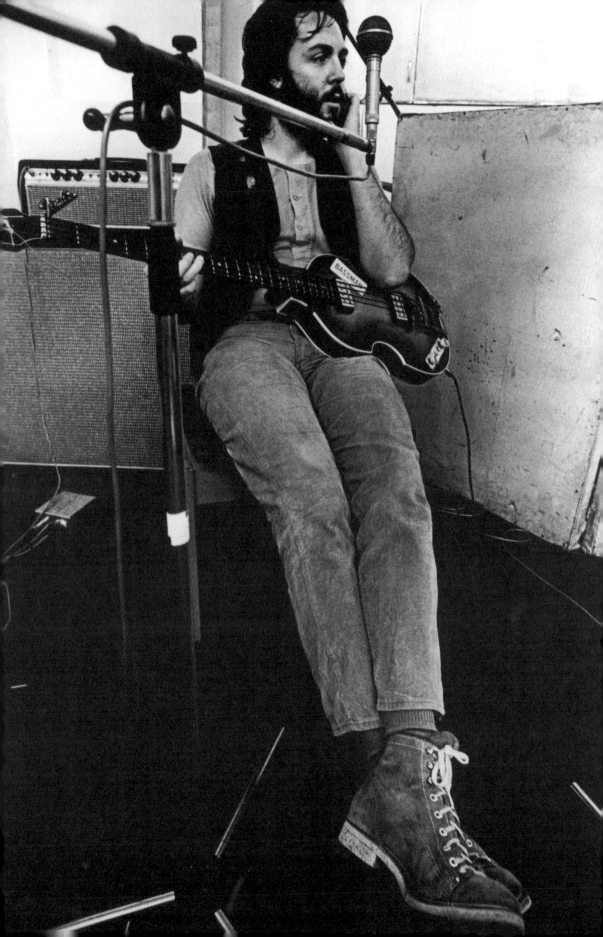

GET BACK
(Lennon/McCartney)

The last full original Beatle single was another victory for Paul over John. And this historic *Anthology* release comes from the final occasion that The Beatles performed together as a group in public. The original plan had been to film the group playing in an exotic location – a Tunisian amphitheatre, the newly-launched *QEII*, or the rather more mundane Chalk Farm Roundhouse. But in the end, with all the acrimony and ill-feeling, it was as much as they could do to walk up the stairs and out onto the roof of the Apple building in Savile Row.

That landmark 42-minute performance provided a fitting climax to both the *Let It Be* film and album; and here for the first time is the unedited third take of 'Get Back' – the last song The Beatles performed live, up on the roof. You can hear McCartney singing about Loretta "singing on roofs again..." and with one eye on the police presence, he ad-libs about "having you arrested".

In the end the police did stop the show, the plugs were pulled, and – some seven years after they invented them – The Beatles brought the Swinging Sixties prematurely to a close, on a windy London rooftop, on a blustery winters day, January 30, 1969. So iconographic did the Apple roof performance become, that U2, Paul Weller, James, Blur and Echo & The Bunnymen are only some of the bands who have subsequently adopted the rooftop-gig tactic.

OLD BROWN SHOE
(Harrison)

Along with 'All Things Must Pass' and 'Something', this was the third George Harrison solo demo recorded at Abbey Road on February 25, 1969 – presumably his colleagues decided to indulge him as it was his birthday. The song is one of George's insistent rockers, and three months later a group recording of the song appeared as the B-side to 'The Ballad Of John & Yoko'. But the version here was already a fully-realised demo, with George accompanying himself on piano and then elaborately overdubbing two separate guitar tracks. The song was proof that Harrison too had fallen under Dylan's spell, and the line "for your sweet top lip, I'm in the queue" has a nice Dylan-esque ring to it.

OCTOPUS'S GARDEN
(Starr)

This was the 'Yellow Submarine' of the *Abbey Road* album. Written by Ringo while he was in Sardinia with Peter Sellers during a break in recording *The White Album*, the released version suffocated under the sound effects which were used to beef up this children's favourite. This *Anthology* variant is Take 2, a far simpler interpretation, but already showing all the signs that the group had the song in hand. All in all though, this is one of *Anthology*'s less distinguished moments.

MAXWELL'S SILVER HAMMER
(Lennon/McCartney)

Of all the late-period McCartney songs, this one particularly got Lennon's goat: "I hate it... Paul made us do it a million times. He did everything he could to make it into a single. It never was, and it never should have been." Certainly as a Beatle song 'Maxwell...' does struggle, lacking both the wit and vivacity of 'Rocky Racoon' or 'Yellow Submarine'; strangely though, stripped of its effects – as here on Take 5 – the song actually sounds more charming. Paul busks the lyrics, and wings it with electric guitar impersonations but for all the lyrical fluffs, this is a good example of how, occasionally, an alternate take on Anthology can actually improve on the released version.

SOMETHING
(Harrison)

When Frank Sinatra calls this "the greatest love song ever written" you know you're doing something right. Inspired by James Taylor's 'Something In The Way She Moves' from his 1968 Apple album, George took the first line away with him and weaved

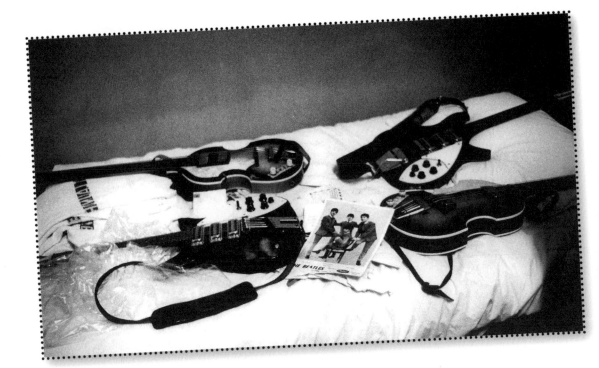

a love song to his wife Patti. While nowhere near as lavish as the produced version which graced Abbey Road, the solo demo here is marvellously frail and fragile. This would become the only George Harrison song to grace the A-side of a Beatle single, and this touching demo acts as a fine counterpoint to the familiar group version.

COME TOGETHER
(Lennon/McCartney)

One of the most troubled songs in Beatle history, this began life as a campaign anthem for acid guru Timothy Leary until John decided to keep it for himself. Freely adapted from Chuck Berry's 'You Can't Catch Me', a borrowing which later landed Lennon in a legal quagmire, the track was chosen to open *Abbey Road*. The version you hear on *Anthology* is the rare and raw Take 1, with John fronting and the remaining Beatles backing him on basic bass, drums and guitar – Ringo's drums particularly are bang on the mark. At Lennon's request George Martin overlaid later takes with echo, but this is the basic, un-dubbed, stripped-down anthem John had originally envisaged in his Toronto hotel room. But the prospect of anticipated "bo-bo" here reduces John to hysterics, and the take winds down.

COME AND GET IT
(McCartney)

An undoubted highlight of the *Anthology* trilogy, this track had previously been intended for release on the earlier *Sessions* album. In less than an hour one July afternoon, during a break from recording Abbey Road, McCartney laid down this astonishingly confident and cohesive demo, playing everything (drums, bass, piano) himself. Apple-signings Badfinger would record this jaunty theme for Ringo's film of *The Magic Christian*; but it is remarkable to hear just how on the button Paul's solo demo is – Badfinger's version was virtually a note for note copy. Badfinger's terrible story eventually culminated in the suicides by hanging of both Tom Ham and Pete Evans (the joint composers of Nilsson's huge hit 'Without You'); while long-time Beatle compadre Mal Evans, who had taken Badfinger under his wing at Apple, died in a tragic police shoot-out in Los Angeles. But all that was still a long way down the line in the summer of Paul's stunning solo demo.

AIN'T SHE SWEET
(Ager/Yellen)
The spontaneous jams which had been so much a part of the January 1969 sessions at Twickenham and Savile Row were a thing of the past by the time The Beatles returned to EMI's Abbey Road studios. But during the recording of 'Sun King' for the album that would become *Abbey Road*, the group once again unwound by running through a trio of Gene Vincent hits.

'Ain't She Sweet' – popularised by Al Jolson back in 1927 and rocked up 30 years later by Gene Vincent – was a regular feature of The Beatles' Hamburg performances, and in 1961 the group had recorded it with Tony Sheridan (See *Anthology 1*). The song was also played as part of their unsuccessful Decca audition, and it now seemed as though the group had finally come full circle. Despite John's croaky vocals, the take here is a rare, together and surprisingly soft moment from a very difficult period – hearing this, it is hard to believe that The Beatles would soon cease to exist.

 BECAUSE
(Lennon/McCartney)
With none of the embellishments of the album version, these spellbinding three-part harmonies were recorded in Abbey Road's smaller No 1 studio, rather than The Beatles' preferred No 2. John, Paul and George clustered around a microphone, and then further vocal tracks were recorded and overdubbed to create a mesmerising, densely packed layer of voices – evoking an illusion of harmony, something which was sadly lacking in the group's lives at the time.

 LET IT BE
(Lennon/McCartney)
Paul knew that he was onto something here, promising his fellow Beatles "this is gonna knock you out". But this was just the kind of cockiness which really grated with John and George at the time; and in turn Paul found their indifference and outright hostility incredibly dispiriting. It was during this period of confrontation and disillusion that Mary, Paul's late mother, appeared to him in a dream and provided the inspiration for probably his best-loved Beatle song.

This take from the Apple basement finds Paul delivering a simply spellbinding performance. You do miss George's vibrant guitar solo, which so enhanced the familiar *Let It Be* version, but it makes a pleasant change to hear the song without John's mocking intro which Paul always loathed – convinced that it was deliberately placed there to undermine his ballad.

The *Anthology* take does however include some Lennon dialogue from later sessions, in which he makes much of the group's new determination to record without the benefit of studio trickery. John's throwaway remark at the end: "let's track it" is immediately met by the self-mocking comment "you bounder, you cheat" as he recalls that such methods had now been consigned to the past. At the time the group were intending their next LP to be the "new phase Beatles album" which the sleeve of the finished *Let it Be* boasted. But all that was soon to end in a messy divorce.

I ME MINE

(Harrison)

Ironically John was away on holiday in Denmark when George, Paul and Ringo got together at Abbey Road's No 2 Studio on January 3 1970, to record the version of George's nice little waltz which would appear on *Let It Be*. George laconically announces John's absence: "You will have read that Dave Dee is no longer with us. But Micky and Tich and I would just like to carry on the good work that's always gone down in Number 2". (Dave Dee, Dozy, Beaky, Mick & Tich were a popular singing group of the period, m'Lud.)

And so it was that The Beatles' final sessions at Abbey Road were conducted without John, whose original Quarrymen were the original foundations for the group. Sadly, twenty-four years later when Paul, George and Ringo reconvened to record 'Free As A Bird', John was once again missing – this time for ever.

THE END

(Lennon/McCartney)

Presciently, the final track on the final album The Beatles recorded together was called 'The End'. In spite of the rancour of the group's final split, Paul singing "the love you take is equal to the love you make" provided an appropriately optimistic note on which to conclude The Beatles' career.

This Anthology version is a George Martin remix of bits and pieces which were left off the familiar Abbey Road conclusion – notably more pronounced guitar parts and an extra helping of the enormous orchestral sweep which Martin had arranged. Anthology concludes most appropriately, with a final solo from each of the three guitarists and, ironically, Ringo's first-ever drum solo. And then with one mighty bound, they are gone...

1

Capitol/Apple CDP724352932528
November 2001

Love Me Do, From Me To You, She Loves You, I Want To Hold Your Hand, Can't Buy Me Love, A Hard Day's Night, I Feel Fine, Eight Days A Week, Ticket To Ride, Help!, Yesterday, Day Tripper, We Can Work It Out, Paperback Writer, Yellow Submarine, Eleanor Rigby, Penny Lane, All You Need Is Love, Hello, Goodbye, Lady Madonna, Hey Jude, Get Back, The Ballad Of John And Yoko, Something, Come Together, Let It Be and The Long And Winding Road.

Although the premise of the disc was to contain all The Beatles' single sides that reached No. 1 in either England or the United States, George's 'Something' only made No. 4 in the UK and No. 3 in America. Many fans were concerned over the omission of both 'Please Please Me' and 'Strawberry Fields Forever', with UK fans in particular questioning the inclusion of 'Eight Days A Week' and 'Yesterday', neither of which were released as singles in the UK during the Sixties.

It was explained that EMI Records together with Capitol Records in the USA chose the songs that were either No. 1 in the *Record Retailer* chart in the UK (the only independently-audited UK chart throughout the Sixties) or in the *Billboard* chart in the USA. The Beatles achieved 17 No. 1 hits on the *Record Retailer* singles chart between May 1963 and July 1969. In the USA, The

Beatles had a total of 20 No. 1 singles between February 1964 and June 1970.

Priced as a regular album this long playing CD had over 79 minutes running time and represents good value – far better than the red and blue albums. It sold in enormous quantities and seems likely one day to become the biggest selling CD of all time.

LOVE

Apple/EMI 3798082 / 0946 3 79808 2 8
Released November 2006

Because, Get Back, Glass Onion, Eleanor Rigby/Julia, I Am The Walrus, I Want To Hold Your Hand, Drive My Car/The Word/What You're Doing, Gnik Nus, Something/Blue Jay Way, Being For The Benefit Of Mr Kite/I Want You (She's So Heavy)/Helter Skelter, Help!, Blackbird/Yesterday, Strawberry Field Forever, Within You Without You/Tomorrow Never Knows, Lucy In the Sky With Diamonds, Octopus's Garden, Lady Madonna, Here Comes The Sun/The Inner Light, Come Together/Dear Prudence/Cry Baby Cry, Revolution, Back In the USSR, While My Guitar Gently Weeps, A Day In The Life, Hey Jude, Sgt. Pepper's Lonely Hearts Club Band (Reprise), All You Need Is Love

Incorporating elements from 130 individual Beatle recordings – the full list has never been disclosed – Love was created as the soundtrack to a nightly performance by the acrobatic team Cirque de Soleil in Las Vegas. Many of the songs are segued together with

recognisable solos and fills cropping up in places where you don't expect them. While purists might have frowned on this tampering with The Beatles' legendary catalogue, the general opinion that was that Love, in effect a Beatles symphony, was a job well done and a joy to listen to.

Produced by George Martin and his son Giles, the music was remixed and had the complete co-operation of McCartney, Starr, Yoko and Harrison's widow Olivia. Said Giles Martin: "What people will be hearing on the album is a new experience, a way of re-living the whole Beatles musical lifespan in a very condensed period."

At the 50th annual Grammy awards on February 10, 2008, the album won Grammys in two categories – Best Compilation Soundtrack Album and Best Surround Sound Album.

McCartney and Starr, the only surviving members of The Beatles at the time of its release, responded positively to Love. McCartney noted that "This album puts The Beatles back together again, because suddenly there's John and George with me and Ringo." Starr said that the album is "really powerful for me and I even heard things I'd forgotten we'd recorded."

Ringo is correct in that the remixed tracks offer glimpses of things on backing tracks previously unheard, or at least unappreciated, on the original recordings. A perfect example of this is Paul's bass playing during the second half of 'Hey Jude', the long chorus in which his part skips along majestically in a high register that was all but inaudible before. The juxtaposition of 'Within You And Without You' and 'Tomorrow Never Knows' was particularly effective, and Lennon would surely have approved of 'Sun King' being remixed backwards.

The album closes on a poignant note with the voices of George – "Put the red light off" – and John: "This is Johnny rhythm just saying good night to you's all and God bless you." Many fans' eyes would have watered slightly when they first heard it.

REMASTERS

With great fanfare and an advertising campaign that must have cost millions, digitally remastered versions of all of The Beatles' studio albums were released on September 9, 2009. Each album featured the track listings and artwork as it was originally released in the UK and came with expanded booklets including original and newly written liner notes and rare photos.

The rereleases included The Beatles' 12 studio albums, together with *Magical Mystery Tour* as well as *Past Masters Vol. I* and *II*, which have been packaged as one collection. For a limited period, each CD was

also embedded with a brief documentary film about the making of the album. This was also the first time The Beatles' first four LPs (*Please Please Me, With The Beatles, A Hard Day's Night, Beatles For Sale*) were made available in stereo CD format. These 14 albums, along with a DVD collection of the documentaries, were also available for purchase together in a box set.

The Beatles In Mono, a second collection, gathered all of the group's recordings in their original mono mixes. It featured 10 of the band's albums and a further two discs in the *Past Masters* mould. The mono *Help!* and *Rubber Soul* reissues also included the original 1965 stereo mixes (not been previously released on CD). All appeared in mini-vinyl CD replicas complete with original sleeves, inserts and label designs.

Virtually every critic who reviewed the remasters commented that it was like hearing the songs again for the first time.

FURTHER READING

Of the estimated 2,000 book titles available on The Beatles, a handful proved invaluable in writing this book.

Anyone who ventures into Beatle waters would be rash to go without the works of Mark Lewisohn. For me, *The Complete Beatles Recording Sessions* (Hamlyn, 1988) is the definitive Beatle book, chronicling just how the group did it. *The Complete Beatles Chronicle* (Pyramid 1992) is an astonishing tour-de-force of research, uncontaminated by idle speculation.

The Beatles' BBC recordings are ably documented in Kevin Howlett's *The Beatles At The BBC* (BBC Books, 1996).

Barry Miles' authorised biography of Paul McCartney, *Many Years From Now* (Secker & Warburg, 1997) is revealing as the first inside-looking-out Beatle book.

Bill Harry's *Ultimate Beatles Encyclopedia* (Virgin, 1992) is an indispensable guide, covering everything Fab from Abbey Road to the Zodiac Club.

Finally, as an analytical guide to the music of The Beatles, Ian McDonald's *Revolution In The Head* (Vintage, 2008) is highly recommended.